AMERICA
A Place Called Hope?

To Zhanna

AMERICA

A Place Called Hope?

CONOR O'CLERY

THE O'BRIEN PRESS
DUBLIN

First published 1993 by The O'Brien Press Ltd., 20 Victoria Road, Dublin 6, Ireland

10 9 8 7 6 5 4 3 2 1
British Library Cataloguing-in-publication Data
O'Clery, Conor
America, A Place Called Hope
I. Title
320.973
ISBN 0-86278-342-9
Typesetting and layout: The O'Brien Press
Cover design: Graham Thew
Cover separations: Lithoset, Dublin
Printing: The Guernsey Press Co. Ltd., Channel Islands

CONTENTS

PREFACE

THIS IS A REPORTER'S BOOK. I am not a critic, nor an economist nor a political scientist nor a historian, but I believe I know a good story when I see one. What is happening in the United States today is one of the best stories around and deserves fuller treatment than is possible within the confines of a newspaper. In *America, A Place Called Hope?* I set out to describe and put in context some of the dramatic events and changes which I have witnessed at a time when the first Democratic president in twelve years was taking the road to the White House, and to convey the excitement, fear, hopes, and dreams of people living in Clinton's America.

Of all the debts incurred in writing this book, the largest is to *The Irish Times* which sent me to Washington, and to its chairman Major Tom McDowell and editor Conor Brady who gave me the means and the freedom to travel around the United States to record the events for *The Irish Times* – a writer's newspaper for which I am privileged and proud to work.

I would like to thank all those people who gave me interviews, some of whom are quoted, and the officials in government and independent organisations who helped me with research and statistics. Most of the book results from personal observation and reporting, but I must record my indebtedness for additional material to the published works listed in the bibliography and to contemporary political chronicles of the United States, in particular the *Washington Post*, the *New York Times*, the *Los Angeles Times*, the *New Yorker*, *Vanity Fair*, *The New Republic* and *Newsweek*, the latter being the only journal permitted to have a reporter behind the scenes in the Clinton campaign.

A special word of thanks must go to Martin Sixsmith for taking time to read the proofs at a critical stage and offering exceptionally useful suggestions, to Brendan Scannel for his helpful comments, and to Andrew Stephen, who gave invaluable stylistic advice. I am grateful to Michael O'Brien for helping me see beyond my daily horizons and conceive of the book, and the unfailingly courteous and helpful staff at O'Brien Press. Ide ní Laoghaire's creative editing skills and superb advice kept me on the right track and made this a better book. My wife Zhanna was partner and adviser in the whole enterprise from beginning to end.

I still believe in a place called Hope

BILL CLINTON
Democratic Party National Convention,
16 July 1992

INTRODUCTION

Lift up your eyes upon
This day breaking for you.
Give birth again
To the dream.

MAYA ANGELOU, 20 JANUARY 1993

THE ELECTION OF BILL CLINTON as the forty-second president of the United States generated an atmosphere of hope and stimulated vigorous debate about the country's future. The new administration in the White House began its four-year term full of optimism that it could bring real change. After twelve years of hands-off Republican leaders, the Americans had chosen a loquacious president with poetry in his soul and an economic plan in his hand. The sixties generation, which was shaped by civil rights, Vietnam and rock 'n' roll, took the torch from the generation which fought in World War Two.

On assuming office, this assertive, intelligent politician and one-time Oxford scholar from a place called Hope, Arkansas, spoke to the nation in words of optimism. In his State of the Union message on 18 February 1993, he said: 'We can still enter the twenty-first century with possibilities our parents could not even have imagined, and enter it having secured the American Dream for ourselves and future generations.'

It has been three decades since an American leader called on his people with such stirring rhetoric to join him on a great national journey. Clinton's greatest challenge is to prove himself worthy of his role as national icon by keeping this new hope alive. Hope is a tender plant in an America where, during the past few years, people have felt increasingly that they have lost direction as a nation. The world, too, hopes that the United States under Bill Clinton will respond with enlightened leadership to the enormous challenges of the post-Cold War era.

There was considerable pessimism about the future when I arrived in the United States more than a year before the 1992 presidential election, after witnessing the decline and fall of the Soviet Empire as Moscow correspondent of *The Irish Times*. It wasn't obvious at first.

Seen from the blighted landscape of Russia, the United States was very much Thomas Jefferson's 'Arcadia' and Abraham Lincoln's 'the last, best hope on earth.'

It is still the world's greatest economic and military and cultural superpower but anyone arriving in the United States today finds a country trying to haul itself out of a period of doubt and uncertainty. At the end of the 'American century' there is a widespread feeling that the country is in decline. Much has gone wrong with the American Dream. For the first time in memory, Americans face lowered expectations about the future. Unlike the generations before them, which could expect to double their living standards every twenty-five years, today's citizens of the United States do not assume that their children's lives will be better.

In the richest and most abundant country on earth, there is violence on an unprecedented scale and accelerating social decay. The United States is alone among developed countries in not having a proper health-care system. The US comes twentieth in the world between Italy and Greece in child mortality rates. More than fourteen million children live in poverty, an increase of 50 percent in a decade. A family earns one-third less, in real dollars, in 1993 than twenty years earlier. The nation is heavily in debt and the gap between rich and poor is growing. While middle-class incomes declined in the last fifteen years, the average income of the richest 1 percent of Americans has doubled.

The United States is the only industrialised country in the world whose production workers experienced a drop in hourly pay in the 1980s. From 1977 the average pre-tax earnings of the poorest 20 percent of Americans declined by 5 percent. At the same time the salaries of chief executives in the top one hundred American companies jumped from twelve to seventy times higher than the wage of the average factory worker. The decade of Reagan-Bush economics was one of corporate greed, leveraged buy-outs and bankruptcies, financed largely by depressing the wages of the workers. Deregulation and the shelving of anti-trust laws provoked a merger mania on Wall Street and corporate acquisitions and take-overs, many of them paper manipulations designed to make financiers richer, brought about the closure of thousands of successful companies and the devastation of whole communities. At the same time, in the space of ten years, the US has become the world's largest debtor nation.

The United States is still the greatest industrial power, but clothes stores are full of cheap clothes made in sweat-shops in South America and the best-selling cars are Japanese. The great bulk of electronics, machine tools, cars, semiconductors, steel and textiles used in the United States is imported. The growth rate has steadily declined as that of Japan has risen. Professor Paul Kennedy in his 1993 book *Preparing for the Twenty-first Century* notes that the Japanese economy is expected to grow faster than America's for the rest of the century, despite its current problems. At present rates the US could lose its status within twenty years as the world's biggest economic superpower.

Hope is a scarce commodity among the vacant lots, empty buildings and graffiti of the inner cities where the social system has collapsed in violence and despair. In Washington, areas of the city are killing zones, to be avoided at all costs. There are more homicides – almost a thousand – each year in the nation's capital than in Northern Ireland. It is a shock to Europeans coming from a society where weapon sales are largely banned to find that liberty in America means the right to possess the most advanced and lethal weapons.

The level of violence in the United States indicates a fundamental and worsening cultural problem. Automatic weapons and hand-guns are used to settle disputes among young men in the inner cities. A huge drugs trade drives an underground economy with a turnover of $50 billion a year, feeding the habits of 1.8 million cocaine addicts. Crime has overwhelmed the forces of the law. In the last decade the prison population of the United States increased by 130 percent, and the rate of imprisonment of offenders rose to the highest in any industrialised nation.

In all my reporting career, in Northern Ireland, Afghanistan, the Middle East, South Africa and the Soviet Union, I have rarely seen people as afraid as those on the streets of Los Angeles during the four days of insurrection in April 1992, following the acquittal of four white policemen on charges of beating black motorist Rodney King. The angry and isolated African-Americans, unable to escape from poverty and violence, cry out for action rather than rhetoric from a federal government which for a decade devoted 25 percent of its budget to military expenditures and only 1 percent to urban projects. America has become two nations: one the sprawling suburbs of shopping malls, gardens, country clubs and barbecues; the other the inner city wilderness of dereliction and crime where a minority of dedicated people struggle to keep hope alive.

But everything is a matter of perspective. Going from the chaos of Moscow to the relative order of the United States, my friends told me, would be like going from the ridiculous to the sublime. In fact, the extremes and idiocies of the social and cultural conflicts which dominated contemporary affairs in the US for the last two years often made me feel I had come from the sublime to the ridiculous.

While Boris Yeltsin was declaring the Soviet Union dead from the top of a tank in Moscow, America was indulging in self-obsessed debate about abortion, homosexual rights, women's rights, date rape and sexual harassment. People clashed in the streets over abortion and gay rights. The country was transfixed by two sensational public events concerned with sexual behaviour – the Clarence Thomas nomination hearings and the William Kennedy Smith rape trial. As the former Yugoslavia descended into civil war, America agonised over Anita Hill's charges of sexual harassment; while Ukraine was declaring itself to be an independent nuclear power, America focussed on lurid courtroom arguments about an alleged rape at the Kennedy Palm Beach compound.

These unsavoury episodes are part of a struggle for the soul of a society where moral absolutes are in permanent conflict. America is the only country in the world defined not by language, ethnicity, colour or religion but by the notion of personal freedom and individual liberty, and these issues are at the heart of a spiritual and social crisis over how such liberties should be defined. To set the parameters for human liberty, American pioneers framed a Constitution infinitely more protective of human freedom than Magna Carta. The US Supreme Court interprets the Constitution and decides the issues when moral absolutes collide. For twelve years Republican presidents packed the Court so that it has become a vehicle for conservative ideology. The tide of civil rights which flowed during Lyndon Johnson's 'Great Society' has ebbed. There is a mean edge to the way modern America interprets its much-praised Constitution. America does not even debate the death penalty any more and, in the most enlightened and politically correct country in the world, executions are commonplace, setting it apart from other developed nations.

The end of the Cold War helped intensify the struggle for the soul of America. The United States won the confrontation with Soviet communism but in doing so it lost the rationale for everything it did in the last forty-five years. The Cold War, directly or indirectly, determined defence, industrial, trading and foreign policy. It was a unifying force inside the country and the determinant in all its foreign alliances. For the first time in over half a century, domestic reform must be tackled without the national incentive of a foreign policy crisis. Daunting as is the task at home, it is matched by the need to define a new role for the United States as the lone superpower in the wake of the collapse of the Soviet empire. The ties America formed with sometimes unsavoury allies on the basis of shared anti-communism are weakening. As George Bush's hope of a new world order have faded, US strategic goals have become ill-defined, raising questions which have yet to be answered about involvement in the world's regional conflicts.

This, then, is the background against which the presidential election of 1992 was fought. The year was, as George Bush said, a 'weird year', one of the strangest in American political history. The aim of this book is to convey some of the sound and fury of the presidential election, to explore the personalities of the new First Couple in the White House and to explain the great debates which are reshaping America. It attempts to bring to the reader some of the flavour of a dramatic political season starring a host of colourful characters, from Ross Perot and Edward Kennedy to Gennifer Flowers and Anita Hill, and to explain why America turned to a young leader who began his campaign as an outsider and ended winning an electoral college landslide against a president who had achieved the highest popularity rating in living memory.

Chapter 1

A PLACE CALLED HOPE

Happen! Happened in Arkansas! Where else
could it have happened but in a creation state,
the finishing-up country.
It's airs. Just breathe them and you will
snort like a horse.

THOMAS BANG THORPE, 1852

WITH EXTRAORDINARY FORESIGHT, Bill Clinton's mother arranged for him to be born in a place called Hope, a town in southern Arkansas, not far from the Louisiana and Texas borders. Hope is noted for its annual watermelon festival and not much else, unless you count the fact that the Bowie knife was invented here in the blacksmith's shop at the Old Tavern sometime around 1830 and that it was a convenient stop on the South-West Trail for such famous Americans as Davy Crockett and Sam Houston. Music-lovers also say that the best speakers come from Hope: they refer not to politicians but to stereo loudspeakers from Klipsch and Associates who have a factory in Hope employing 150 people.

People living in Hope seemed a bit bemused when visitors like myself began turning up on their main street in the hot summer days of 1992 to follow another well-worn trail, that of the journey from log cabin (well, almost) to White House on which Bill Clinton had embarked, and to find out just who was this hand-shaking, redneck, Bubba politician who had come as if from nowhere to challenge George Bush for the leadership of the post-Cold War world. The definition of a Bubba, I was told, was a southern white male who, if his front porch collapsed, would lose at least three dogs and whose wife smoked, drank and ironed, all at the same time. To most people from the East Coast, Hope was a typical backwoods hick town buried in the pecan and soya bean and cattle fields of the Deep South. 'We're at, well, the centre of nowhere, some people might think,' admitted Mary Neill Turner of the Hemstead County Historical Society in Hope. It is a God-fearing community of 9,643 souls in which the tallest building is the Baptist Church. Like many other southern towns, Hope is 'dry', which means residents have to drive fourteen miles to buy a bottle of Jack Daniels or a six-pack of Budweiser at a licensed liquor store in a 'wet' county. Bona fide travellers like myself could, however, order drinks at the hotel bar in the Best Western Hotel as long as we promised to stay overnight, or we could pay five dollars to join a members-only 'club' which in every other respect was a regular bar. There is no bookstore or music shop in Hope. But appearances can be deceiving. The little redneck town has a thriving would-be cultural life. It boasts an arts council and a theatre whose run that summer included *The King and I*, *The Mousetrap* and *Oklahoma*, and performances by the Shreveport symphony orchestra from Louisiana.

The future US president was born in Hope's Julia Chester Hospital on 19 August 1946 and given the name William Jefferson Blythe IV after his father, William Jefferson Blythe III, a tall young farmboy from Texas who sold cars. His mother was Virginia Cassidy, a striking, vivacious and witty woman, who worked as a nurse at the Tri-State Hospital in nearby Louisiana. William and Virginia married and planned to move to Chicago but, three months before Bill was born, his father's car left Highway 61 as he drove home one night and crashed into a rain-filled ditch in which he drowned.

Virginia Blythe was left a widow and penniless. She moved to New Orleans to train as a nurse-anaesthetist and left baby Bill in the care of her parents, the Cassidys, who owned a provisions store in the black section of town. Bill Clinton recalled years later how he would be taken to visit his mother in New Orleans and remembered seeing her 'kneeling at the railroad station and weeping as she put me back on the train to Arkansas with my grandmother.'

Grandfather Cassidy believed in the Christian virtues of discipline, education and fairness and the infant president-to-be got early training in Bible study. He was taught to respect the African-Americans who came to the store. A fierce tolerance set old man Cassidy apart in the Arkansas of those days where racial feelings ran high. This was the state which gave its support to the segregationist George Wallace of Alabama, when he ran for president in 1968 and 1972.

One of the white kids in Hope with whom Bill played in Miss Perkins's kindergarten was Thomas 'Mack' McLarty, son of the local Ford dealer, then a town big shot. Even then Bill Clinton was making friends with those who mattered. Their friendship was to endure. 'Mack' is now Clinton's first White House Chief of Staff.

When Bill was four, his mother Virginia remarried. Bill's step-father was Roger Clinton, a car dealer. This gave the child a nuclear family and a new name and home. They moved from Hope to Hot Springs, a holiday and resort spa in a forest park in the Ouachita Mountains, an hour's drive to the north.

In this cosmopolitan oasis Clinton grew up, went to high school, graduated and dated his first girlfriends. He actually spent his most formative years here, though in the flowering of his political career he preferred to remind people that he came 'from a place called Hope'.

There were good reasons for this, aside from symbolism. Hot Springs was a shady place. Its casinos and slot machines and hot baths attracted mobsters like Lucky Luciano and Meyer Lansky and Al Capone in the pre-war days. The town to which Bill Clinton was brought by his step-father was a rhinestone of corruption on the southern Bible Belt.

Roger Clinton's brother, Raymond, worked in a drugstore on Central Avenue in the 1920s and recalled in an interview he gave in 1980 how 'Al Capone used to come down, walk down the street with his hat ... turning his hat down ... and he would have two men behind and two men in front and two on each side. You couldn't miss him ... four or five doors above me was the Southern Club and that's where they hung out when gambling was going on.' Prostitution was conducted openly. The municipal authorities, riddled with corruption, imposed a 'pleasure' tax of sorts on the brothels; once a month the whores were brought to the courthouse by the police, and the judge fined them five dollars each and their madames ten.

In those days the town was run by a dictatorial Irish-American called Leo McLaughlin, who toured the streets in a buggy pulled by two horses called 'Scotch' and 'Soda'. McLaughlin was twice indicted on corruption charges, though never convicted, but it was well known that bribes were paid down the line to keep the illegal rackets going smoothly.

Mayor Melinda Baran, a contemporary of Clinton's, described Hot Springs as the sort of town where every family had a skeleton rattling around in a closet. Her own grandfather was a member of the political machine that made the city safe for gamblers in the 1930s but somehow, despite a modest salary, he managed to acquire a handsome hillside property outside town.

The author Shirley Abbot wrote a poetic memoir, *The Bookmaker's Daughter*, about her father who ran a betting shop in Hot Springs. She described the resort as a place that 'deconstructs and demolishes the American dream of virtue and hard work crowned by success, as well as all the platitudes and cant about the democratic process and small-town American life.'

The gambling joints, all of them illegal, were abruptly closed by Arkansas Governor Winthrope Rockefeller in 1967. I found the modern Hot Springs (population 32,462) to be a quiet, genteel, rather run-down town, more like an English spa than an American city. As I drove down Central Avenue on a July afternoon, I had to give way to horse-drawn tourist carriages and gaudily-painted amphibious trucks taking day-trippers for rides on the nearby lake. The gracious thoroughfare is lined by nineteenth-century bath houses, elegant examples of Renaissance Spanish and Victorian architecture with names like Fordyce, Magnesia, Ozark and Lamar. The town had decided to renovate and reopen the bath houses after a quarter of a century of neglect, and once again visitors were taking the waters from some of the town's forty-seven thermal springs, immersing their sweating bodies in hot tubs, sitz baths and vapour cabinets in water which bubbles up at a temperature of 143 degrees Fahrenheit.

Across the way from the bath houses, where the gambling houses once flourished, there are now cafés, art galleries and souvenir shops. One store displayed on the sidewalk T-shirts which made fun of Arkansas's redneck image; printed on the front were several answers to the question: How do you know you are from Arkansas? 'If Jack Daniels makes your list of most admired people'; 'If directions to your house include "turn off paved road"'; or 'If a six-pack and a bug-zapper is your idea of holiday entertainment.' The Southern Club has been turned into a wax museum. On a gable wall someone had painted a huge mural of a city on a hill, and, in giant blue letters, the words: 'The Great American Dream'. Café-owner Dennis Magee had erected a plaster plaque to 'Bill Clinton, Presidential Candidate 1992' on the wall of his coffee-house.

His neighbour, Carolyn Taylor, an artist and gallery owner from Oklahoma who gushed with enthusiasm about Bill Clinton, told me she had fallen in love with Hot Springs, though as a child she thought backward Arkansas would be the last place on earth where she would come to live. 'I know it sounds dah-dee-dah-dah, but there's an energy here artists can pick up on,' she explained in the shaded Italianate brick patio behind her studio on Central Avenue. Artists from France, Italy and China have come to live in Hot Springs. 'Isn't it a joy that there is such a town in Arkansas where people from all over the world can feel at home?'

Before World War Two, Raymond Clinton left the drugstore to run the Buick dealership in Hot Springs. In his showrooms he encountered some of the notorious gangland figures, including Owney Madden, a mobster exiled from the East Coast in a deal with federal agents, who often came in to buy cars. Raymond brought in Bill's step-father, Roger, to run the parts department.

The Clintons fitted easily into the shadowy life of this gangster hang-out in the Ouachita Mountains. Roger and Virginia liked the good time. They hung out a lot at the casinos and Virginia Clinton enjoyed the jazz at the Vapours Club. She became a familiar figure on Central Avenue in her Buick convertible, with her heavy make-up and her hair dyed with a white streak. Bill Clinton's mother also frequented the Oaklawn race track where her standard wager was, and still is, two dollars at the pari-mutuel window, the American equivalent of the Tote. She never had much luck. In her house by the lake today is a framed needle-work reminder that 'A Race Track is a Place Where Windows Clean People.'

Her flamboyance and love of nightclubbing inevitably caused some gossip. The waitress in the Arlington Hotel dining room whispered to me darkly: 'I could tell you some stories about her' – but she never did. One critical tale about Virginia did appear in the *Los Angeles Times* during the presidential election. It alleged that in 1981 a seventeen-year-old white girl, injured when a stone was thrown through a car window by a black youth, died on the operating table when Virginia had problems inserting an oxygen tube in her throat, and that, as governor, Clinton had protected from dismissal an allegedly incompetent medical examiner who had exonerated his mother from any blame. Virginia Clinton says today the issue was phoney, dragged up by her son's enemies.

The story did, however, draw attention to a nasty underside to Hot

Springs life: the stone had been thrown when the girl's teenage boyfriend deliberately drove through a predominantly black area of town to shout racial insults at people in the street.

The schoolboy Bill Clinton had little contact with this seamier side of the city of secrets and vapours. The family, however, had its own secrets. Roger Clinton, the 'Dude' to his friends, was a decent man when sober, but when he drank his mood became ugly and abusive. His first wife had divorced him for heavy drinking and assault. In Hot Springs he subjected his second wife to the same treatment. Once he fired a gun into a wall of the house in a shouting match with Virginia and sometimes in a drunken temper he would order Virginia, Bill and Bill's younger half-brother, Roger Jr., who was born in 1956, out of the house, and they would have to walk a mile to a motel to stay the night.

Clinton has related in interviews how he stopped the regular beatings of his mother by bursting into the bedroom one night and ordering his step-father never to touch Virginia again. When Bill was fifteen, his mother and step-father divorced and in the record of the official divorce proceedings the youth described the scene rather differently. 'The last occasion on which I went to my mother's aid,' he said, 'he threatened to mash my face in if I took her part.' Virginia and Roger remarried two months later despite Bill's objections, but he was reconciled with his step-father before he died of cancer in 1968.

'What moulds character,' Virginia said later, 'is not the strength you talk about but the strength in your everyday living.' She said she believed the experience made Bill Clinton more determined than ever to be in control of the family's lives. He acquired a life-long distaste for excessive drinking; his mother said she had seen him drink only an occasional beer and never hard liquor.

'I was forty years old by the time I was sixteen,' Clinton recalled many years later, explaining how his penchant for compromise arose from his difficult family background. 'I think that my desire to accommodate is probably due in part to the sense that I had from my childhood that I was the person who had to hold things together in my home, to keep peace. I mean, basically we're living in a world where co-operation is better than conflict.' He also admitted that a side effect was that he sometimes acted sixteen when he was forty, which caused problems of a different kind.

Wanda Thompson, who works in the visitors' centre on Central

Avenue, was a classmate of the future president in high school. She also knew some big secret about Bill Clinton but, like the waitress in the Arlington, was not telling. When I asked what she remembered about him, her colleague behind the counter giggled and teased her, saying: 'Go on, tell him what you told me about him.' But Wanda wouldn't. But she did say that there was something different about Bill Clinton at school. He wore overalls when the fashion was Levi's and T-shirts and he was always the cleverest in class. He was pleasant, smart, good at debating and always involved in school politics.

Although she was a Baptist, Virginia sent Bill at age seven to St. John's, a Catholic school, where he stayed for two years. A nun there once gave him a D for conduct instead of his usual A. When Virginia went to the school to complain, the teacher explained it was a ruse to get him to stop jumping up first to answer every question, he was that competitive. It worked. The boy was so anxious to do well he could not bear to get a bad mark. Clinton later went to Hot Springs High, where he was regularly first in Latin, maths and music. Bill Clinton was the type of student whose best friends were the teachers. He was the winner of so many awards that the head introduced a regulation limiting the number of competitions a pupil could enter. Even at that time Clinton loved rhetoric. He memorised the speeches of Martin Luther King as well as the words of Elvis Presley's hits. A school companion remembered him cruising round town crooning 'Love Me Tender' in a husky voice. He also learned how to play the sax. In his high school year-book, Clinton is pictured playing the saxophone as one of the Three Blind Mice, a jazz combo whose members wore dark glasses. 'He was a cool dude,' said one of his contemporaries, 'and always had a bunch of girls around him!'

The town of Hot Springs attracted not just gamblers but visitors from far afield in America and some from Europe, and those growing up with Clinton recall a feeling of being apart from the rest of Arkansas. It was a town of contradictions, a gambling mecca with a middle class which attracted good teachers. 'We were the Chosen Ones,' Bob Haines, another of Clinton's classmates told a reporter. 'We were the ones who were going to do better than our parents did. It was a small town but a very liberal town in a sense. We always felt different from the other people in Arkansas, who were hicky and redneck.'

The biggest event in Clinton's life at this time was his visit to

Washington in 1963 as a delegate for Boys' Nation, a youth movement to encourage political development. When they arrived at the White House, President John F. Kennedy walked outside to greet the boys. An ecstatic Clinton stepped forward to shake his hand, and a brief film was taken by cine-camera of the thirty-fifth and the future forty-second United States presidents greeting each other, one aged forty-six, the other sixteen. Clinton himself would be forty-six when he succeeded to the White House. It was like a laying-on of hands by JFK, or so it would be portrayed later. Clinton fell in love with the world of politics, abandoning thoughts he had of becoming a Baptist minister.

Clinton left Hot Springs in 1964 to enter Georgetown Catholic University in Washington, which he chose for two reasons: to get to Washington to be near the centre of power and to learn international politics. He was in Washington when riots erupted over the assassination of Martin Luther King. A friend recalls Clinton reciting passages from King's 'I have a dream' speech as he drove her across town to bring supplies to people affected by the riots.

The Vietnam draft was then in operation, but Clinton avoided the call-up by getting himself signed on for reserve officer training at the University of Arkansas, though he then went to Oxford and did not attend the training courses either. At Oxford he had problems with his conscience and, on 3 December 1969, he wrote a letter to Colonel Eugene Holmes, head of the Reserve Officer Training Corps at the university, thanking Holmes for saving him from the draft, apologising for misleading him and saying he had decided to accept the draft after all. By this time he must have known his chances of call-up were slim. He confessed also that he was not a fit candidate for reserve officer as 'I have written and spoken and marched against the war.' After he left Arkansas the previous summer, he said, he had gone to Washington to work in the national headquarters of the anti-war organisation, the Vietnam Moratorium, then to England to organise American students for demonstrations.

The letter was an extraordinary attempt to balance radical views with ambition and showed that even then Clinton had his eye on getting to the top in politics.

'I decided to accept the draft in spite of my beliefs for one reason: to maintain my political viability within the system,' he wrote. 'For years I have worked to prepare myself for a political life characterised by both practical political ability and concern for rapid social progress. It is a life I still feel compelled to lead.' He had suffered anguish and loss of self-regard because of opting out, he said. 'I hardly slept for weeks and kept going by eating compulsively and reading until exhaustion brought sleep.'

Clinton drew a high number in the draft lottery and was not called upon to serve in Vietnam. He went instead to Yale and, after getting his law degree, returned to seek his political fortune in Arkansas. To tide himself over until the opportunity arose, he took a teaching job in Little Rock, the state capital, an hour's drive north-east of Hot Springs.

Little Rock at this time was recovering from an episode in the city's history which made it a byword across the world for racial intolerance. In 1957, Arkansas Governor Orval Faubus tried to hold back the tide of desegregation in southern states by ordering out the National Guard to prevent nine black students from entering the all-white Little Rock Central High School. President Eisenhower sent a thousand troops of the 101st Airborne Division into Little Rock to enable the black kids to register and begin their studies. Faubus backed down and withdrew the National Guard, but for months the world saw newsreel film of soldiers patrolling Little Rock school corridors as whites jeered their black classmates. Like everywhere else in the Deep South, acceptance of desegregation eventually came as parents were forced to choose between integration or no education for their children, and with the passing of time came enlightenment.

Little Rock today I found to be more integrated than most American cities. The power elite, both black and white, send their children to Central High. Black, white, Asian and Hispanic live together, especially in the working-class and middle-class south-east suburbs, and they mix easily in the streets, the malls, bowling alleys and restaurants. But the Arkansas capital, like other small American cities, is a violent place. Black youths calling themselves 'Crips', 'Bloods' and 'Folk' in imitation of their Los Angeles gang counterparts engage in turf wars over crack cocaine which, in a city of only 176,000 people, pushed up the homicide rate in 1992 from fifty-two to sixty-one. This is as high a killing rate in relation to population as New York or Los Angeles. At the intersection of 15th and Oak Street, a placid-looking area of trees and wooden frame houses near the city centre, where drugs are sold to 'friends', i.e. customers, both black and white, there were three separate killings in 1992. Some murders result from gang bravado – a teenager can get killed if his cap is tilted to the wrong side, a sign of 'Crips' or 'Folk' loyalty.

Despite this, Little Rock still manages to combine a rustic life-style with a high degree of sophistication. Restaurant menus include traditional Dixie fare – blackeyed peas, fried catfish, barbecue, grits and jalapeno hominy casseroles. 'Your Mama's Best Food' downtown, run by Fleming and Barbara Stockton, does lunch of chicken and creamed corn and purple-hull peas, served at tables with plastic cloths.

Many patrons of more upmarket restaurants would, of course, describe such fare as 'hokey'. There is money and sophistication in Little Rock. Mercedes cars and BMWs jostle in the streets with four-wheel-drive jeeps. The money is local, much of it connected with the chicken industry, which has provided thousands of jobs but has crippled many working women with repetitive strain injury and polluted some rivers. When an American eats a chicken it most likely comes from Arkansas.

New money tends to live in West Little Rock which has several large new mansions, and the old elite live in The Heights in the western suburbs where the mock Georgian and Tudor homes are furnished with English antiques. They go to Episcopal, Presbyterian and Methodist, rather than Baptist, churches and dress themselves from city fashion stores with names like Barbara/Jean, Barnett, Mr Wicks and Baumans. They play golf in the Country Club of Little Rock, where the initiation fee is $20,000 and which has yet to admit any black members. It is patronised by the 'FFLRs', as local people call them, the 'First Families of Little Rock', a version of the better-known East Coast acronym 'FFVs', the 'First Families of Virginia'. When he arrived to make his mark in Little Rock, Clinton took up golf – the one sure way to meet the rich and influential in every American town – and occasionally played a round at the all-white Little Rock Country Club as a guest.

People are defined in Little Rock by their access to power and money. The city is dominated by politics, a game which residents say is open to anyone. It is a 'great recreation', Kay Arnold, a vice-president of Arkansas Power and Light once said. 'It's the most fun you can have with your clothes on.' When Bill Clinton arrived from Yale, long-haired and liberal, he could hardly wait to get into the game. He saw all around him the need for reform. Arkansas, with its mostly rural population of 2.3 million, was a depressed, backward state, where people said, 'Thank God for Mississippi' – the underdeveloped condition of Mississippi meant there was at least one of the other forty-nine US states that ranked lower in social and economic indicators.

Still only twenty-seven, Clinton cheekily ran for an Arkansas seat in the United States Congress in 1974 as a Democratic candidate against a popular Republican, John Paul Hammerschmidt. 'The only reason I ran for Congress is because they couldn't get anyone else to do it,' Clinton said later. In fact he had to beat three Democratic hopefuls in a primary election. He drove round the state campaigning in a Chevelle truck with AstroTurf in the back 'and had a hell of a time.'

During the campaign a rumour went around that he was the 'man in the tree'; in 1969 a protestor at Arkansas university said he would not come down from a tree until the Vietnam war ended. Clinton insisted it wasn't him, he was in Oxford at the time. The protestor later confessed to his identity, but the legend persists to this day in Arkansas.

The young man from Hot Springs thrived on the handshaking and backslapping. His strapping figure would unfold out of his car at traffic lights to pump a passer-by's hand to gain one more vote. Clinton lost narrowly but he made a huge impression as an articulate liberal, not only daring to venture into conservative backwaters but managing to win friends and supporters at the same time.

In 1975, Bill Clinton married Hillary Rodham, whom he had met at Yale. She had come up to him in the library in the law school and said: 'Look, if you're going to keep staring at me and I'm going to keep staring back, I think we should at least know each other. I'm Hillary Rodham. What's your name?' Clinton was so embarrassed he couldn't remember for a few moments what he was called. She came to teach law in Little Rock but, undecided about marriage, returned home to Chicago to talk to her parents. When she arrived back, Bill met her at Adams Field airport and said: 'You know that house you liked?' 'What house?' she asked. He took her to a pretty little glazed-brick residence with beamed ceilings and a bay window on California Drive which Hillary had casually admired. 'I've bought it,' Clinton said triumphantly. He had also installed an antique bed and flowered sheets from Wal-Mart. 'So you're going to have to marry me,' he said. She did. Being an independent-minded liberal, she kept the name Rodham rather than adopt the surname Clinton.

Hillary Rodham shared Bill Clinton's political ambitions and when he fought his next political battle, to become Arkansas attorney general in 1976, the pair of Yale graduates gained a reputation as crusaders against the establishment. He won this contest and in 1978 stood for Governor of Arkansas.

With the stakes higher, the opposition was tougher. Clinton was accused of having liberal views on gun control, on marijuana use and on capital punishment – and of being the man in the tree. But he portrayed himself as a compromise progressive candidate, and pulled off a shock win to become, at thirty-two, the nation's youngest governor. The *Arkansas Gazette* acclaimed the victory as the end of the old-style political bosses and concluded that 'the old demon [of racial hatred] is nearly gone.' The theme of his inaugural ball, 'diamonds and denim', reflected Little Rock's growing wealth and egalitarianism. Clinton invited former Governor Orval Faubus. This did not go down well in urban black areas but it showed a remarkable openness to old political enemies which would manifest itself through Clinton's political career.

The Clintons moved into the Arkansas governor's mansion, a two-storey red-brick Georgian-style house on six acres in the historic Quapaw quarter. He thought he was invincible. In his first two-year term Clinton nonchalantly took on powerful trucking and timber interests, and introduced reforms with liberal exuberance. He was aided by bearded young aides and by Hillary Rodham, who defied tradition and wore shapeless sweaters and no make-up to emphasise her liberal credentials. He also applied the ideology of the sixties in commuting around seventy prison sentences.

Early success went to the head of the Arkansas *wunderkind*. He earned a reputation for youthful arrogance and for listening only to his own advice. He imprudently increased the licence tax on cars and trucks from $15 to $30 to pay for new roads. Poor people, the real Bubbas and the black farmworkers who drove their pick-ups until they fell apart and then replaced them, felt betrayed. Clinton was also criticised for allowing President Carter to relocate at Fort Chaffe in

Arkansas nineteen thousand Cuban criminals, misfits and psychiatric patients who had been taken out of the Caribbean island's penal institutions and dumped by Fidel Castro in the United States. When they rioted and broke free, threatening to besiege the town of Baring, Clinton's popularity plummeted.

Worse – in the eyes of the state's conservatives – was to come. On 27 February 1980, when the Clintons' daughter, Chelsea, was born by caesarean section, the formal announcement the parents inserted in the newspapers said: 'Governor Bill Clinton and Hillary Rodham had a daughter.' This public disavowal of a husband's name was not what was expected from Arkansas's First Lady. Hillary made fun of convention, once saying, when asked what she should be called: 'I'm the first lady, Bill is the first man and Zeke is the first dog.' Adding to his reputation for arrogance, the young Governor was caught speeding at eighty miles an hour during an Arkansas state highway safety campaign.

The inevitable happened. When the next election came round in 1980, Clinton was defeated by Republican candidate Frank White and had to leave the governor's mansion. Clinton wept openly at his defeat and, almost inconsolable, withdrew from view. The boy wonder of Arkansas politics could not bear the idea that he was not liked. 'After that loss he was one humble son-of-a-bitch,' said an acquaintance from Texas. Rumours surfaced for the first time about troubles in his marriage.

But as another two years went by and the next election approached, Clinton was to be found in his car again, driving all over the state, shaking hands, begging forgiveness, asking people where he went wrong, promising to listen next time. He ran a television advertisement saying he had taken his mistakes to heart. One of the lessons he had learned was to rein in his progressive impulses in order to retain a broad constituency of popular approval. Clinton apologised over the high number of prisoners whose sentences he had commuted. Hillary, who had become a lightning-rod for anti-Clinton sentiment, dyed her hair, exchanged her glasses for contact lenses and announced that she was changing her name to Clinton.

The couple were forgiven and they won back the governor's mansion. At the inauguration, Hillary wore a beaded gown of silk and lace. Little Rock society smiled and nodded approval, and the band played 'Happy Days Are Here Again', the traditional Democratic Party song of solidarity. Her name in future, she let people know, however, would in fact be Hillary Rodham Clinton.

While chastened, Clinton had not lost his concern to reform Arkansas and he turned his attention to the state's backward education system. Schoolchildren in Arkansas scored well below the national average in school tests. Clinton set up an education standards committee and made Hillary its chairperson, with a mandate to improve the level of education throughout the state. He imposed a $180 million sales tax to pay for the subsequent education reform, the most controversial part of which was a requirement that all teachers take a competency test.

The state's teachers rebelled. There were marches and demonstrations. When Clinton came to address eight hundred teachers in a hall he was warned that he would get the silent treatment. His mother, Virginia, who was in the audience, described later how her son walked onto the stage, gave his speech and walked out of the building. A professor said: 'So help me, I ain't gonna take no damn test.' She retorted: 'Sir, that's a double negative and that means you will take the damn test.'

In the end the teachers backed down. In 1985, more than twenty-five thousand took the test. Some 2,500 failed and had to sit again. It meant the end of the careers of over a thousand teachers, of whom a disproportionately high number were black.

Clinton won re-election in 1984 and soon found himself facing one of his biggest personal tests. A state police colonel telephoned his chief of staff, Betsey Wright, to say that Clinton's half-brother, Roger, aged twenty-seven, had been observed selling cocaine. She told Hillary, who broke the news to her husband. Clinton had little option but to tell the officer: 'Do what you normally do.' The police set up a sting operation and Roger was caught. He was sent to prison for a year. When he came out, Virginia and Bill joined him in intensive family therapy sessions. Clinton said later he could help because he understood addictive behaviour, having grown up with an alcoholic step-father.

It was a traumatic time for him. He told writer Joe Klein that he spent days in agony over the police operation as he couldn't tell his mother what was going on. 'It was a nightmare, but it was the right thing to do. He had a four-gramme-a-day habit ... he would have died.'

Despite his troubles and rumours of marriage problems which kept surfacing in the editorial offices of Little Rock's two daily newspapers, Clinton was a hardworking and successful governor. The *Wall Street Journal* assessed his economic performance as 'particularly good'. By the time Clinton left the governor's mansion in January 1993, Arkansas ranked forty-seventh in per capita income. Utah and West Virginia now joined Mississippi at the bottom of the table below Arkansas. More important, Clinton had helped bring Arkansas into modern, enlightened America. He had elevated women and blacks in his administration, and their presence in high office had come to be regarded as almost commonplace.

The way Clinton did business as governor revealed a politician prepared to accommodate the forces with which he had to contend. An example of this was the deal he made with the International Paper Company (IPC). In 1985, IPC, a major state employer, was preparing to move its operations out of Arkansas. Clinton telephoned its chairman in New York and in the course of an hour worked out a massive tax break. The company stayed. Clinton's supporters said the tax credit led to the modernisation of industry in Arkansas. Critics said he almost gave away the store; it meant cutting spending for six quarters to balance the books.

Other people who dealt with him found his combination of charm and openness hard to take. Clinton liked to see both sides of an argument and remain friends with his protagonists. Bill Becker, president of Arkansas AFL-CIO, the big, nation-wide union, issued an oft-repeated denunciation of Clinton at a labour gathering. The Governor, he said, would 'pat you on the back and pee down your leg.'

Clinton's indecision was also becoming legendary. He once agonised over a state bill, decided to veto it on the evening of the last day before returning it to the Arkansas legislature and had it pushed through the door of the clerk's office at the House of Representatives. He then changed his mind and had a state trooper retrieve it with the aid of a coat hanger.

In July 1987 he signalled he was about to declare his candidacy for the presidential race the following year. A press conference was called. TV crews arrived. Crowds of supporters gathered for the expected announcement in Little Rock on 15 July. Again Clinton underwent a last-minute change of mind. He appeared, looking glum. With tears welling up in his eyes he said he would not be running. He had just told a group of close friends over lunch that he could not face the prospect of the national media spreading rumours of his infidelities. Gary Hart was being hounded from the Democratic field of candidates because of sexual indiscretions. Clinton had been badly shaken at the merciless dissection of Hart's character. He asked a friend, Max Brantley: 'Is there a point ever in a person's life, a political person's life, when the things you've done in the past are forgotten?' But he confessed to the *New York Times*: 'It hurts so bad to walk away from it.'

It was inevitable, nevertheless, that Clinton's ambition would one day propel him towards the presidency. In 1987 Clinton was rated by *Time* magazine as one of the country's top fifty leaders. In 1988 the National Governors' Association voted him best governor in the US. The young man from Hope had become a leading member of a new generation of young Democrats, mainly from southern and western states, looking for a way ahead for the party, searching for a new, practical vision to replace the noble but outdated civil rights idealism of Lyndon Johnson's Great Society. That same year he got his first nation-wide political break. Democratic Party presidential candidate Michael Dukakis asked Clinton to make the nominating speech at the Democratic Party National Convention.

But it turned out to be a disaster. The crowd, eager for a stirring oration, got a long, pedestrian lecture. The only cheer Clinton received was when he said the words, 'In conclusion ...'. His boring performance became a national joke. Talk-show host Johnny Carson said the surgeon general had approved Governor Clinton as a sleep-aid. Clinton salvaged his reputation by appearing on the Carson show a few nights later, and playing 'Summertime' on the saxophone. 'I just fell on my sword,' he admitted to Carson. 'It was a comedy of errors.'

Rumours that Clinton would run for president in 1992 surfaced in 1990 when he campaigned again for election as governor. However, he promised voters that if elected he would not seek any other office for four years, the new term length for Governor of Arkansas. 'Will you guarantee it?' asked a reporter. 'You bet,' he replied. 'I'm gonna serve four years.'

It was not to be the last time Clinton would break an election promise. Editorial writer Paul Greenberg of the *Pine Bluff Commercial* had taken to calling him 'Slick Willie', the name of a café in Little

Rock, because of the way he appeared to slide out of commitments, and the name had begun to take on.

Clinton won again, but he had accumulated enemies during his tenure of the governor's mansion, particularly in the press, and it was a nasty campaign, during which Hillary Clinton interrupted a televised news conference held by her husband's Republican opponent, Tom McRae. McRae was attacking Clinton as a candidate exposed as having no policies, a charge he illustrated by showing a drawing of Bill Clinton naked with his hands over his crotch. Suddenly the governor's wife, in hound's-tooth suit and with a file of documents in her hand, appeared and began reading from reports, which McRae had written as head of a policy institute, praising Clinton's work as governor. McRae was crushed.

As the time for declarations in the 1992 presidential election drew near, local reporters began to pressurise Clinton about his four-year promise and about allegations of extra-marital affairs and smoking marijuana. In September 1990 Clinton told reporters asking about his private life: 'It's none of your business', and accused the press of being the 'morals police' of the country. A week later he denied using these words. When an *Arkansas Gazette* reporter asked if he had used marijuana as a college student he said: 'The answer to that question is no.'

Clinton told friends he agonised for a long time over breaking his election pledge in the governor's race to run for president. During the summer of 1991, he and Hillary, who were overnighting in a guest house while the governor's mansion was being painted, discussed the proposition endlessly. One night Bill slept badly, then suddenly sat upright in bed, waking his wife. 'You've got to run,' said Hillary, when she saw the look on his face.

Clinton warned her that it would be a dirty campaign. Hillary said they should still go for it. Friends believe that by then Bill Clinton had levelled with his wife and that if the newspapers started investigating his private life she would not hear anything new, something which would have destroyed them both. In any event, Hillary was fairly sure that Governor Mario Cuomo would enter the race and probably take the nomination. This would be, perhaps, no more than a rehearsal for 1996.

After driving round Arkansas asking people to release him from his four-year pledge, Bill Clinton made his move. On 3 October 1991, with his now-greying hair styled like Robert Redford's in *The Candidate*, he appeared at the Old State House in Little Rock, where a high school band, a college choir, 4,500 people and dozens of reporters had gathered, and announced the decision which would conclude his odyssey through Arkansas. He declared that he was running for president.

Chapter 2

THE MANHATTAN PROJECT

Till their own dreams at length deceive 'em
And oft repeating, they believe 'em.

MATTHEW PRIOR, *ALMA*, 1718

IT WAS WITH MORE HOPE THAN CONFIDENCE that Bill Clinton set out on the year-long road to the White House that bright October day in 1991. For most of the year, George Bush, who achieved the highest popularity ratings of the century after rallying the world behind the American-led attack on Iraqi forces in Kuwait, had been regarded as a 'shoo-in' for the 1992 presidential election. It was conventional wisdom to say that Bush could win by simply showing up.

With the incumbent Republican president apparently invincible, many leading Democratic figures like Al Gore, Dick Gephart, Sam Nunn and Jay Rockefeller had declined rather prematurely to enter their names for the Democratic nomination. The popular favourite, Governor Mario Cuomo of New York, was still agonising, Hamlet-like, over whether to throw his hat in the ring. Clinton was one of half-a-dozen relatively unknown Democratic hopefuls who stepped in where others feared to tread and who prepared to do battle for the Democratic nomination in the primary elections, the state-by-state selection by the Party faithful of committed delegates for the annual Convention at which the candidate would be nominated.

Former US Senator Paul Tsongas from Massachusetts was the first to declare. A self-deprecating lawyer of Greek background, Tsongas had successfully fought off lymphoma, a cancer of the lymph nodes – at least he appeared to have until the symptoms re-emerged in 1993. He has a persistent little cough, the result of radiation treatment. Just as he had recovered from his ills, he said, so could the nation – if it was prepared to endure harsh treatment like a gasoline tax to reduce the $4 trillion national debt and adopt his 'aggressively pro-business' policies.

The second Democratic candidate, former California Governor Jerry Brown, aged fifty-three, sometimes known as 'Governor

Moonbeam' because of his spiritualism – he spent some time studying Buddhism and had trained to be a Jesuit priest – promised a genuine if quixotic insurgency against the system. Brown maintained the obvious – that big financial contributions from special-interest groups corrupted the political system – and announced he would take no contribution of more than a hundred dollars. He set out on his campaign in a van, sporting a white turtle-neck jumper which he wore even at black-tie dinners to prove his outsider credentials.

Also in the line-up was Senator Bob Kerrey, a Vietnam war hero with wispy blue eyes who had lost part of a leg in combat but had two valuable campaign assets – a Congressional Medal of Honour which proclaimed him a national hero and a former association with Hollywood actress, Debra Winger, which gave him an intriguing aura of glamour. Kerrey, who campaigned on the one issue of health-care reform, entered on impulse and never seemed fully engaged in his campaign.

Senator Tom Harkin, an old-style prairie populist from Iowa, belonged to a different era and was not seen as a likely winner outside his home state.

Nobody held out many hopes either for Virginia's conservative Governor Douglas Wilder, the nation's first-ever black governor and the only African-American to enter the contest. Wilder hoped for moderate white backing but was to be sadly disappointed in his quest to rise above the politics of race. When focus groups of voters in New Hampshire were shown all the candidates' programmes anonymously, a majority backed Wilder's, but when they were identified, somehow Wilder's candidacy was no longer popular. Sadly disillusioned, the Virginia Governor cut his losses and got out quickly.

Heading a group of no-hope candidates was one well-known Democrat, former Senator Eugene McCarthy, aged seventy-seven, a silver-haired poet-politician whose strong showing in an anti-Vietnam war campaign in New Hampshire in 1968 drove President Johnson into retirement and energised a whole new generation of young people.

Clinton was a favourite from the start. He had established a solid foundation of support for his candidacy within the Democratic Party by an astute reading of the political landscape. Along with other moderates like Senator Sam Nunn of Georgia and Senator Al Gore of

Tennessee, he had formed the Democratic Leadership Council in 1985, designed to pull the Party away from the left and towards the centre. These were Democrats who had seen the light after Walter Mondale, the Democrats' liberal candidate, had been whipped by Reagan who won forty-nine out of fifty states in 1984. The Council was dominated by middle-aged centrist politicians from the Deep South and the West and on Capitol Hill was sometimes referred to as the 'white boys' caucus.' It was the Bubba club. Many of its backers were corporate lobbyists and its donors included conglomerates like Dow Chemical, the American Petroleum Institute and Georgia Pacific.

At the annual meeting of the Council in Cleveland, Ohio, in May 1992, Clinton impressed his colleagues as a consummate politician with a mastery of position papers on every subject. He was among those who proposed a new covenant, one which would combine concern for business and the poor, and also speak for the middle classes. He spoke about the need to get people off welfare and back to work, an idea which would enable a Democratic candidate to outflank a Republican from the right.

The expression of such aspirations thinly disguised a coolness towards the Democratic Party's core constituencies, liberal and labour groups led by such figures as the Rev. Jesse Jackson who had a political-social agenda which championed the poor, both black and white. Said Clinton to his fellow moderates: 'Too many of the people who used to vote for us, the very burdened middle class we're talking about, have not trusted us in national elections to defend our national interests abroad, to put their values on our social policy at home or to take their tax money and spend it with discipline.'

They should lay claim to two groups of voters, he said. One comprised the suburban 'independents' living among the avenues and malls of America's 'edge cities' who resented federal spending and thought themselves recession-proof. The other consisted of the 'Reagan Democrats', the blue-collar ethnic voters earning from $20,000 to $40,000 a year, who had been born and raised in local Democratic politics but whose unhappiness with the Democratic Party, for raising taxes and paying court to Jesse Jackson, had driven them into the arms of Reagan and Bush.

After he announced his candidacy, backed by $3 million raised by the Democratic Leadership Council, Clinton made his first campaign pledge, aimed at winning back Democratic voters. In a speech in Chicago he promised that he would work for a 10 percent tax cut for the middle classes. It was a commitment he would not keep and which he would soon drop. But it helped win attention.

The Arkansas Governor began attracting big crowds when he arrived in New Hampshire. Weighing 16 stone and standing 6 foot 2 inches, he cut an imposing figure. He was a Dixie version of John F. Kennedy with a touch of Elvis, though up close his appearance was more human and flawed, with baggy eyes and a red nose brought on by a recurring cold. He brought sophisticated techniques to his campaign. Clinton purchased television time for half-hour town-hall chat shows where he took questions from members of the audience rather than from reporters. He criss-crossed the New England state in a chartered plane and distributed twenty thousand videos of 'Clinton, the Man and the Candidate' to any hapless voters who opened their doors and admitted to owning a video-recorder.

The closing date for entering the first Democratic primary in New Hampshire was 20 December. That day Governor Cuomo paid for two charter planes to stand by at the New York state capital of Albany to fly himself and a posse of officials to New Hampshire to lodge the necessary papers, if he should decide to run. The other Democratic candidates, already campaigning hard in the small New England state, held their breath. But Mario Cuomo ended the great debate with himself at literally the last minute, announcing he would not run as he had yet to balance the New York state budget. Clinton was in an aeroplane putting the finishing touches to a statement welcoming Cuomo to the race when he heard about the New York Governor's decision by portable telephone from his aide, George Stephanopoulos. A press secretary reached Hillary at the mansion in Little Rock and gave her the news.

'Oh, my God,' she said. It was now serious.

Clinton began contacting old allies for advice. A year earlier he had called in Frank Greer, a Washington political consultant, and Stan Greenberg, a Yale academic and pollster, to advise him on how to win a record fifth term as Governor of Arkansas. They had helped get Clinton re-elected by urging him to campaign as an agent of change, even though he was a long-standing incumbent. He invited Greer and

Greenberg to join him for a round-table conference to discuss the bigger campaign which lay ahead.

They knew that the issue of Clinton's womanising would inevitably come up and at that meeting they agreed what their tactics would be – the Clintons would admit that there had been problems in the marriage but that they loved each other and were committed to their daughter, Chelsea, then eleven years old.

The issues arose almost immediately in New Hampshire. The first of what Betsey Wright, Clinton's chief of staff, called 'Bimbo eruptions' came when a rock groupie called Connie Hamzy told *Penthouse* magazine that she had had a tryst with Clinton in a Little Rock motel. Hillary furiously demanded that they go after the woman and discredit the story but Clinton urged caution. He related over dinner that evening to his aides what had happened. He had been at a meeting in the hotel when the woman turned up in a swimsuit and invited him up a staircase. He refused, whereupon she pulled down her top and said: 'See what you're missing.' There were three eyewitnesses to discredit her account, but CNN ran the story. Clinton's controversial marriage was rapidly becoming a topic for debate. A television interviewer in New Hampshire asked him if he had ever committed adultery. 'If I had I wouldn't tell you,' Clinton replied. In a televised forum with the other Democratic candidates, the moderator, Cokie Roberts, asked if he was hurt by rumours of affairs with women. 'I think the American people are sick and tired of that kind of negative politics,' he said. 'They want somebody who can lead.'

Teams of reporters from the national media, digging into Clinton's past in Little Rock, soon discovered that there were allegations on public record that the Governor had extra-marital affairs with five women. They were contained in a suit filed by former Arkansas state employee, Larry Nichols, on 12 September 1990 in Little Rock circuit court. In it he sought damages from Clinton for wrongful dismissal; Nichols had been sacked for using state telephones to make international calls. One of the women he named was a former Miss Arkansas who had become Miss America. Another was cabaret singer, Gennifer Flowers, who had been given a minor state job by Clinton, and who had been a rock and blues singer of modest talent on the Little Rock circuit. Flowers was born Eura Gean Flowers in 1950 in

Oklahoma City and had adopted Gennifer as a professional name – 'Gennifer with a G' as she would often say.

All of the five women had been approached by Little Rock reporters at the time the suit was filed and they had denied the allegations. The local newspapers had refrained from printing their names but a Little Rock radio station, KBIS-AM, did broadcast the list in full. Gennifer Flowers professed to be outraged and sent a lawyer's letter threatening a libel action over 'wrongfully and untruthfully' saying she had had an affair with Clinton. Thus when the national newspapers came across the list, they too decided there were no justifiable grounds for publication. There was one exception – *The Star*, a 95-cent weekly scandal sheet sold at supermarket check-outs.

On 28 January 1992, as Clinton was surging ahead against his four rivals for the Democratic nomination in New Hampshire, *The Star* appeared with a headline saying: 'DEMS' [Democrats'] FRONT-RUNNER BILL CLINTON CHEATED WITH MISS AMERICA'. It named the five women, while admitting that none had told *The Star* the story was true. But, encouraged by a large payment estimated at between $130,000 and $150,000, Gennifer Flowers decided to give her explicit story to *The Star* in time for its next edition on 4 February.

The headline this time was 'MY 12-YEAR AFFAIR WITH BILL CLINTON – Mistress tells all!' From 1977 to 1989, said Gennifer Flowers, she and Clinton regularly made love all over her apartment, 'not just in the bedroom, but on the floor, in the kitchen, on the couch, even in the shower.' He called her 'Pookie' and once tried to have sex with her in the men's room in the governor's mansion. 'I'm so tired of all the lying and hiding,' sighed Flowers, who was shown lying on bed revealing an ample bosom. 'For twelve years I was his girlfriend, and now he tells me to deny it, to say it isn't true. Well, I'm sick of all the deceit, of all the lies. The truth is I love him – and yes, we did have an affair. Sometimes Bill would jog the couple of miles from the mansion. I admired his stamina, being able to make love with such enthusiasm after running – I used to tease him about running back much slower.'

Gennifer Flowers also supplied *The Star* with tape recordings of telephone conversations she had had with Clinton late in 1991 in which he had said, referring to reporters following up Nichols's allegations: 'If no-one says anything, then they don't have anything.

If everyone is on record denying it ... no problem.' Clinton complained in one excerpt from the tapes that he might lose the nomination to Bob Kerrey, saying: 'Because he's single, nobody cares who he is screwing.' In another he grumbled that '[Mario] Cuomo's at 87 percent name recognition and I have 54 percent.' Flowers reacted to the Cuomo remark by saying: 'I wouldn't be surprised if he didn't have some mafioso major connections,' to which he replied: 'Well he acts like one.' Clinton never admitted the authenticity of the tapes, but later he apologised to Governor Mario Cuomo for what he had said.

When the colour pages of that edition of *The Star* arrived in black and white on the fax machine at Clinton campaign headquarters, campaign manager David Wilhelm telephoned Frank Greer in Washington. 'Our smoking bimbo has emerged,' he said. Clinton's chief election strategist James Carville confronted the candidate and asked him what no-one else dared. Was it true? Clinton said he and Flowers had not had sexual intercourse.

Hillary Clinton, campaigning alone in South Dakota, turned on her television in a motel on Monday, 27 January, and saw Gennifer Flowers playing the tapes at a chaotic press conference in New York. Reporters were shouting questions such as 'Did the Governor use a condom?' The whole thing was becoming farcical. She rang her husband. He told her: 'Hillary, who's going to believe this woman? Everybody knows you can be paid to do anything.' She replied: 'Bill, people who don't know you are going to say – why were you even talking to this person?' Later she called Little Rock and heard that another young woman had been offered half-a-million dollars to say she had once made love to the Governor. 'My God! What next?' she asked.

On her six-seater charter plane that evening she vented her frustration to Gail Sheehy of *Vanity Fair*. 'If we'd been in front of a jury I'd say: "Miss Flowers, isn't it true you were asked this by AP [Associated Press] in June of 1990 and you said no? Weren't you asked in the *Arkansas Democrat* and you said no?" I mean I would crucify her.' She went on: 'I'm just not going to sit by any more and say, "Well, it's the press's responsibility." If we can destroy people with paid stories, what next? ... I don't think Bill appreciates how TV doesn't really give the other side.' She said she had 'absolutely no doubt' that her husband had told her everything she needed to know. There had been, over the years, a development of trust. Reflecting on how the

Republicans had used paroled rapist Willie Horton to discredit Michael Dukakis in 1988, she exclaimed in a moment of inspiration: 'This is the daughter of Willie Horton!'

The mainstream US media, which had declined to publish the allegations, saw no reason to suppress the fact that *The Star* had published them, and made the story front-page news. Nichols, horrified, withdrew his suit and apologised to all concerned for promoting rumours, but it was too late. Overnight, Clinton dropped twelve points in opinion polls in New Hampshire. James Carville asked angrily: 'Is a bought story in a supermarket tabloid going to drive the presidential campaign?'

The Arkansas Governor decided to follow through with a daring extension of the strategy worked out with Greer and Greenberg: he would face down the allegations on prime-time television. Clinton arranged to appear with Hillary on a special *60 Minutes* interview on CBS, shown at peak viewing time after the Super Bowl, the big game of the American football season which attracted an audience of twenty-four million households. A studio was fixed up in Boston, with Hillary organising the colours and camera angles, and the interview was pre-recorded the evening before. Everyone on the set realised the importance of the moment. This could make or break Clinton's candidacy.

Interviewer Steve Kroft began by asking Clinton if he had had an affair with Gennifer Flowers. He said he had not. Had he ever had any extramarital affairs? 'I have acknowledged wrongdoing,' Clinton replied. 'I have acknowledged causing pain in my marriage ... I'm not prepared to say that any married couple should ever discuss that with anyone but themselves.' He said he knew Gennifer Flowers, and had talked to her on the phone, but again denied, when pressed, that there had been an affair.

'You said that your marriage has had problems,' said Kroft. 'Does it mean adultery?' Clinton paused, with Hillary's cool eyes upon him. 'I think the American people, at least people who have been married a long time, know what it means,' he said.

When Kroft framed a question referring to his relationship with Hillary Clinton as an 'arrangement', the Arkansas Governor interrupted him angrily.

'Wait a minute,' he said. 'You're looking at two people who love each other. This is not an arrangement or an understanding. This is a marriage.'

Hillary Clinton added: 'I'm not sitting here because I'm some little woman standing by my man, like Tammy Wynette. I'm sitting here because I love him and I respect him and I honour what he's been through, and what we've been through together. And you know, if that's not enough for the people, then, heck, don't vote for him.' She brought the discussion sharply to an end. 'There isn't a person watching this who would feel comfortable sitting on this couch detailing everything that ever went on in their life or their marriage,' she said. 'And I think it's real dangerous in this country if we don't have a zone of privacy for everybody ... We've gone further than anybody we know of, and that's all we're going to say.'

Carville, a tall, balding Cajun from Louisiana with an infectious grin, succumbed to emotion and frustration as he watched the recording and wept. 'We may go down,' said Carville, 'but at least that's behind us.' But the interview, conducted before a log fire with brass fireguard and with Hillary's arm casually thrown along the back of a sofa behind her husband, brought the couple to national attention, and focussed on the fact that they had stayed together and saved their marriage rather than get divorced. Under the circumstances their performance was masterly. To many, Hillary Clinton had saved the candidacy.

Tammy Wynette, naturally, was not amused. The country singer wrote an open letter to Hillary Clinton that said: 'You have offended every woman and every man who love that song – several million in number. I believe you have offended every country and music fan and every person who has made it on their own with no-one to take them to the White House.'

Clinton watched the showing of the programme in Little Rock with Hillary and Chelsea. Afterwards he complained bitterly that the most emotional segments had been left out. 'It was a screw job,' he said. 'They lied about how long it was going to be. They lied about what was going to be discussed ... it couldn't have been worse if they had drawn black Xs through our faces.' Carville angrily accused CBS of 'screwing' Clinton by editing out his best moments. From this minute on, relations between the Clintons and the media began to deteriorate markedly.

In the snows of New Hampshire the voters were not quite as concerned as the press about Gennifer Flowers. At a rally in Portsmouth, people shouted down a man who tried to ask Clinton a question about his personal life. Clinton told him: 'This election is far more about you than about me, and you should be hiring the person who can do the best job for you to turn the country round, to turn this state around, to put the people back to work, to save our jobs and our future.' Clinton had guessed correctly that people were impatient with such distractions and wanted to hear what candidates proposed to do about the economy.

The press was in a bind. The failure by prominent American journalists in the 1960s to follow up reports of President Kennedy's affairs, which had had implications for national security, had created a climate where it was argued that the private lives of presidential candidates should be rigorously investigated. Unfaithfulness in private life, it was widely said, reflected on character and fitness to rule. Now the public was refusing to accept that past unfaithfulness was a disqualifying character trait. They were in effect saying that now-forgiven marital indiscretions should be ignored in the case of a new, energetic and intelligent leader of high-minded ambition who could set high standards of culture and style, inspire people with visions of a new America and engage them in a serious dialogue about the economy. Many people did see Clinton in these terms. They were saying that the true test of a leader was not whether he had moral failings but whether he was prepared to sacrifice personal indulgences in the service of higher national priorities.

The press backed away from the Gennifer Flowers story as rapidly as it had picked it up. Attacked by voters for prurience, slightly ashamed of its role in muckraking, and reluctant to bring down their favourite Democratic candidate, the mainstream media let the story drop. Columnists agonised instead about the media's right to pry. They reflected on the Gary Hart episode, when the 1988 Democratic Party hopeful had recklessly dared the media to catch him with a woman who was not his wife and they had done just that, with blond model, Donna Rice. Clinton by contrast was saying that his 'troubled' days were behind him. The polls also showed that the Clinton damage control exercise had been successful and that most voters remained unaffected by the sex scandal.

On the campaign plane the mood changed. Clinton seemed serene the evening after the television appearance on *60 Minutes*, according to one of his travelling companions. He did an Elvis impersonation and took time out to smoke a cigar.

The episode had the effect of focussing national attention on Hillary Clinton, who had dropped the Rodham for the duration of the campaign (it was to appear again when they got to the White House), apparently for the same practical reasons she dropped it in 1980. Twice voted one of the nation's top one hundred lawyers in America by the *National Law Journal*, and a former chairman of the Children's Defence Fund, she had shown herself to be a formidable asset to the campaign, someone who brought northern city sophistication to the ticket of the 'good ole boy' from Dixie. Once a bookish-looking woman with spectacles and brown hair, she had transformed herself into a stylish blonde. In intellectual terms, Bill Clinton, said some of his closest friends, married above himself.

Hillary Clinton's poise and assurance were on display when the couple attended a dinner in Washington for Democratic governors, held the same week as the Gennifer Flowers episode. Everyone was seated when they arrived at the ballroom of the Sheraton Hotel but all eyes turned to the door as they strode in, as always hand-in-hand. In those days they presented a picture of a couple in love and Bill Clinton even made it look sometimes as if they were just married. The hands parted and both Clintons started working the floor, moving separately from table to table. They were charming, confident, smooth and, most important, presidential – Hillary as much as Bill. To those of us watching that evening, one thing was clear. This was a co-campaign, a joint ticket. On occasions when admirers told Hillary they wished she was the candidate, Bill would jokingly say: 'Buy one, get one free.'

The daughter of a Republican draper in Chicago, Hillary had broken with family political tradition in 1968 to campaign for Eugene McCarthy on his anti-Vietnam war crusade. When she graduated from Yale she worked on the staff of the congressional committee set up to impeach Richard Nixon. She read widely in religion and once toured Arkansas to give lectures on 'What it means to be a Methodist'. Aged forty-four, she had a portfolio five pages long, including a partnership in the Rose Law Firm of Little Rock which brought her a salary and commission of $120,000 a year, four times what Bill Clinton earned as governor. She also had a track record as a reforming politician willing to take the heat for her husband on controversial issues like education reform.

Acquaintances found the woman behind the public image elusive and, for all her self-confidence in public, occasionally vulnerable. When someone asked her how it felt to be subjected to the media frenzy, Hillary Clinton recited an old nursery rhyme: 'As I was standing in the street as quiet as can be/A great big ugly American came up and tied his horse to me.' She could be caustic too. Encountering an unexpectedly large crowd in Nashua when Clinton was down in the polls, she said to an aide: 'They may just want to see the freak show.'

Bill Clinton's troubles in New Hampshire were not over after Gennifer Flowers was dismissed from the front pages. A few days later, the *Wall Street Journal* resurrected an old story about how Clinton had dodged the Vietnam war draft by agreeing to enter the Reserve Officer Training Corps in exchange for deferment, then backing out of the commitment. This had also been investigated by Little Rock newspapers during elections for Governor in Arkansas. What was new was that Colonel Eugene Holmes, once non-committal when approached by journalists, had told the *Journal* that 'Clinton was able to manipulate things so that he didn't have to go in.' A few days later ABC television got hold of the letter Clinton had written to Colonel Holmes thanking him for 'saving' him from the draft.

Clinton now looked decidedly shifty. This made the earlier explanations look disingenuous. The draft issue unsettled him more than Gennifer Flowers. He gave impatient and evasive replies to questions. The dynamic policy-master began to look more like 'Slick Willie', the name his opponents used against him in Little Rock and, in the space of one or two days, Clinton went into freefall. On 17 February, the day before the primary election, Greenberg did a tracking poll. It showed Clinton, who had been comfortably in the lead, now trailing the dogged Paul Tsongas by eighteen points to thirty-four.

'I'm dropping like a turd in a well,' said Clinton. But in a final appeal to New Hampshire voters, he vowed: 'I'll fight like hell. I'll fight till the last dog dies.'

The result was better than he had anticipated. 'St Paul', as Clinton's team derisively called Tsongas, got 33 percent of the vote, but Clinton took 25 percent, a creditable showing. Kerrey got 11 percent, Harkin 10 and Brown 8. Eugene McCarthy got a mere 211 votes. 'New Hampshire has made me the Comeback Kid,' Clinton boasted at an election night rally. Next day he asked his wife: 'You don't think I should congratulate Tsongas?' 'No,' replied Hillary. 'We're declaring victory.'

Just before the Clintons' *60 Minutes* television interview, at the most vulnerable moment of his reach for the highest office in the land, Clinton had to confront another crucial question of conscience, also with political implications. This was whether to use his powers as Governor of Arkansas to stay the execution of a black convict, Rickey Ray Rector, from Cummings, Arkansas.

In 1981 Rector had cold-bloodedly shot dead Patrolman Robert Martin. Before being captured, Rector had put a gun to his own temple and fired, destroying some of his brain tissue. The operation to save his life had left him a mental defective. Rector had nevertheless been sentenced to death and the Supreme Court had rejected final appeals lodged by his lawyer. Only one justice, Thurgood Marshall, dissented on the grounds that the Court had once before invoked the Eighth Amendment to prohibit a state from executing an insane prisoner.

Conservative voters were not in favour of pardoning black killers, and Clinton had learned not to wander too far from the national consensus. The date for the execution of Rector arrived and Clinton flew home from the crisis over Gennifer Flowers in New Hampshire to respond to any last-minute appeals. As governor, Clinton had already refused to commute the death penalty for two white killers. This time his political career was possibly at stake. If he commuted Rector's sentence he could be depicted by the Republicans as soft on crime, a charge which had helped sink Michael Dukakis four years previously. He could on the other hand have stayed away from Arkansas and delegated his authority to his deputy, the lieutenant governor, who was in favour of the execution.

Some saw his return to Little Rock as a cynical act designed to confirm his conservative credentials to blue-collar 'Reagan Democrats'. It was certainly at odds with his own progressive, compassionate image not to show clemency to a pathetically brain-damaged convict, and it raised questions about Clinton's readiness to suppress his real beliefs and intentions in pursuit of political ambition. The *Houston Chronicle* said: 'Never – or at least not in the recent history of presidential campaigns – has a contender for the nation's highest elective office stepped off the campaign trail to ensure the killing of a prisoner.'

Rector did not know what was happening to him and saved the pecan pie from his last meal to eat later, according to Marshall Frady who published a study of the episode in the *New Yorker* in February 1993. Almost his last words, after watching election news on television two hours before his execution, were: 'I'm gonna vote for him, gonna vote for Clinton.'

The next big electoral test for the Democratic hopefuls came on Super Tuesday, 10 March, the day eleven states, mostly in the South, held their Democratic Party primaries. These elections would produce more than a third of the committed delegates to the Democratic Convention in July which would select the party's presidential candidate. Bob Kerrey and Tom Harkin were forced to withdraw, their campaigns out of money. But Clinton surged ahead, benefiting from his southern roots and his enhanced conservative record, to win Texas, Florida, Oklahoma, Mississippi, Louisiana, Tennessee and Missouri. Exit polls showed that he had achieved the southern politician's dream, a bi-racial vote from a populist coalition of middle class and poor whites, blacks and Latinos. Clinton also made inroads among blue-collar Democrats when the contest moved to a new series of primaries in the rust-belt states of the north. To their surprise, big crowds turned out for the Clintons in Chicago. 'Who are all those people?' asked Hillary. 'Get used to it,' said a reporter.

It was Hillary's turn next to get a bad press. The *Washington Post* raised questions about the relationship between Clinton's administration in Arkansas and his wife's law firm, though Hillary said she received no share of the firm's profits from state contracts. Before a television debate in Chicago, Clinton's aide, George Stephanopoulos said: 'If you hear the word Hillary, don't let him finish.' Jerry Brown, who had acquired a version of the *Post* story by telephone, told the audience that Clinton had got a 'big electability problem – he is funnelling money to his wife's law firm for state business.'

'That is a lying accusation,' retorted Clinton. 'You're not fit to be on the same platform with my wife.' The reaction afterwards favoured Clinton. 'I figure, in a deal like that, no-one remembers the specific words. They just remember if you stuck up for your wife,' he told his friends.

Afterwards in a corridor, a reporter asked Hillary Clinton about criticism of her professional life. She let her pique with the whole affair dictate her reply. 'I suppose I could have stayed at home, baked cookies and had teas,' she said, 'but what I decided was to fulfil my profession, which I entered before my husband was in public life.'

The remark provoked protests across the United States from women who had chosen to or had no alternative but to stay at home. Suddenly it was open season on Hillary. There had already been something of a backlash against her from the conservative right, which saw her as a dangerously politically-correct liberal. The *American Spectator* had called her the 'Winnie Mandela' of American politics. The Republicans were also infuriated by a remark she had made to Gail Sheehy about double standards in the media, which she accused of pursuing her husband while ignoring a long-rumoured affair between George Bush and his former head of protocol, Jennifer Fitzgerald – referred to by those in the know as 'Jennifer with a J' to distinguish her from Ms. Flowers. 'I just don't understand why they think they can get away with this,' she had said. 'Everybody knows about George Bush's carrying on.'

This seemed to be a deliberate attempt to put the heat onto George Bush and a signal to his aides to lay off, while leaving Bill Clinton with clean hands. It came across as underhand. Hillary Clinton withdrew into herself. Realising that her assertiveness was not always an asset to the ticket, she lowered her profile and curtailed her public remarks. She apologised for the remark about George Bush, saying: 'Nobody knows better than I the pain that can be caused by discussing rumours in private conversation.' The cookie remark was also causing her some pain. The magazine *Family Circle* organised a cookie recipe contest between Hillary Clinton and Barbara Bush which both found distasteful but which neither could ignore. (Readers favoured Hillary's recipe which used vegetable shortening instead of butter.)

After Clinton won the next two big states, Michigan and Illinois, Paul Tsongas dropped out. He was broke, his financial plight considerably worsened by a $1 million fraud by an aide which would not come to light until a year later. With only the iconoclastic Jerry Brown left, the nomination battle was all but over – but Clinton had been badly mauled. It was time to take stock.

A *Los Angeles Times* survey of 1,395 voters showed that more than half of the people in three key groups of voters – suburban, lower middle class and those voters aged twenty-five to forty-four – had an unfavourable impression of the front runner. The turnout at primary elections had been the lowest ever. A private Democratic National Committee poll showed that Clinton trailed Bush twenty-four points in honesty and trustworthiness. Clinton's negative rating in key states like Connecticut was 41 percent. One of the constant complaints Democratic Party pollsters heard when they carried out surveys was that no-one knew why Bill Clinton wanted to be president.

Carville and Greenberg drew up a memo in mid-April in which they concluded that the central problem the candidate faced was 'trust'. The answer was the Manhattan Project, a top-secret plan aimed at finding out how to recast Clinton to remove the 'Slick Willie' image and make him appear trustworthy and electable.

In the making of a president in modern America, policies and postures are decided according to the perceived concerns of the voters. The most advanced democracy in the world has produced the most advanced techniques for perfecting populism. Central to this development is the focus group, small gatherings of voters who act as guinea pigs for campaign engineers who watch them through one-way mirrors so as to remain unobtrusive. The Manhattan Project, as it was named by Clinton's image-making adviser, Mandy Grunwald, was a carefully-planned operation to discover from focus groups across the country what precisely it was that triggered negative and positive responses to Clinton.

The first focus group consisted of ten white women aged over forty-five in Allentown, Pennsylvania. Sitting round a table, five said at first they were for independent candidate Ross Perot, three for George Bush and two for Clinton. 'He just goes with the flow,' explained one woman. 'He wouldn't steal, but he'd shade the truth,' said a second. 'If you ask his favourite colour, he'd say "plaid",' said another. (For a long time afterwards, whenever Clinton sounded slick, his aides accused him of 'going plaid'.) Greenberg used the group to test a hypothesis that if people knew more about Clinton as a person they would have more positive feelings about him. He distributed a biography listing thirty-five personal items covering Clinton's life from his birth in Hope to his time as Governor of Arkansas. Opinions slowly changed round the table. Some had thought Clinton was rich and privileged like the Kennedys; others that he had no children. By the end of the session seven voted for Clinton, two for Bush and one for Perot.

Some groups were hard to turn around. In one gathering of middle-class women in suburban New Jersey, several described Clinton's message as glib and insulting. Seven men in another session voted five for Perot, one for Bush and one for Clinton. Clinton was 'Slick Willie' who 'plays both sides of the street' and who 'won't look you straight in the eye,' said two of the men. But they also used words like 'forceful' and 'creative' and refused to criticise him on moral grounds. After the personal biography was distributed, they voted Clinton six, Perot one, Bush none.

The message was clear: negative ratings could be brought down if the candidate was repackaged. Clinton's problem was not so much Gennifer Flowers or draft-dodging, Greenberg concluded, it was 'the belief that Bill Clinton is a typical politician.' To win, they had to 'depoliticize' the candidate, make him a person with a history rather than just a master of policies. The campaign would succeed, said his press secretary, Dee Dee Myers, 'when Hot Springs and Hope prevail over Oxford and Yale.' At the same time, Clinton's candidacy would not catch on unless voters became convinced that he wanted to change America. They had to be persuaded to jettison the image of Clinton as a philanderer and depict him as a thoughtful, well-intentioned outsider.

Greenberg also turned to the 'dial-group' method of obtaining public reaction. In 'dial-groups', people are asked to move an electronic needle along a calibrated scale from zero (cold) to 100 (hot) to express approval or disapproval as they watch a video of the candidates. In Dayton, Ohio, twenty-six politically moderate women, initially unenthusiastic about Clinton, began to push the needles towards 'hot' when he said things like: 'No more something for nothing' and 'We must get welfare recipients back to work.'

As the first findings from the Manhattan Project came in, it was evident that Clinton, with his outgoing, naturally friendly character, had the potential to come across as warm and committed to change, in contrast to Bush who had no core beliefs and to Perot who was cold and impatient. But it was another thing to translate this into action and get the negative ratings down.

In the meantime, Clinton was fading in national opinion polls and in May he dropped to third place behind Bush and Perot. Clinton was in despair. 'So far as I'm concerned we're at zero,' he told a Little Rock meeting of campaign strategists in May. 'We're a negative, we're off the screen. We don't exist in the national consciousness. We might as well have been like any member of Congress and kissed every ass in the Democratic Party ... I have busted my butt for seven months and the American people don't know crap about it after I poured $10 million worth of information into their heads.'

Around this time, Greenberg, Carville and Greer produced a fourteen-page interim report on the Manhattan Project. Clinton had to identify with the rage of the electorate, they said; he should say at every opportunity that Reagan-Bush trickle-down economic policies had failed and that he had a plan to improve schools and make health-care accessible; the Clintons should make every effort to appear as a loving couple; they should exchange intimacies in public to provide opportunities for pictures of domestic sharing; they could create a family vignette where 'Bill and Chelsea surprise Hillary on Mother's Day'; Hillary Clinton should arrange joint appearances with friends where she 'can laugh, do her mimicry' and recreate her image to remove suspicions of her 'being in the race for herself' or 'running the show'. 'The message,' Greenberg said, 'would change the dynamics of the race.'

In pursuit of a new image, Clinton appeared on Music TV, the channel for rock and rap music-lovers, to answer questions from teenagers. He donned dark glasses and played the saxophone on the Arsenio Hall Show. He telephoned New York's Rockline radio station to talk to a programme guest, Bono of U2. 'How do you want us to call you?' asked Bono. 'Shall we call you Governor or Bill?' 'Naw, you call me Bill,' Clinton said. 'All right,' said Bono, 'and you can call me Betty.' At the end of the conversation the lead singer of U2, the most popular rock group in America, gave what amounted to an endorsement of the Democratic candidate. 'I must say from all of us – you sound like a president,' he said.

Clinton still had to face the crucible of the New York primary election to tie up the nomination. The city's non-stop media treated the competition between Clinton and Brown in the Big Apple as a gangland war. Clinton was tense and on edge as he began campaigning in the city. His frayed nerves showed when a member of the militant gay organisation ACT-UP called out to him at a fund-raiser in a Manhattan nightclub: 'What are you going to do about AIDS? We're dying!'

'That's why I'm running for president, to do something about it,' Clinton replied. But when the questioner persisted, he snapped: 'You do not have the right to treat any human being, including me, with no respect because of what you're worried about. I did not cause it. I'm trying to do something about it ... I'm sick and tired of all these people who don't know me, know nothing about my life, know nothing about the battles that I've fought, know nothing about the life I've lived, making snotty-nosed remarks about how I haven't done anything in my life ... that's bull and I'm tired of it.' (The forty-six-year-old heckler, Robert Rafsky, a senior vice-president of Howard J. Rubenstein & Associates, a public relations firm, died from complications brought on by AIDS on 22 February 1993.)

In New York, Clinton was again involved in controversy, admitting after years of evasive answers that he had experimented with marijuana at Oxford 'a time or two, but I didn't inhale', a remark that was to haunt him for months to come. He faced once more the question of adultery on the Phil Donahue television show. 'Are you denying the allegations or are you saying it's not fair?' Donahue asked him bluntly. A young woman stood up and sharply criticised the talk-show host. 'We've wasted half an hour attacking this man,' she said. 'I think it's ridiculous.' The audience applauded enthusiastically and the topic was not raised again.

The surprise in the New York primary was not that Clinton won but that non-runner Paul Tsongas came second. Brown's insurgency had finally peaked, with voters doubtful about a proposal he put forward for a 13 percent flat tax. The vote was seen as a protest by New York Democrats who did not like either Clinton or Brown. It was a vote for 'none of the above'.

After New York, Clinton's campaign analysts urged him to consolidate the vote of the 'Reagan Democrats'. Previous Democratic contenders for the White House – in particular Jesse Jackson, leader of the Rainbow Coalition, a multi-culture pressure group – had lost the allegiance of many natural blue-collar followers because of their identity with liberal, minority interests.

Jackson, who ran for the Democratic Party nomination in 1988, is an inspiring leader in whom the two traditions of black American politics merge – the drive for black integration and self-reliance and the urge for black solidarity to fight against injustice. When he articulated the politics of togetherness in the 1988 Democratic primaries, Jackson rallied support from blacks and whites alike. As a champion of inner-city blacks, however, he was deeply unpopular with working-class whites, resentful of his assertiveness and fearful for their status and jobs. In addition, as a liberal, he was a hate-figure for the conservative right.

To a centrist populist like Clinton, Jackson was bad news. Clinton calculated that he did not need Jackson to win the black vote. As a southerner, he was more comfortable with blacks than many more politically-correct northern liberals, and he instinctively knew that he would get their support in a fight with an unpopular Republican tied to big business. Unlike the two previous Democratic candidates for president, Walter Mondale and Michael Dukakis, who were white liberals from the north, Clinton felt he could dispense with Jackson as an ambassador to the black community. He could scorn the minuet of courtship Jackson demanded during every presidential election without being tarnished as a racist. Clinton's record on affirmative action in promoting blacks in Arkansas was good. He had close ties to a new generation of powerful, sophisticated politicians who were displacing Jesse Jackson as African-American leaders, men like Vernon Jordan, who would later head Clinton's transition team, and Ron Brown, chairman of the Democratic Party, who would become Clinton's Commerce Secretary. A decision was taken that Jesse Jackson should be marginalised by the Clinton campaign. It was only a matter of finding an opportunity.

The antipathy which developed between the two men was clear for all to see. At a black women's function which they both attended, Clinton kept to the back of the stage to avoid even being photographed with the black leader. Jackson called mockingly: 'Hey, Mr. Bill, come and shake the folks' hand.'

'It seems,' Jackson told me in Detroit one day during a voter registration drive, that Clinton's 'first pre-occupation was to regain the

"Reagan Democrats", and there is not enough time to spend nurturing and inspiring those who had never left.'

Jackson, a dapper figure with neat moustache, gold-buttoned blazer and tasselled shoes, who relished the reputation of power broker in the Democratic leadership, was reduced in 1992 to trying to persuade blacks to register to vote in rust-belt cities like Detroit. The task was made palatable by a $1.5 million grant to the Rainbow Coalition from the Democratic Party National Committee and by the knowledge that it would assist black candidates running for Congress or the Senate.

Most blacks in the United States do not vote and Jackson had a formidable task. In Detroit only 12 percent of African-American adults turned out to vote in the 1988 presidential election. Inner-city blacks believed that the American system was loaded against them. Two in five black children live in poverty in the United States and African-Americans are three times more likely than whites to live in a single-parent family. Infant mortality among blacks is higher than in Malaysia. Blacks account for 12.1 percent of the US population but 28.8 percent of AIDS cases. Homicide is the leading cause of death among black males between fifteen and thirty-four, of whom one in five has a criminal record.

In Detroit, Jackson reminded rallies of the struggle for black rights, of how twenty-nine years earlier, when civil rights supporters travelled to Washington to hear Martin Luther King, 'we had to relieve our tired bodies in humiliation behind cars and trees as the Holiday Inns and the Howard Johnsons were closed to us.' They must 'do what Mandela cannot do.' He asked people if they would like to serve as a juror in the Rodney King case, when four white policemen were found not guilty of beating a black. After a chorus of 'Yes', he reminded them that only registered voters could sit on a jury. Only by voting could they influence the political process and address the crisis of poverty in the black community and keep hope alive, he said. It was his constant refrain – 'Keep hope alive! Keep hope alive!'

Jackson also attacked the popular perception of the poor as welfare cheats. 'Most poor people are not on welfare,' he said. 'They put food in hamburgers. They change beds in hotels. They work in the hospitals. They wipe the bottoms of those that are sick. When they get sick they cannot afford to lie in the beds they make up each day.' He would raise up his audience, begging them to look after children and stop violence. 'Dogs raise their puppies,' he told one meeting. 'Cats raise their kittens, cows raise their calves. Surely men and women, just a little lower then the angels, must raise the babies that they make. You are not a man because you make a baby. You've got to raise the baby.' Amid a chorus of 'Yes' from young women, he cried: 'You've got to break the cycle of babies making babies'. In the old days, he said, 'the big threat was the rope, now we lose our lives through dope.' 'Stop the violence,' he would cry. 'Stop the violence,' they would reply. 'Save the children.' 'Save the children.' 'Down with dope.' 'Down with dope.' 'Up with hope.' 'Up with hope.' 'Keep hope alive.' 'Keep hope alive.' As if it was an afterthought, Jackson would tell his listeners that it was 'in their objective interests' to vote for the Democratic candidate for president.

Clinton's opportunity to demonstrate his independence from Jackson came at a June conference of the Rainbow Coalition in Washington where both men shared the programme with a little-known rap singer called Sister Souljah, real name Lisa Williamson. Sister Souljah had been quoted shortly after the Los Angeles riots in April as saying: 'If black people kill black people every day, why not have a week and kill white people? ... So if you're a gang member and you would normally be killing somebody, why not kill a white person?'

Instead of ignoring her presence and paying lip service in his speech to Jackson's ten-year, trillion-dollar plan to rebuild America, as Dukakis or Mondale might have done, Clinton attacked the rap singer. 'If you took the words "black" and "white" and reversed them, you might think David Duke was giving that speech,' he said, referring to the former Ku Klux Klan leader running for the Republican presidential nomination.

Jackson, who had been sitting stony-faced at the table beside Clinton with his chin resting on the palm of his hand, straightened up abruptly, his eyes narrowing at what he interpreted, correctly, as an attempt to embarrass him. Clinton's ploy worked. Jackson accused him afterwards of exploiting the rap singer to appeal to conservative whites, but it mattered little. Clinton had pulled off a tactical coup. His remark was popular with white voters and with blacks who did not like Jackson. It put Clinton on the side of the majority in an angry debate which happened to be going on over soul music. At the time, police all over America were protesting about Time Warner's release of a song called 'Cop Killer' by Ice-T which included the words 'I'm 'bout to bust some shot off/I'm 'bout to dust some cops off.'

Just before the Democratic Convention in July, Clinton named Al Gore, a Tennessee senator with the respectability of a suburban high school principal and a record of service in Vietnam, as his running mate. Gore had run for president in 1988 as a conservative southern Democrat with a strong record on the environment. Privately a lot of fun, his wooden, self-righteous public performances failed to impress voters.

He tells a joke against himself. 'How can you tell Al Gore from a roomful of Secret Service agents? Answer: he's the stiff one.'

Gore was an inspired choice for Clinton – he helped consolidate conservative voters. The Tennessee senator had broken with his party to vote for the MX missile, the B-1 bomber and the Gulf War. He epitomised secure, middle-America family values. Al Gore was married happily without a hint of scandal. In 1985, at the initiative of his wife Tipper, he had organised Senate hearings on rock music lyrics that the Gores felt glorified casual sex, violence and satanic worship. The result was the appearance of warning labels on US music products so that parents could monitor what their children were buying. At the same time, Gore was in favour with politically-correct liberals because of his strong record on the environment. The Clintons and Gores lined up at the governor's mansion in Little Rock to present the new, wholesome Democratic Party ticket to the nation.

The image here was the message – two youthful-looking high achievers, safe southern centrists rather than east-coast liberals, with behind them, in a line, their good-looking families, all of them blond (or almost) and winsome: Hillary Clinton, her daughter Chelsea, three of the four Gore children, Kristin, Albert and Sarah, and Tipper Gore.

On the calibrated scale in the dial-groups, the needles moved upwards. The positive ratings began to prevail over the negative. The stage was set for a successful Democratic Party Convention where the findings of the Manhattan Project could be put fully into operation.

The Convention began on 14 July in a stifling hot New York. Standing on the floor of the immense auditorium in Madison Square Gardens and gazing up (in awe) at the stage constructed for the four-yearly event, arriving guests realised that this was going to be as

THE MANHATTAN PROJECT 55

much showbiz as politics. The stage was on five levels, painted in pastel shades of blue and pink and curved as if designed for a Fred Astaire and Ginger Rogers dance spectacular. It seemed appropriate when I looked in on the morning of the grand opening that there should be a chorus line rehearsing for a Convention musical interlude, kicking their legs in the air. As they finished, a producer's voice called from the empty stalls: 'Hold it, that's right, applause, applause, more applause, now exit.'

The Convention was to be a Broadway spectacular, a carefully-scripted show with dancing, singing and less real debate than a Soviet Communist Party Congress. Reality would merge with fantasy: the auditorium was dominated by a mammoth TV screen made up of sixty-four individual screens so that delegates could watch the action live or on TV. The purpose of the four-day extravaganza was clearly to ensure that everyone would know 'A Star Is Born.'

When delegates crowded in, it was evident that the only items on the programme which mattered were the nomination of Bill Clinton and his prime-time televised acceptance speech. No-one listened to routine addresses from the podium. Wandering around the floor during debates, I encountered a man ringing a bell, another with a false nose, a third cradling a sleeping baby. Men in baggy shorts and ten-gallon hats argued and joked with women in business suits. People talked, gossiped, waved placards and looked for celebrities.

Among the famous faces in the California section was Oliver Stone, director of the controversial film *JFK* about the death of President Kennedy. He wore a button saying: 'Paranoids have the facts.' Asked if he had yet established Ross Perot's whereabouts on the day Kennedy was assassinated, he replied: 'Give me a break. We still haven't found out where George Bush was.' All around him, Jerry Brown supporters kept up a chant of 'Let Jerry speak!' in protest against a ruling that no-one could speak without endorsing Clinton, which the former California Governor was unwilling to do.

Brown was nowhere to be seen. He was staying in a shelter for homeless people in New York, people said. He got Clinton on the telephone at the Intercontinental Hotel, then put him on hold. After five minutes waiting, the Arkansas Governor hung up.

Outside, there was madness. Madison Square Garden is surrounded by streets which cater for all tastes. On one side is the Capuchin church of St. John and the Blarney Stone pub. On another, beneath a ten-storey advertisement for Camel cigarettes, is a peepshow with 'live girls' and a row of porn shops where drug dealers trade openly. A drug gang was broken up by the Guardian Angels, the swaggering New York vigilantes, just before the Convention opened on 14 July. Several Guardian Angels in red berets loitered on the crowded pavement, looking tough for the benefit of delegates. People shouted at their leader Curtis Silwa: 'Curtis, good to see you!' Not long before, he had been shot and wounded, or so he claimed. He held court on the kerb with a live iguana perched on his beret, placed there by a cackling old Japanese woman.

The committed and the crazies were out in force to welcome the Democrats. On Eighth Avenue, protestors lined up behind barriers to shout about Haiti, Croatia, Kosovo, animal rights and abortion. Young men from the 'No Greater Love Ministry' handed out leaflets, shoulder to shoulder with touts distributing flyers for the topless bars.

Into this cauldron of heat and noise came several thousand women in one of the biggest-ever demonstrations for abortion and women's rights in the city's history. Black and white, young and old, they chanted in unison: 'Not the Church, not the state, women must decide their fate,' and 'Hey! Hey! Ho! Ho! George Bush has got to go.' One woman carried a placard saying: 'Free Barbara Bush!' As they passed Madison Square Garden they chanted: 'We're women, we're angry, we vote.'

These words were echoed inside by the silver-haired Democratic Governor of Texas, Ann Richards, who cut through the uproar on the floor to bring the Convention to its feet by declaring: 'My name is Ann Richards and I'm pro-choice and I vote.' Barbara Mikulski, the first woman to be elected as a Democratic senator, followed her to say: 'This is the year of the woman. Never again will a woman come before a committee of the United States Senate and then be assaulted for telling the truth.' The Democratic Party was clearly the beneficiary of the anger of women over the treatment of the law professor, Anita Hill, when she testified at Senate committee hearings the previous autumn that she had been sexually harassed by George Bush's Supreme Court nominee, Clarence Thomas.

There was excitement in the air – Clinton's approval ratings were rising sharply in the polls – and growing hope of a new Democratic era.

The Clinton programme was designed to have broad appeal. Called 'Putting People First', it proposed a programme to rebuild America's roads and transportation systems, affordable health-care for all and higher taxes on the rich.

The programme stated: 'We will lower the tax burden on middle-class Americans by asking the very wealthy to pay their fair share. Middle-class taxpayers will have a choice between a children's tax credit or a significant reduction in their income tax rate.'

Former Congresswoman Barbara Jordan, a gifted and powerful black orator, hunched down over the microphone to warn the Democratic Party not to desert its liberal traditions. 'The American Dream is not dead. It is not dead, it is gasping for breath but it is not dead,' she said. 'But there is no time to waste because the American Dream is slipping away from too many. It is slipping away from too many black and brown mothers and their children ... When you talk about change,' she asked, 'what do you mean? Change from what to what?'

An answer of sorts was given by New York Governor Mario Cuomo – the mafioso remark by Clinton forgiven if not forgotten – who nominated Governor Clinton as Democratic candidate for president with the words: 'It's time for change. It's time for someone smart enough to know, strong enough to do and sure enough to lead. The comeback kid. A new voice for a new America.'

Here in Manhattan, the Manhattan Project finally triumphed. The focus groups had warmed to Clinton when they were told of the hardships he had to overcome in his life, of the loss of his father and of his problems with his alcoholic step-father and of his marriage and daughter. Now a biographical video was shown to the hushed Convention as it waited for his acceptance speech, emphasising with soft focus the sacrifices and the tragedies and the family values which had moulded Clinton's career along the road from Hope to Broadway. In the video, Clinton described how, when Chelsea was born, 'I stood in that delivery room. I was overcome with the thought that God had given me a blessing my own father never knew, the chance to hold my child in my arms.' He related how during the New Hampshire primary he and Hillary sat with Chelsea to watch the pre-recorded television interview in which he admitted to marriage problems and how he had asked Chelsea afterwards: 'What do you think?' to which she replied:

'I think I'm glad you're my parents.'

Everyone craned to look at Hillary and Chelsea in the VIP seats. Since her assertive personality had become a problem, Hillary Clinton had transformed herself from an assertive career woman into a coy, wide-eyed mother figure, red-cheeked with excitement over her cookie contest with Barbara Bush. She was referred to now in campaign releases as Hillary Clinton rather than Hillary Rodham Clinton, and she talked in interviews about child-rearing and recipes. 'I'm just an old-fashioned patriot,' she said. 'I cry at the Fourth of July when kids put crepe paper on their bicycle wheels.' She had to 'pinch herself' to believe she was going to see her husband nominated for president. Her role in the White House would be as 'the voice for children'.

When Al Gore addressed the delegates he, like the presidential candidate, dwelt at length on family tragedy. He described how his six-year-old son, Albert III, was hit by a car in front of the Memorial Stadium in Baltimore and how he and Tipper had spent a month in hospital with their son, nursing him back to health. 'I ran to his side and held him and called his name, but he was limp and still, without breath or pulse,' he said. 'His eyes were open only with the empty stare of death, and we prayed, the two of us, there in the gutter, with only my voice.' Again the cameras turned and necks twisted, to look at the boy squirming in embarrassment in his seat.

At the grand finale of this slick, sentimental Broadway show, the Clinton and Gore families paraded around the stage and gathered for a tableau of happy domesticity. The use of children in the presentation of the Democratic ticket to win electoral support was exploitative, a cynical exercise in image manipulation. But in the country which gave the world the situation comedy and the soap opera, few objected to what was, in popular parlance, a 'defining' moment for the potential new leader of the Western world.

We were watching a political ritual of modern America, a bid for power by a gifted and intellectual leader who felt it necessary to package himself first and foremost as a loving and beloved family man who could be trusted to keep alive the American Dream of a happy and wholesome future. The tableau on the stage in Madison Square Garden also, of course, helped to lay the ghost of Gennifer Flowers.

Clinton did not forget that the Manhattan Project had underlined the need to make change and hope the theme of his speech. 'Our values – freedom, democracy, individual rights and free enterprise – they have triumphed around the world,' he said, accepting the nomination. 'And yet, just as we have won the Cold War abroad, we are losing the battles for economic opportunity and justice here at home. Now that we have changed the world, it's time to change America. I have news for the forces of greed and the defenders of the status quo: your time has come and gone. It's time for change in America.' He finished to a huge roar of cheering with words suggested by Hillary: 'I end tonight where it all began for me: I still believe in a place called Hope.' To enhance the feeling of buoyant optimism, the music which filled the arena was 'Can't Stop Thinking About Tomorrow', displacing for the first time the traditional 'Happy Days Are Here Again'.

A few hours earlier, as Clinton was putting the final touches to his acceptance speech, James Carville, his chief strategist, had come rushing into his room. 'AP is reporting that Perot is dropping out,' he announced. The Dallas billionaire who had put himself forward as an independent candidate had quit the race, he said. 'Damn,' replied Clinton, 'Perot is my main man.'

Chapter 3

INSPECTOR PEROT

I'm mad as hell, and I'm not going to take it anymore.

PADDY CHAYEVSKY, *NETWORK*, 1976

LARRY KING IS A FIFTY-EIGHT-YEAR-OLD, five-times-divorced, nice-guy interviewer from Brooklyn whose real name is Zeiger. He hosts the *Larry King Live* talk show on CNN Television. To enhance a sense of intimacy on his show, King appears in shirt-sleeves and braces and his guests, personalities who range from presidents to pop stars, are always shown in close-up, sitting across a narrow desk. The guest on the night of 20 February 1992, two days after the New Hampshire primary election, was Ross Perot, a short, skinny Texas billionaire with jug ears. King opened his show with the words: 'About a third of the voters in the New Hampshire primary said they wished somebody else was running, and some undoubtedly have this guy in mind.' He turned to Perot. 'Are you going to run?' he asked.

'No,' said Perot.

'Is there any scenario in which you would run for president? ... Can you give me a scenario in which you'd say – OK, I'm in?'

'No, no, I don't want to,' replied Perot.

'I know, but is there a scenario?' asked King.

'I've got all these everyday folks ... writing me in longhand,' replied Perot '... I would simply say, all those folks who are constantly writing and calling, if you feel so strongly about this, number one, I will not run as either a Democrat or a Republican because I will not sell out to anybody but the American people –'

'So you'd run as an independent?' interrupted King.

'Number two – if you're that serious – you, the people, are that serious – you register me in fifty states, and if you're not willing to organise and do that –'

'Wait a minute. Are you saying ...? Wait a minute.'

'– then this is all talk.'

'Hold it, hold it, hold it, hold it.'

'Now stay with me, Larry.'

'Wait, wait, are you saying ...?"

He was. Ross Perot was declaring his willingness to run for president, with the condition that people who wanted Perot in the race put his name on the ballot in every state, a task involving the collection of millions of signatures.

Many people had for years been pressing the cocky computer tycoon to stand for president. In 1987, the chairman of the National Governors' Association – his name was Bill Clinton – had suggested he run for the White House. In November 1991, Tennessee Democrat, John Jay Hooker, long an admirer of Perot, had managed, after several attempts, to get him on the telephone and urged him to run. Hooker thereafter rang almost daily to plead and cajole, convinced that only someone like Perot, a self-made billionaire with a simple faith in his ability to get things done, could save America from debt and decline. Hooker, knowing that his man was on the verge of succumbing, had primed Larry King with the right questions. It still took King fifty minutes to draw out the right response.

Perot's declaration was like a spark in dry brush. The next day the switchboard of his computer company in Texas, Perot Systems Corp., seized up as people rang from all over the country to volunteer to help. A telephone bank with a hundred lines and a small army of volunteers was quickly installed on a floor of Perot's Dallas tower in Merit Drive. As the draft-Perot movement took off, the number of lines was increased to 1,200. The calls kept increasing at an amazing rate. On one single day, a quarter of a million calls were logged. Within a few weeks there were Perot volunteer organisations in every state.

What was it about this folksy billionaire with a high-pitched Texan twang that made him so appealing? Perot's story was, as he put it himself, the fulfilment of the American Dream. 'I have lived that dream,' he often said. His story was one of hard work and good fortune. He was born in Texarkana, a town which straddles the Arkansas-Texas border, where his father was a cotton-broker. As a boy he broke horses and sold newspapers. From Texarkana junior college he graduated to the US Naval Academy in Annapolis, served in the navy for four years, then left to sell computers at the Dallas office of IBM.

In the late 1950s, selling computers was, in his words, like selling umbrellas on a rainy day: everyone wanted them. IBM at the time was retailing only computer hardware, which meant that clients had to hire groups of programmers to tailor the machines to their needs. Better to offer customers a package of computer services, said Perot. IBM wasn't interested so, with $1,000 from his wife's savings, he left in 1962 and set up his own company, Electronic Data Systems Inc. (EDS).

He struck it lucky almost immediately, winning huge contracts from the federal government which was being swamped with health-care claims from new welfare programmes, Medicare and Medicaid. Perot needed a highly-disciplined workforce for his EDC operations. His men sometimes had to take over computer systems in the face of hostile staff who feared they would be made redundant. He turned to 'Uncle Sam' for his recruits. Ex-Marines and army officers formed the backbone of his computer hit-squads, which took on names like 'First Wave', 'Dirty Dozen' and 'The Wild Bunch'. They were disciplined, hard-working and ruthless. After local operators sabotaged the computers in a Jan Juan company, pouring sand on the disc-drives before the EDS men could get at them, take-overs were conducted like military operations. Executives would meet with local programmers in one office while the hit men were sealing off the machines elsewhere in the building.

Perot maintained an atmosphere of militarism by banning facial hair and insisting on suits and white shirts. His crews of young, driven executives became known as the 'Dallas White Shirts'. He sacked any male employee guilty of marital infidelity. 'If she can't trust him, how can I?' he said.

EDS was a huge success. When the company went public in 1968, Perot's share was valued at a phenomenal $1.5 billion. Overnight, the man who looked like he should be behind the counter of a hardware store became a cult figure in corporate America and the Perot legend was born. In 1984, after a near-disastrous venture into Wall Street, Perot sold EDS for $2.55 billion to General Motors which was streamlining its data-processing operation, and he joined the GM board. Later, after an acrimonious public feud with GM chairman Roger Smith, Perot accepted a $700 million settlement and pulled out. He then founded Perot Systems Corp. to fight his former firm, EDC, for its health-care business.

Ross Perot ruled his empire from an office in Dallas where Norman Rockwell pictures hung on the walls and the fangs of a rattlesnake were displayed in a glass bowl. He was a complicated figure, a loner in politics who saw himself as the champion of the little fellow. He is the classic outsider, but at the same time a consummate insider who lobbied and rewarded Congress members for helping to push through tax breaks which brought him even greater wealth. He was a frequent visitor to the Nixon White House two decades earlier where he offered to spend millions of dollars to organise America's 'silent majority' in favour of the Vietnam war. Charles Colson, special counsel to Richard Nixon, recalled to a reporter that Perot never made good on his promises. One day Colson told him in his White House office: 'Ross, it's time to put up or shut up. If we don't see some money within a week, I'm going to decide you're nothing but a phoney.' Perot left and never spoke to him again.

Perot also tried unsuccessfully in 1969 to persuade Nixon to give the silent majority a voice through the concept of the electronic town hall – televised meetings at which the president would chat with hand-picked voters. He was ahead of his time. It was to be nearly a quarter of a century later before another president, Bill Clinton, would make the electronic town hall a valuable tool to maintain a cosy relationship with the American public.

Impatient and wilful, Perot was also capable of acts of great kindness. When a Dallas policeman was paralysed in a skiing accident in Colorado, the computer billionaire had him brought home in his private plane and he paid all medical expenses. He flew an executive's wife to an eye specialist at his own expense. He financed a school for inner-city kids.

Perot also inspired intense loyalty, and went to great lengths to protect his executives. When two Perot emissaries were jailed in Teheran's Gasr prison in 1978 over a contractual dispute between EDS and the Shah of Iran, Perot sent a paramilitary team to Iran under Colonel Arthur 'Bull' Simons to organise their escape. Conveniently, the Khomeini revolution provided a riot which freed the two men along with the rest of the inmates. The episode became the subject of a book, *On Wings of Eagles*, by British writer Ken Follett.

Such stories helped to enhance and build the legend. Rescuing Americans abroad became an obsession with Perot, who put up money for an abortive attempt by Colonel Oliver North, the figure at the centre of the 'Irangate' scandal, to ransom US hostages in Beirut. He also financed some bizarre ventures by mercenaries into south-east Asia in search of missing POWs. He has always maintained, on slim evidence, that the US government needlessly abandoned men missing in action.

There was a dark side to Perot, as those who crossed him found out. Law-school student Jan Scruggs, a co-founder of the Vietnam Memorial Fund, approached Perot and solicited $160,000 to finance a design competition for the nation's Vietnam war memorial to be erected beside the Lincoln memorial in Washington. The entries were unveiled on 6 May 1981 at Andrews Air Force Base. The winning design, by twenty-one-year-old Yale student, Maya Ying Lin, had two black granite walls starting at ground level and gradually sinking ten feet into a depression to meet in a V, with the name of every American who died engraved in the stone. Conservative veterans were infuriated. They thought the V shape was an allusion to the hippies' anti-war salute and that the colour black signified that the war was a national disgrace. Perot took their side. He had made Vietnam veterans his cause, adopting the 1,400 prisoners of war who returned in 1973, throwing parties for them and finding them jobs.

Perot called Scruggs and demanded that the design be changed and a flag and statue be added as a heroic counterpoint, as many veterans were demanding. The committee of the Memorial Fund refused. Today the wall, one of the most haunting war memorials in the world, is a place of daily pilgrimage for Americans. But Scruggs has only unhappy memories of his entanglement with Perot. The despotic tycoon had him investigated by several agencies and demanded an audit of the memorial to try to prove misuse of funds. Nothing was found. Scruggs said he never wanted to go through anything like that again.

Perot's total confidence that all problems had a solution conjured up the can-do spirit of America. He was a problem-solver with a gift for sound-bites. 'You can't get pearls without irritating the oysters,' he would say. The patriotic billionaire was good at portraying himself as a little-guy populist and volunteers saw him as a political faith healer, the embodiment of the national will, Huckleberry Finn in a business suit leading a revolt of the colonies against the distant and uncaring centre. A cartoon by 'Rogers' in *The Pittsburgh Press* expressed the contradictions of the Perot revolution: it showed a middle-aged man with a can of beer saying: 'I'm sick and tired of politicians who are out of touch with the common man. I'm voting for that Texas billionaire.'

People seemed to believe that Perot truly could do something about the economy and the paralysis of national politics. At the point when he entered the campaign, neither of the main parties inspired hope for the future. Bush lacked vision and could offer only a lacklustre economic programme, and the Democrats appeared to be a hopeless bunch led by 'Slick Willie'.

Third-party candidates have rarely done well in American politics but never before had an independent with a reputation for taking on the system come along prepared, as Perot claimed he was, to spend $100 million of his own money. All over the country volunteer Perot committees were formed. What happened in Annapolis, capital of Maryland, was typical. Joan Vinson, aged sixty-one, prominent in the bay-side town's public life, began telephoning friends to get together a 'Perot for President' committee. She was one of many people across the US who had come in contact with and admired Perot. Her husband, F4 pilot Bobby G. Vinson, was shot down over North Vietnam and had never returned. She had first met Perot in 1969, she told me, when he took up the cause of Vietnam combatants missing in action. Joan Vinson booked a room in the Ramada Inn for a hundred people. Word got out and 750 turned up, causing chaos in the hotel where a Miss Maryland contest was under way. 'They stormed in with the intensity of a Tornado,' she recalled. 'They were one-third Republican, one-third Democrat and one-third people who had never been involved in politics. There were well-to-do people and union workers with the Teamsters. Perot was saying to us what was in the hearts and minds of the American people. What Perot said about honesty and integrity in government, about jobs leaving the country, struck a chord with us. People with a good income, looking forward to a peaceful retirement, were facing a future where pension funds had no money. Younger people looking to the future were saying, I don't know what it holds for me. In all walks of life people were looking at the collapse of America. People think an individual can make a difference. As Ross Perot said: "If you have problems with the government look in the mirror."'

From an office overlooking the harbour on Chesapeake Bay donated by Bennett Crain, an Annapolis lawyer, volunteers set forth to shopping malls to gather 63,169 signatures, the 3 percent of the Maryland electorate needed to get Perot on the ballot for the presidential election. A 'Perot-meter' shaped like a giant thermometer was set up in the corner of the office to show the latest count. Posters were distributed with Uncle Sam pointing his finger outwards, with the words 'AMERICA NEEDS PEROT'.

Perot shunned conventional campaign tactics, preferring to appear on talk shows or to go on highly-publicised visits to accept the completed ballot petitions. When 150,000 signatures had been collected in Maryland, more than twice the number needed, he came from Texas to receive them at a rally at the picturesque Annapolis harbour. Perot made the last part of the journey across Chesapeake Bay in a crab boat, the *Ada Marie*, accompanied by a flotilla of small craft trailing banners saying 'Vote Ross for Boss.' When I came alongside in a fishing boat on which I had been given a ride, Perot, standing under the sun roof flanked by four unsmiling men in suits and ties, lifted a crab and waved it, laughing merrily. At the Annapolis pier, Colonel Mustard's Ceremonial Brass Band played and a woman sang 'Wake up America, Perot's the way to go, / Workin' for the people, working for Perot.' A crowd of several thousand cheered. Perot mounted a paddle boat and declared: 'Everywhere I go there are people like you with stars in their eyes who are excited about taking their country back.'

At such appearances, Perot avoided any statements of policy. He freely admitted he had no detailed plans, only a faith in his ability to tackle problems like a mechanic by 'lifting the hood and fixing it.' The way to make the economy work was to stabilise the job base 'because that will stabilise the tax base.' On business – 'there are industries we've got to keep in this country and we're losing them right and left. We've got to target them; we've got to make sure that we're first and best. In Japan they have an intelligent supportive relationship between government and industry. Study it. Analyse it. Improve on it, instead of trying to dismantle our companies.'

The tax code was a mess, he said. 'We should replace our tax system and with these criteria; it's got to pay the bills, it's got to be fair, and it should generally be paperless for most people. You bring together the people with the most experience, put together two or three plans, explain them to the American people in detail over television, get a consensus from the American people about what the new tax plan should be.' It was their fault that the country was in a mess. 'The first thing you have to do in our country is blame somebody, right? Well, go home tonight and look in the mirror. You and I are at fault because we own this country and there is the problem in a nutshell. We have abdicated our ownership responsibility ... We own this country. We've got to put the country back in control of the owners. In plain Texas talk, it's time to take out the trash and clean the barn, or it's going to be too late.'

Such populist, common-sense language from a man who epitomised success had enormous appeal to disillusioned voters. The recession and the national debt as well as the bipartisan gridlock in Washington had left voters contemptuous and distrustful of both parties. Perot was pointing to a way out. 'He's got common sense and leadership and brains; my goodness, what more do you want?' exclaimed Earl Greer, a retired naval officer at the Perot Annapolis headquarters. Among the crowd in Annapolis was William Ozkaptan, a thirty-four-year-old travel agent with a minor role in history – as a US military employee in Germany he had written on the Berlin Wall: 'THIS WALL WILL FALL, BELIEFS WILL BECOME REAL'. The graffito had inspired Ronald Reagan, when he saw it on a visit to West Germany and thought it was written by a German, to make his famous plea: 'President Gorbachev, tear down this wall.' Said Ozkaptan: 'I'm sick and tired of politicians not doing what's right. Ross Perot will win this election. The political system will fall just like the Berlin Wall.'

In the days after the Larry King show, Perot climbed steadily in the polls. The high point of his popularity came in the second week in May when a *Time*/CNN poll showed him leading the field with 33 percent approval rating compared with 28 percent for Bush and 24 percent for Clinton. His army of volunteers had grown in every state. But its commanders in the field were amateurs. They were without direction. Perot did not want outsiders coming in to tell him what to do, but, political professionals were badly needed to give the campaign coherence. They appeared in the shape of Ed Rollins, a campaign strategist who had managed Ronald Reagan's landslide victory in 1984, and Hamilton Jordan, President Carter's chief of staff, a charts-and-graphs expert regarded as one of the best political professionals in the business. They were drawn to Perot by the energy and originality of his movement. 'I too was frustrated with the political system,' said Rollins, who had also served Presidents Nixon and Ford.

'I had been around politics and campaigns for thirty years and I saw a system that wasn't working.'

Rollins and Jordan were at first cordially welcomed and made co-chairmen of the Perot campaign. Rollins, a balding, bearded political pro with the same highly-tuned instincts as James Carville of the Clinton camp, immediately saw the dangers ahead. He believed the free ride Perot was getting from the media would not last. He told Perot: 'Ross, you have to understand, this is war; no one's going to get murdered, but don't think it's not every bit as tough. The weapons are lethal in a different way.' He tried to convince Perot of the need to define himself, rather than let the media depict him for what he was – an eccentric little rich man.

'Ross, there's two words I want you to write on your mirror every morning,' Rollins told Perot. 'One is KOOK and the other is HOPE. If they make you into a kook, or if anything you do makes you into a kook, you lose. The second thing is, every single day you've got to go out and be the candidate of hope – the person who can change the direction of this country.'

Rollins had instinctively judged the mood of the electorate – without the benefit of a Manhattan Project. People wanted to be given hope that real change was possible by an assault on a political system which had failed them. The two imported political professionals also organised their own focus groups, and these also suggested the need for more personal information about the candidate, more about Perot the man, his modest beginnings, his family, how he made his money, how he had stood up to the system and taken it on. But the Perot headquarters people lived in a different world, one of corporate ethics and secrecy. Perot had always run his companies like authoritarian nation-states. His executives regarded the professional political cadres as a virus which would destroy their immune system and tarnish their grassroots campaign. When Rollins and Jordan presented Perot with a $147 million budget for research, advertising and campaigning, Perot gave it the thumbs down. He challenged the finding of polls showing that 70 percent of voters wanted to know his specific policy positions. He rejected the notion that he had to campaign to become president.

'The American people don't care about issues,' he said. 'Why do I want to pay for this when I can go to Larry King?' he asked, when presented with prepared TV advertisements he would have to pay for.

Rollins brought in from San Francisco a gifted film producer, Hal Riney, who had made Reagan's 'Morning Again in America' commercials in 1984. Riney prepared a rush of a five-minute biographical film. Perot hated it. 'This is crap,' he said to Jordan after viewing it in his Dallas office. 'You're supposed to be a pro. You tell me this is supposed to be world class, like you know what you're doing. What the hell do I need you for? You've wasted my money. My money! On this crap!' Later, Jordan said to a colleague: 'This is horseshit, I'm getting out of here.' But he changed his mind and stayed on.

Perot seem justified at first in rejecting professional advice. His appearances around the country drew enthusiastic crowds of 'Perotists'. After a five-city, interactive-TV exchange in May, when he addressed his followers from gigantic screens, a crowd in Topeka, Kansas, marched to the state capitol building with six times more signatures than needed. But he peaked as the media began taking a closer and more critical look. The press started to define him in the very way Rollins had warned – as a kook. A series of news reports appeared portraying the Dallas billionaire as 'Inspector Perot', a busybody who investigated his business competitors, political opponents and employees. Critical stories appeared about how he treated his staff. ABC television discovered that an EDS employee, Bobby Joe King, had been fired in 1986 after he told his supervisor that he had been in hospital with pneumonia as a result of contracting the AIDS virus; he had lost all his medical benefits and had filed a suit against the company which was settled out of court. Perot used off-duty policemen to monitor his telephone calls. He also paid $76,000 to a San Francisco firm, partly to investigate campaign workers whom Perot suspected of fraud.

Washington Post reporter David Remnick reported how in 1987, when interviewing Perot in his office, the diminutive billionaire had shown him a photograph of Richard Armitage, a defence official in charge of the POW issue, along with a Vietnamese girl, implying that he had been compromised by her. One story alleged that Perot had hired a private investigator to check out a Jewish literature professor at Vanderbilt whom his daughter Nancy was dating. The most startling revelation was that the independent candidate had once investigated the US president. In 1986 Perot had looked into a deal under which the firm of Pennzoil, headed by a friend of George Bush, received a $48 million tax credit for donating land to the government. Perot tipped off the *Washington Post* anonymously at the time that it was a fraud: the land was worth less than the tax credit. He was motivated, it appeared, by anger at Bush's alleged failure to back up Perot's efforts to locate and rescue POWs in south-east Asia (none of whom was ever found). The same year Perot had also passed on to Bush, then vice-president, word that his two sons may have been engaged in improper business activities. Presented with these stories, President Bush said: 'I'm sick about it if it's true ... If he was having my children investigated, this is beyond the pale ... I think the American people will reject that kind of tactic.' Perot countered by producing a 1986 note from Bush thanking him for the tip-off about his sons. He protested: 'The Republican dirty tricks committee has been carefully putting this together [in] a carefully orchestrated plan to try to damage me.'

Republicans declared open season on Perot. Bush's press secretary, Marlin Fitzwater, called him 'dangerous and destructive' and a 'monster'. Vice-President Dan Quayle described him as a 'temperamental tycoon'. They suggested that his long-standing obsession with POWs had turned him into a conspiracy theorist. The Republican leader in Congress, Bob Michel, described Perot as a mountebank who raised the spectre of 'authoritarianism'. Clinton held back, anxious to pick up Perot voters as the Texan's ratings began falling.

'Is this ever gonna get fun again?' Perot asked Rollins over a lunch in Dallas. 'Fun?' repeated Rollins. 'When I started, this thing was fun,' said Perot. Rollins replied that campaigns were never fun. 'It's like war. It's miserable. Running for office isn't fun. Winning is fun.'

The chances of Perot winning were already looking bleak by the time the Democratic Convention was getting under way in New York. Clinton was beginning to pull away from Bush and Perot in the polls. The more voters came to know about Clinton the person, the more they seemed to like him. The opposite was happening with Perot. As Clinton captured the television pictures and his approval rating climbed above 50 percent, Perot, with no campaign coverage or TV commercials, dropped to 20 percent.

Everything Perot did now went wrong. As the campaign fell apart he travelled to the annual convention of the National Association for the Advancement of Coloured People (NAACP) to secure support from black voters. It was his first address to any group other than his volunteers. He did not consult his professional handlers, and the speech was a disaster. At first he was warmly received. Then he turned to the subject of what happens when the economy goes into recession. 'I don't have to tell you who gets hurt first,' he said. 'You people, you people do.' Perot did not realise how insulting the reference to 'you people' had been to his black listeners until reporters told him.

'I live in a world of set-ups,' he snapped on the plane on the way home. Perot telephoned CNN president Tom Johnson. The master of the sound-bite complained: 'I've been sound-bitten to death,' and said that the sound-bite from the NAACP made him look like David Duke.

At Dallas headquarters Rollins was at his wits' end. None of his advice was heeded. 'I've been in campaigns before when I didn't know what a candidate was going to say. I've never been in a campaign when I didn't know where the candidate was,' he said in an account of his experiences. He had felt uneasy since one of Perot's close advisers had said to him over dinner: 'Ed, we're concerned about you doing this. There's your health to consider and your second marriage.' The remark was puzzling to Rollins. Not many people knew he had married twice or that he had had a mild stroke ten years previously.

After forty-five days his relationship with Perot came to an end. Perot had not entrusted him to run the campaign; worse still, Rollins suspected his employer was probing his loyalty by tapping his telephone. Morale was plummeting all round. High-profile supporters across the country were becoming disenchanted as the campaign lost steam. Katharine Hepburn's agent rang from New York to demand 'What's happening down there?' and warned that Perot was going down the drain in New York.

On 16 June, tight-lipped and scowling, Perot appeared at a press conference in Dallas to announce he was quitting. He explained that the revitalisation of the Democratic Party meant that an independent candidate could cause a paralysis in the electoral system. Everyone knew it was not the real reason. Perot had had enough. His reputation had taken a battering, he was outraged by the unfavourable media treatment and he was falling in the polls. To resurrect the campaign at this point he would have had to spend much more than the $100 million he had spoken about, and immediately.

In the corridors of his campaign headquarters, the Dallas White Shirts with their close-cut haircuts and polyester ties appeared with uniformed security guards. Robert Barkin, a communications consultant, told reporter Marie Brenner: 'It was like the scene in *The Empire Strikes Back* where Darth Vadar steps onto the bridge of the ship, but he is preceded by the surrogates who rush in and secure the area.' They began sealing rooms, shutting down computers and pulling out telephone lines. 'We have orders to turn off the computer,' a guard told Rollins's deputy, Charlie Leonard. 'Get the fuck out of here,' answered Leonard, who complained to Tom Luce, Perot's long-time associate, saying: 'Tom, this is an outrage.' One of the White Shirts told press spokeswoman, Liz Maas, as he turned off her screen: 'I'm logging you off, you no longer have access to this computer.' As guards ushered them out, another professional aide, Joe Canzeri, who had once worked for Reagan, cried out in disgust at the heavy-handed security tactics: 'They're boarding the buses for Buchenwald! They're taking us to Buchenwald!' Full-time paid staff recruited for the petition drive were asked to sign pledges before they left, stating they would 'agree to refrain from making any disparaging remarks or negative comments, either publicly or privately, directly or indirectly, regarding Ross Perot.' They also agreed 'not to disclose any information about ... conversations, interactions and anecdotes deriving from meetings with Ross Perot ... or the personality or management style of Ross Perot.'

Bill Clinton telephoned Perot from the Intercontinental Hotel in New York after Jim Carville broke the news of his withdrawal. 'Ross, no-one in American history ever moved as many people as you did,' he said. Perot's volunteers, who had bathed him in adulation for four months, were now indeed moved – to tears of anger and frustration. They could not believe that the man who had stirred their patriotism and summoned them into action with the promise of a political insurrection had abandoned them. Perot had made the case against George Bush and was now getting out of the way and leaving the field to Bill Clinton. A Perot petition volunteer in the street near Madison Square Garden in New York threw his lined sheets of paper on the ground and stamped on them in fury. 'Personally I feel betrayed and I think we have been victims of the greatest political con job in our lifetime,' said lawyer Matthew Lifflander, standing on a chair at the People for Perot headquarters in Lexington Avenue, New York. 'It simply isn't fair. He has forced the alienated to be even more alienated.'

All over the country the volunteers reacted with disbelief and anger. The Perot supporters I had got to know at Maryland headquarters were heartbroken. They were deeply disillusioned. It was hard not to sympathise with their feeling that they had been cruelly betrayed.

In Ventura County, California, in a scene reminiscent of Eastern Europe, volunteers tied a rope around the neck of an eight-foot statue of the 'Plain Texas Talker' and hauled it away in a dump truck. In north Dallas volunteers showed what they thought of Perot's decision to quit by massing in a formation for air-borne news photographers. The word they spelled out was 'chicken'.

Chapter 4

AMERICA FIRST

Yesterday the bird of night did sit,
Even at noonday, upon the market place,
Hooting and shrieking.

SHAKESPEARE, *JULIUS CAESAR*, ACT 1, SCENE 3

BUT THE JUG-EARED ROSS PEROT was not the only maverick figure to grab the limelight in this extraordinary election year. The first Republican candidate to run for the party's nomination for the 1992 presidential election was David Duke, a former Ku Klux Klan leader who once wore a white hood and carried a burning cross. He was opposed to immigration, free trade, foreign aid, federal assistance for minorities and civil rights, and he strongly favoured a greater use of capital punishment. If he hadn't been a neo-Nazi with a racist resumé, these policies might have got him further than they did, for they were little different from those of a significant section of the Republican Party.

Duke prepared for his attempt to win the Republican nomination by running for governor in the southern state of Louisiana in 1991. The very fact that he managed to get himself put forward by Louisiana Republicans as their only candidate for governor was a sign that, in this part of the country at least, something was seriously wrong in the party headed by the US president.

The Republican Party is a coalition embracing the religious right, blue-collar workers, southern whites, suburban conservatives and big business. It had survived intact throughout the years of the Cold War, thanks mainly to the adhesive of anti-communism. With the collapse of the Soviet Union there was no common enemy to rally the right. At the same time, there was widespread political alienation in the United States. Jobs were being lost. Industries were moving to Mexico. Wages were lower. Immigrants were pouring in. There was little optimism about the future. Voters believed that government had largely abandoned the middle class. There was an anger in the country over gridlock in Washington.

The danger at such a turning-point in United States history was that a demagogue of the right would harness these feelings of discontent and direct them into a campaign to unleash the protectionism and nativism which have always lurked beneath the surface of America. Enter David Duke.

As Duke's campaign for governor got under way, I drove north from New Orleans one chilly autumn day in 1991 and across Louisiana to the town of Monroe, where Duke was due to address a rally of his supporters. I turned on the car radio and tuned in to WWL870 New Orleans. The talk show host, Scoot, was having difficulty getting callers to discuss his topic of the day, which was the announcement by star basket-ball player Magic Johnson that he had contracted the AIDS virus. They wanted to debate only the election for governor, set for a week later on 16 November 1991. Duke was pitted against the Democratic Party candidate, former Governor Edwin Edwards, a silver-haired devotee of gambling casinos who had once turned up in Las Vegas with a suitcase of banknotes and had twice been indicted on corruption charges, though never convicted.

Some of the callers to the radio show said people should vote for the sixty-four-year-old Edwards rather than allow a Ku Klux Klan man to become governor. This was the choice of the driver of the red Cougar in front of me whose bumper sticker declared: 'VOTE FOR THE CROOK, IT'S IMPORTANT.' Others derided Duke's claim to be a born-again Christian who no longer believed in racial and religious hatred. The Holocaust, Duke had said, was a 'historical hoax perpetrated on Christians by Jews'. The Jews 'probably deserved to go into the ashbin of history'. Listeners were reminded of how Duke celebrated Hitler's birthday every year; as with so many zealots of the American right, Duke looked to fascist Europe for his role models.

I pulled into Waffle King for breakfast. At the counter a white salesman in his forties, whom the busty middle-aged waitress fawned over like a teenager, borrowed the business section of my *Times-Picayune* to check a share price.

'Forget the polls,' he said when the conversation came round to David Duke. 'I'd like for you to know this isn't going to the wire. Duke' – he pronounced the name 'Dook' like everyone else in Louisiana – 'will win sixty-forty.' He based his judgement on conversations with those people he met on his travels, small businessmen who worked in seafood, farming and petro-chemicals and who resented their taxes going to pay welfare cheques.

'I travel all over,' he explained. 'I listen to folks talking. They won't say it out but they will vote for Dook. They are fed up with women having babies just to get welfare. It's ridiculous, crazy. And what did Edwards ever do? He just ripped off the state, and he's fixing to do it again.'

All over mid-Louisiana there were Duke posters on sticks in the grassy verge. The biggest I saw, a huge hoarding with the words 'DUKE GOVERNOR', almost hid an advertisement proclaiming 'Sun Belt Exterminators. We Kill Bugs Better'. Along the road there were countless Baptist churches with tiny white spires, half-hidden among magnolia trees and azalea, camellia, redbud and myrtle shrubs. This was Protestant country, settled since the eighteenth century by English, Scots-Irish and Irish, in contrast to the mostly Roman Catholic French bayous of the south.

'Scoot' faded out and the voice of an evangelist came on the radio to say: 'The most wonderful thing about being a born-again Christian is that we can contact the Lord daily. Send up an SOS to the Holy Spirit today. Donations by Visa or Mastercard to the Christian Jew Hour, San Antonio.' On another station I heard: 'Folks, y'all gettin' FALSE INFORMATION about AIDS. They say a famous athlete has got so-called AIDS. Good people, there is NO SUCH THING as AIDS. It's a ruse by LIBERAL homosexuals to get PUBLIC FUNDS. AIDS is a MYTH.'

I stopped at the South of the Border Café where a juke-box, the old kind with moving coloured bubbles in plastic columns, was playing Dwight Yoakam's 'You Are The One'. In the 'convenience room' a long metal trough served as a public urinal. It was filled with hundreds of pennies – cent coins – many green with age. 'Yea, ain't that funny,' said Hilda, the waitress, when I asked her about the coins. As she placed a bowl of shrimp gumbo on my table, she said: 'Do you recall when Superglue first came out? Well, the owner stuck a penny there as a joke, to see who would try to take it. It's become a tradition now.' Sure she supported Duke, she said. 'That's all the talk you hear in the lounge.'

But there were many who hated what Duke stood for. As I drove along the two-lane road, where lorries crawled by with freshly-gathered cotton packed into wire cages, and still-unharvested cotton hung on withered stalks in the flat fields like candy floss, I came across Randy Smith's roadside provision store and poolhall. This was the heart of Dixie. But Randy Smith, the elderly white proprietor of the store, shook his head in despair at the choice offered to Louisiana in the election. 'I don't think most people will support Dook,' he said. 'There is no place for the Klan in modern America.'

Black and white kids, barely teenagers, played together on his two pool tables. It is a paradox that strikes most outsiders visiting the Deep South that small communities appear more integrated at parish level, and black and white people are more at ease with each other, than in many 'Yankee' states. It bears out the saying that in the northern cities they love the race, but hate the people, whereas in the southern states they love the people, but hate the race.

It was evening when I reached my destination, Northeast University outside Monroe, a bleak old industrial town which had been named after the first steamboat, *The James Monroe*, to arrive along the Ouachita River from the Mississippi in 1819. Duke was billed to address an evening rally of his followers in the assembly hall. At the door, tough-looking election workers gave out leaflets attacking the Democratic candidate.

One of these leaflets set the tone for the Duke campaign. It read: 'Edwin Edwards is my shepherd, I shall not want. He leadeth me beside still oil refineries and abandoned rice farms. Five thousand years ago Moses said – pack up your camel, pick up your shovel, move your ass and I will lead you to the promised land. Roosevelt said – lay down your shovel, sit on your ass, light up a Camel, this is the promised land. Edwards will take your shovel, sell your camel, kick your ass and tell you to be grateful.' It concluded: 'I'm glad I live in Louisiana. I'm glad I'm free. I wish I were a dog and Edwin Edwards was a tree.'

A red-faced man signalled the show was about to begin by holding aloft on the stage a coloured picture of Duke. The eight hundred people in the packed hall screamed and waved Duke placards. 'Dook, Dook, Dook,' they chanted, making a rutting, animal sound.

In the audience there were pretty young women, some with babies, dozens of heavily-built men in ten-dollar Duke baseball caps bought at the door, rows of middle-aged couples and an assortment of youths who mostly bunched up at the back. One was a startling Elvis look-alike with sideboards and high shirt collar. Even with people standing at the back, three hundred supporters were left outside in the cold after the hall filled up. The only black person in the hall was a television soundman.

I found myself sitting in the fifth row beside Ann, a young nurse from the village of Columbia, and her two friends. She told me she had come because she wanted Duke to do something to cut welfare payments and benefits which she was convinced were being abused.

'If a welfare baby has a runny nose they run to the hospital,' she said, scornfully. 'You should see them!'

She didn't agree with what Duke had said in the past about Hitler and the Ku Klux Klan, but she believed he had changed. 'To say he can't change is denying the Holy Spirit.'

One of her companions, Mary, also a nurse, leaned over from two seats away and interrupted defiantly: 'And what if he hasn't changed. Who cares anyway?'

'Shush, Mareeeee!' scolded Ann.

Most of the people in the hall were descended from poor white immigrant families who had settled in Louisiana not long after it became the eighteenth US state in 1812, so long ago that nobody much talked about or knew where they originally came from. In these parts of the United States there was no tradition of moving on, or of new people moving in. Nobody travelled much. 'I ain't never even bin in no airplane,' Ann said. They shared a long tradition of opposition by poor and middle-class whites to big government, and a feeling of political alienation when it appeared they had been abandoned by those that governed them. Racism was only one of many factors in their coming together behind Duke.

The appearance of the fair-haired, forty-one-year-old candidate at the back of the stage sent them into a frenzy. His pretty-boy good looks, the result of plastic surgery, brought screams from Ann and Mary. The emcee quietened them down for a prayer. 'Dear Lord, watch over our candidate, in Jesus' name we pray,' he said. Then followed a slide show: Duke with his family, Duke at prayer, Duke with the Stars and Stripes wrapped around him, Duke rugged in shirt sleeves – this produced frantic screams – Duke serious, Duke smiling.

When it was over, Duke came centre-stage to give his speech, flanked by two fat, unsmiling Louisiana state police officers in wide blue hats. When Duke strode to left or right during his oration, they escorted him in step, eyes front, jaws clamped tight and crossing one leg after the other, as if in some pantomime routine.

There was no overt racism in Duke's speech, which was restrained compared to previous racist candidates for Governor in Louisiana, like Willie Rainach who in 1959 declared: 'You don't have to discriminate against negroes. Nature has already discriminated against them.' There were reporters and television cameras in the hall, which meant code words had to be used.

When Duke called for 'equal rights for all', everyone knew he meant an end to affirmative action where job quotas were set aside for racial minorities. 'Welfare recipients' signified blacks. 'Drug dealers' meant blacks. 'New York' meant Jews. He called for a society of 'Christian values' where people could walk the streets without fear. He would ban welfare people from squandering money on lottery tickets, he said. They responded with loud cries of: 'You got it!' 'That's right,' 'Amen,' and 'Hallelujah'. When Duke said, 'We've got the death penalty in Louisiana, we've got to enforce it,' there were one or two shouts of 'Lynch them!'

Duke's anti-Washington message was popular, but his problem was that he was the wrong messenger. As election day aproached in Louisiana, it became clear that many members of the religious right, attracted by Duke's conservative views on welfare, crime and big government, could not stomach his crude attitudes on colour. Some deserted him when his born-again claims proved to be hollow.

The most prominent supporter to see the light was Robert Hawks from Tennessee, who organised Duke's campaign until he encountered the openly racist side of the Republican candidate. Hawks had offered his services to Duke because, he told me: 'He said he had changed his life and had turned over to Christ. As a Christian I said, well, I will go and stand by this young man who has turned his life over to Christ.' But then an incident occurred in Morgan city.

'We were going through black country,' Hawks said. 'About twenty to twenty-five rumbustious blacks began throwing paper cups and gravel. We pushed David down in the convertible and sped away. Afterwards Dook said: "Those niggers nearly went crazy, didn't they!"' Robert Hawks resigned in disgust and went home.

But finally, despite the fervour of his supporters, Louisiana voted for the 'crook' on election day. Edwin Edwards won 61 percent of the vote to Duke's 39 percent. 'Tonight reason and compassion reign in Louisiana,' Edwards told a victory party in New Orleans. 'Tonight Louisiana became first to turn back the merchant of hate, the master of deceit. Louisiana has defeated the darkness of bigotry and prejudice, hatred and division.'

Fear of economic disaster for the state had helped turn the tide. Many other states and industries had threatened a boycott of Louisiana, which could have harmed industry and tourism. Even so, half of the state's whites voted for Duke. Edwards won only because he secured a record turnout of the black voters who make up almost a third of the state's 2.7 million-strong electorate. Thousands who had never voted before lined up at registration booths so they could oppose a white supremacist. Blacks tipped the balance. Nevertheless the depth of alienation among middle-class and working-class white southerners was laid bare and Duke had temporarily gained a national platform for his nativist, hate-filled cause.

The size of his vote was also a blow to the authority of President George Bush who had asked Republicans to ignore Duke's candidacy.

As Duke was heading for defeat, another more serious challenge from the right was emerging to confront President Bush. It came in the form of a fifty-four-year-old, fast-talking, television commentator and former presidential aide called Patrick Buchanan, who announced his bid for the Republican Party presidential nomination three weeks after the Louisiana election and headed immediately from his Washington home to New Hampshire to campaign in the Republican primary election.

'David Duke is busy stealing from me,' Buchanan complained to the New Hampshire newspaper, the *Manchester Union Leader*. 'I have a mind to go down there and sue that dude for intellectual property theft.'

Indeed, Buchanan shared Duke's view of the world. The main difference between the two was that Buchanan was smart and was a Washington insider with a network of connections in the political and media world. Like Duke, he too had praised Hitler in his day, at least obliquely, once describing the Nazi leader as 'an individual of great courage ... extraordinary gifts', and he had suggested that Holocaust statistics were exaggerated. His utterances betrayed a sympathy for the idea of white supremacy. 'Why are we more shocked when a dozen people are killed in Vilnius than by a massacre in Burundi?' he asked. 'Because they are white people. That's who we are, that's where America comes from.' He told an interviewer: 'If we had to take a million immigrants in, say Zulus, next year, or Englishmen, and put them in Virginia, what group would be easier to assimilate and would cause less problems for the people of Virginia?'

He complained that when his wife Shelly was going down Washington's Connecticut Avenue she encountered 'these guys sitting on the corner playing bongo drums. I mean, this is the town I grew up in.' He saw government help for blacks as an offence against conservative principles. The black family that survived segregation, depression and war, he maintained, collapsed under the Great Society, Lyndon Johnson's programme to help the poor and repressed. 'While hundreds of billions have been piled on the national debt, we have created in America's great cities a permanent, sullen, resentful underclass, utterly dependent upon federal charity for food, shelter and medical care with little hope of escape.'

Where Duke was an avowed racist, Pat Buchanan was the authentic voice of angry, white, Christian, American nationalism. If there was to be an upsurge of nativism and protectionism as a result of the end of the Cold War, combined with the recession and the loss of jobs and markets to foreign countries, Buchanan was ideally qualified to be the political vehicle. He had a zealous following among the religious right which had emerged in the previous ten years because of what Buchanan described as the natural, healthy reaction in a once-Christian country that had been 'force-fed the poisons of paganism.'

Buchanan was regarded by his admirers as the guardian of the faith and the conscience of the conservatives. They loved his outspoken comments on matters which troubled them. Buchanan described abortion clinics as 'free-world terminals for the trains that left earlier in the century for Vorkuta and Auschwitz.' He said the Supreme Court had morally contaminated America with 'raw sewage' by unleashing a flood of pornography on the nation, destroying public schools through forced desegregation and tying the hands of police and prosecutors by re-interpreting the Bill of Rights. AIDS was nature's retribution on gays, the result of 'promiscuous sodomy, unnatural, unsanitary sexual relations between males.'

With his razor-sharp intellect, puckish sense of humour and a delight in being politically incorrect, Buchanan was acceptable in circles which would not entertain David Duke. Michael Kinsley, a liberal columnist with whom he sparred nightly on CNN's political soapbox, *Crossfire*, said: 'Give Buchanan this, unlike his rival George Bush he's got principles,' though he added, 'true, they're mostly the wrong principles.'

Buchanan is descended from Protestants from the north of Ireland who first settled in Mississippi. They became Catholic when Patrick Buchanan's grandfather Henry married Mary Agnew Smith, one of seventeen children of an immigrant Irish family. While he attributed his brawling, hard-drinking nature to his Scots-Irish blood, Buchanan maintained that: 'My views, my values, my beliefs, were shaped by being a member of an Irish Catholic conservative family of nine children.' His father's heroes were General MacArthur, Generalissimo Franco and Senator Joseph McCarthy, whose 1950s' witch-hunt against alleged communists made him a detested figure to the liberal left. The young Buchanan was brought up in the Blessed Sacrament parish, a Roman Catholic enclave of Washington. From his youth he was combative. A Jesuit teacher, Father Stephen McNamee, said to him: 'Every time I look over in your direction, you look as though you are going to explode. What is the matter with you? Why are you so angry?'

While he worked off some of his aggression fighting against Protestant gangs as a member of a Catholic gang called the 'Homers', Buchanan occasionally let his attitude problem get him into real trouble. One day in 1959, the twenty-year-old Buchanan honked his car horn at two policemen in Georgetown, the now-fashionable quarter of Washington. They pulled him over and gave him a ticket, and when he protested 'in X-rated language' a fight started in which he was clubbed with batons and his left hand was broken. The two policemen ended up in Georgetown Hospital and he was fined twenty-five dollars and suspended from university for a year.

Buchanan embarked on a career as a sharp-witted polemicist of the right, briefly interrupting an increasingly lucrative profession in writing and broadcasting – once to write speeches for Richard Nixon, the second time to act as communications director for President Ronald Reagan from 1985 to 1987.

Clearly, it would be a bitter fight. Buchanan believed the Republican President had betrayed the Reagan revolution. 'George Bush,' he said, 'is the biggest spender in history and the highest taxer.' Given his well-publicised views, no-one was surprised when Buchanan announced that his campaign slogan in his fight with George Bush would be 'America First'.

'When we say we will put America first,' he explained, 'we mean our Western heritage is going to be handed down to future generations, not dumped onto some landfill called multi-culturalism.'

New Hampshire, a slab of northern granite bordering on Canada's Quebec province, is a bell-wether for candidates and an early indication of the mood of the country in an election year when a president is involved. It sends strong signals to Washington indicating how Americans feel about the way the country is being run. In the New Hampshire winter snows, people would judge whether George Bush's victory in the Gulf War, his claim to have won the Cold War and his laissez-faire approach to the economy were sufficient to ensure re-election.

The state was the opposite of Louisiana in geography, climate and temperament, but it had a traditional conservative base and a nativist tradition dating back to the 'Know Nothing' movement of the nineteenth century which advocated a prohibition on new immigration. Republicans in New Hampshire were also in an angry mood as they went into the primary election. The state was enduring its third year of recession. Seven banks had gone bust in 1991. Personal bankruptcies had doubled. Unemployment lines were lengthening. Much of the blame was directed towards Bush for letting the economy slide and for paying too much attention to foreign affairs while people suffered at home. With the Cold War over, many New Hampshire voters were also tempted, like Buchanan, to look inward. The worse the recession got and the more the communist threat receded, the more, it seemed, people were becoming protectionist and isolationist.

Buchanan worked hard on the theme. He described President Bush's 'New World Order' as 'globalist nonsense'. 'George Bush wants to be president of the world. I want to be president of America,' he told people as he started the round of petrol stations and roadside diners. He called for the phasing out of foreign aid, the withdrawal of all US troops from Germany, Japan and South Korea and the building of a fence along the US border with Mexico to keep out illegal immigrants.

One of the biggest crowds of the New Hampshire campaign turned out on a frosty evening in January to fill the vast auditorium at Dartmouth College in Hanover, a neat university town almost on the Vermont border and a half-hour ride by propeller plane from Boston.

It seemed that every conservative student and supporter for miles around had donned suit and tie to come out that night and cheer on the Republican challenger. A few dozen demonstrators, including a man dressed in concentration-camp uniform to protest against Buchanan's views on the Holocaust, also turned up and milled around in the corridor outside with posters describing Buchanan as a fascist, but they were kept well back by Secret Servicemen.

Buchanan spoke in a cold, compelling, acid-sharp voice. He blamed the nation's woes on foreign aid, immigrants and unfair trade practices by foreign countries.

'The Japanese are led by some tough-minded economic nationalists who are looking out for Japan's number one,' he said. 'This country needs to be led by some tough-minded nationalists who will put America first ... In the last three years the regime in Beijing got three and a half billion dollars in loans. Do you think the eighty-five-year-old, chain-smoking, communist dwarf, Deng Xiaoping, is ever going to pay that back?'

The students lined up to ask questions. 'Did you not say,' asked one, 'that AIDS is God's retribution on homosexuals?' 'I don't believe any individual knows the mind of God,' replied Buchanan to loud applause.

'What is the place for blacks and Asians in your vision of America?' asked another undergraduate. 'All Americans have the same constitutional and God-given rights as Patrick Buchanan,' the candidate said. 'But I'll tell you something, my friend. If you are getting into the area of quotas, I believe in merit across the board.'

This brought loud cheers. Affirmative action to promote disadvantaged minorities was a favourite target for right-wing conservatives in New Hampshire no less than Louisiana.

'Would you disown your son if he told you he was gay?' another undergraduate asked. 'What exactly could you do about something like that?' Buchanan replied with a thin laugh.

As the New Hampshire campaign got under way, it became clear that Buchanan was going to inflict damage on an unpopular President. Buchanan mocked Bush's broken campaign pledge 'Read my lips, no new taxes' so many times that I heard children chanting it in the streets of New Hampshire towns. Bush had said during his acceptance speech at the National Republican Convention in 1988: 'The Congress will push me to raise taxes and I'll say, "No". And they'll push and I'll say, "No". And they'll push again and I'll say to them, "Read my lips, no new taxes".'

Congress had pushed in 1990 and Bush had said 'Yes' and raised taxes.

Buchanan was an ideal agent to send a message to Washington, or as the candidate put it, a 'wake-up call'. 'At least Pat Buchanan has a point of view, which one cannot say for other candidates,' Joseph McQuaid, editor-in-chief of the *Manchester Union Leader*, told me.

The *Union Leader*, one of the few American small-city newspapers which has any real impact on elections, came out in support of Buchanan in its editorial columns. It had a record of upsetting candidates it didn't like. (The 1972 Democratic hopeful, Senator Edward Muskie, was so angered by its editorial attacks on him and his wife that he turned up outside the paper's offices in a heavy snowfall to challenge its publisher, William Loeb, to come out and fight. As Muskie well knew, Loeb, a relic of the knife-and-kill journalism of the nineteenth century, was not on the premises but reporters on the scene observed that Muskie appeared to cry with rage. This emotional outburst severely damaged Muskie and helped lose him the nomination.)

Bush's 'key problem is credibility; he hasn't got an ideological rudder,' said McQuaid in his office in the *Manchester Union Leader* building where photographs on the corridor walls showed Colonel Oliver North, a hero of Pat Buchanan's, posing with smiling *Union Leader* executives.

On polling day, 18 January, New Hampshire Republicans gave Buchanan 37 percent of their vote and Bush 53 percent. This was an astonishing achievement for a maverick. Nearly half of Republican voters plumped for someone other than the incumbent Republican President. One in ten registered Republican voters, who couldn't bring themselves to vote for either Bush or Buchanan, wrote in the names of Democratic candidates.

It was a major humiliation for President Bush. Buchanan, born in Washington, raised in Washington, a consummate Washington insider most of his life, had almost beaten him by running as an anti-Washington outsider.

Chapter 5

FESTIVAL OF DARKNESS

1992 ... has turned out to be an annus horribilis

ELIZABETH II, QUEEN OF ENGLAND

WHAT GEORGE BUSH WOULD LATER DESCRIBE as the most miserable year of his life began when he was sick over the trousers of Japanese Prime Minister Kiichi Miyazawa at a state dinner in Tokyo in January 1992.

The dinner, planned as the high point, became the low point of a two-week, mid-winter tour of the Far East with American businessmen in search of jobs and investment. The sixty-seven-year-old President first became ill during a doubles tennis match with the Emperor of Japan and excused himself from a receiving line to go to the lavatory and be sick. Rejecting medical advice to retire to bed, a pasty-faced Bush took his seat at the top table beside the unfortunate Mr. Miyazawa. After the second course of raw salmon with caviar and just before the grilled beef with pepper sauce, the US President fell towards his host's lap, threw up and passed out. A Secret Service man vaulted over a table to stop him falling and Barbara Bush wiped his lips and covered his face with a serviette to hide his embarrassment. He was laid out on the floor and a moment or two later opened his eyes. 'Roll me under the table until the dinner's over,' muttered the President miserably to his physician, Dr. Burton Lee, as he regained consciousness.

It was only a stomach bug, but for American people watching on television it was a metaphor for a failed presidency. What they saw was a president who suddenly could do nothing right.

The trip had been a public relations disaster, with both the US and Japanese press mocking Bush as a travelling car salesman. Bad news awaited the President at home where he learned that his approval ratings, slipping for some weeks, had dropped to 48 percent, a dramatic collapse in public esteem.

At the end of the Gulf War only nine months earlier, Bush's popularity had stood at 89 percent, an all-time record high for a president in the history of Gallup polls. Over 80 percent of Americans were now saying they were dissatisfied with the state of the nation, the highest since 1979. The euphoria of victory in war had been replaced by a mood of frustration. Unemployment had risen to 7 percent, the highest for six years. People were afraid to spend money. There was growing impatience with a recession which had already lasted eighteen months, the longest in a decade, and which showed no signs of ending.

There was anger, too, at political paralysis in Washington where the President regularly vetoed legislation from the Democratic Congress to produce legislative gridlock. Neither the Republican President nor the Democrat-controlled Congress appeared to have any answers to a worsening recession. To many, the President was part of a cynical inner circle which allowed S&L crooks to clean out savings banks: the bail-out of S&Ls, savings and loans institutions, whose money had been siphoned off by land developers, had cost taxpayers $150 billion. A series of scandals on Capitol Hill, where members had been found repeatedly bouncing cheques in the House bank and running up unpaid restaurant bills, had contributed to a feeling that Washington had become a place where complacent politicians indulged themselves at the taxpayers' expense.

The first proof that Bush was vulnerable came in a fight for a vacant Senate seat in the State of Pennsylvania at the end of 1991. Harris Wofford, a little-known Democrat, ran against the hot favourite, Richard Thornburgh, Bush's former attorney general who had resigned from the cabinet to secure this 'safe' seat. Thornburgh, who started his campaign with a forty-four point lead in the polls, emphasised to voters his insider status in Washington and his closeness to Bush.

It was the wrong message. Wofford, a sixty-five-year-old visionary, campaigned on a theme much closer to the hearts of the voters, the lack of affordable health-care. His most popular line at election rallies was: 'The Constitution says that if you are charged with a crime you have a right to a lawyer. But it's even more fundamental that if you're sick you have a right to a doctor.' Health-care in America was the most expensive in any industrialised country, he said, yet the US was the only advanced nation in the world which did not provide a basic package of health-care benefits for all its citizens. Medical insurance costs were so high that 37 million people were no longer covered and another hundred thousand were dropping out of the system each month.

The Democratic candidate also voiced a deep disdain for Washington politics with its perks and privileges and gridlock. Thornburgh, he told voters, was part of the gang which helped create the mess in Washington. Wofford's campaign was run by James Carville, the strategist who would later help propel Clinton to the White House. He presented Wofford as an outsider prepared to fight for change and instilled in him a faith that the Republican favourite could be whipped.

'The idea of Dick Thornburgh coming to Pennsylvania and saying: "Send me to the corridors of power because I know Washington",' Carville noted dryly, 'is like running on a pro-leprosy ticket at the time of Jesus.' Wofford won the seat by ten points in a shock anti-Republican landslide. It was the first 'wake-up call' for George Bush.

When Pat Buchanan challenged Bush for the New Hampshire primary and began to draw big crowds there, the President decided it was time to leave Washington and pay a visit to the little state which had made and broken so many presidential candidates.

On a night of blinding sleet he came to rouse his supporters at a hastily-arranged rally in the basketball gymnasium of Pinkerton Academy near the New Hampshire town of Derry. Before he arrived, I strolled through the sparse crowd milling around on the wooden gymnasium floor to find New Hampshire voters and ask their opinions of the President.

The first person I talked to, a retired civil servant named Bob Boilard, turned out not to be from New Hampshire; he was one of Mr Bush's sailing companions from the neighbouring State of Maine where the President, a 'wonderful man,' had a holiday home at the seaside town of Kennebunkport. The second was Emile Roy, the President's holiday barber, also from Maine, who had made the two-hour drive across the state line to support his client, who was a 'fabulous person.' The third, a young woman waving a Bush-Quayle banner, became coy when I asked where she was from. 'Connecticut,' (Bush's real home state) she eventually replied, then refused to give her name.

It was beginning to look like rent-a-crowd. However, the fourth person I spoke to, a gangling teenager called Vinni Pappalardo, was indeed from New Hampshire.

'Why do you support Bush?' I asked.

'I don't,' he replied. 'I'm for Mario Cuomo, I'm just here to see what the President looks like.'

It turned out that many others had come just to see the two crowd-pullers Bush had brought along, his popular wife Barbara and the Hollywood actor, Arnold Schwarzennegger, whose message for Buchanan was: '*Hasta la vista*, baby.'

This was clear evidence that Bush was in deep trouble and that wide fissures had opened up in Republican ranks. The President was perceived as out-of-touch, the candidate of the status quo in a year when people yearned for change, a man who derided the 'vision thing' when people craved a leader with vision.

Despite nearly thirty years in public life, the Yale-educated Bush remained an elusive figure. He clumsily tried to redraw his image, crying out at an Exeter town hall rally after a glance at his cue card: 'Message – I care. We're trying. I need help.' At ease in a gangly way with world leaders and courteous and kindly in private, his body language betrayed deep embarrassment when mixing with voters. Eating once with construction workers in Los Angeles, Bush continually patted their arms and talked to them with a huge lump of chicken in his cheek, in a clumsy attempt to appear a regular guy. In California even his mentor, Ronald Reagan, remarked of Bush: 'He doesn't seem to stand for anything.' Bush had served as the youngest wartime navy pilot of his day, ambassador to the UN and China, head of the CIA, vice-president and president, yet, in the often-quoted words of his speechwriter Peggy Noonan, he remained 'famous but unknown'.

Now as he struggled to regain popularity it seemed he could do nothing right. He was televised insisting there was no recession while standing on a golf course, the playground of well-to-do Americans. He betrayed his ignorance of everyday shopping at a convention of grocers in Florida where he expressed amazement at how a supermarket price scanner worked; the President passed a drink carton and a bag of sweets over the glass through which price codes are scanned, shaking his head in wonder as the price appeared with a beep. When he made a stop-over in Panama in June to remind voters of how he had liberated the central American country from the tyranny of Manuel Noriega, over-enthusiastic police fired teargas at counter-demonstrators and the US President had to flee with his eyes streaming and guns in the hands of his Secret Service agents. His frustration with critics showed when he was heckled by a group of POW families in Crystal City, Virginia. 'Would you please shut up and sit down,' he cried.

His problems with syntax became a national joke. The weekly magazine *New Republic* began collecting 'Bushisms' of his most tongue-tied moments. (They were eventually published in a book.) In New Hampshire, when trying to sound defiant, he cried: 'Remember Lincoln, going down on his knees in times of trial and the civil war and all that stuff. You can't be, and we are blessed. So don't feel sorry for – don't cry for me, Argentina.' On the economy he said: 'We're enjoying sluggish times and not enjoying them very much.' At a function in Ridgewood, New Jersey, he remarked: 'I don't want to run the risk of ruining what is a lovely recession.' He meant to say reception. Bush's attempts at indignation usually ended in metaphorical disaster. 'I am sick and tired ... hearing those carping little liberal Democrats jumping over my you know what,' he cried at a rally. 'The Democrats want to ram it down my ear.'

The President invoked the Gulf war to stop his slide in opinion polls; if he had listened to the Democratic Congress, he told a rally, 'Saddam Hussein would be in Saudi Arabia and you'd be paying twenty bucks for gasoline – now try that for size.' He used the end of the Cold War to paint himself as a victor-statesman and to impress upon voters his promise: 'If we can change the world we can change America.'

'We liberated the entire world from old fears, fears of nuclear holocaust,' he said. 'And now our children grow up freed from the looming spectre of nuclear war. And having won the cold war, we did more. We led nations away from ancient hatreds and towards a table of peace. And we did still more than that. We forged a new world order, an order shaped by the sweat and sacrifice of our families, the sweat and sacrifice of generation upon generation of American men and women.'

Fired-up by world politics, Bush had no stomach for the domestic fray. His appetite had been dulled by guilt over the mean way he had won the 1988 campaign, in which Michael Dukakis had been defeated in a barrage of negative Republican advertising. 'I'm not looking forward to this,' he said before the election process began. It didn't help that his most trusted 1988 campaign strategist and close friend, Lee Atwater, had since died of brain cancer, aged forty. Bush felt humiliated at the insistence of his advisers that he should kowtow to the conservative right over his broken promise not to raise taxes. He finally said publicly it had been a mistake. 'I thought that this one compromise – and it was a compromise – would result in no more tax increases,' he blurted out at a rally. 'And so I'm disappointed. And given all that, yes, a mistake.' The mistake, few doubted, was in its electoral rather than its fiscal outcome.

The Buchanan challenge to the President continued after the New Hampshire primary and dragged on from winter into late spring. While never able to win a primary, Buchanan's Rottweiler style of attack inflicted wounds on Bush which would not heal before the November presidential election. Desiring to appear presidential, Bush refused to get drawn into a slanging match with his tormentor, and Buchanan was given a free run to drive the debate and re-define the right in nativist and nationalistic terms. He had the President on the run. The day after Buchanan turned his fiery oratory on the federally-funded National Endowment of the Arts for allegedly financing pornographic art, for example, Bush sacked its liberal chairman, John Frohnmayer.

At the same time, the struggle between Bush and Buchanan squeezed out David Duke. Right-wing conservatives were happy to endorse Buchanan as a more respectable flag-carrier. Duke was unable to get his name on the ballot in several Republican primaries, even in the Deep South, and faded into obscurity. Bush got in a last-round jab during the Republican primary in Michigan, home of the American automobile industry, where his campaign broadcast a television advertisement drawing attention to the fact that Buchanan drove a German-built Mercedes. The point was hammered home with the message: 'It's America First in his political speeches but a foreign car in his driveway.'

Bush received little help in rallying the Republican Party from his Vice-President, Dan Quayle. Boyish and enthusiastic, a C student with few obvious qualifications for the job, Quayle never outgrew the image of a deer caught in the headlights when George Bush picked him out of the Senate to become his running mate in 1988.

In almost four years in the White House, Dan Quayle never displayed the intellectual depth or leadership qualities necessary to take over the nation in an emergency. The President's understudy was the butt of the nation's stand-up comics and political commentators. The historian Arthur Schlesinger said of him: 'Quayle is a vice-president who fully lives up to the inconsequentiality of the office.'

Dan Quayle, too, was having a miserable campaign. During a televised visit to a school in Trenton, New Jersey, he asked sixth-grader William Figueroa to spell the word 'potato'. When the little boy spelled the word correctly on the blackboard, Quayle said: 'That's fine phonetically, but you're missing just a little bit,' and coaxed William into adding an 'e'. For the remaining months of the campaign, political posters made fun of the spelling error.

Quayle's wife, Marilyn, the dominant, smarter partner, engineered a chance for her husband to seize the initiative during a visit to Los Angeles after the riots in April 1992. The Quayles were Reagan-type conservatives whose favourite theme was that permissive attitudes in American popular culture promoted by Hollywood liberals were responsible for the break-down of society.

'We have to fight the entertainment industry,' said Marilyn Quayle to advisers as she accompanied her husband to Los Angeles aboard Air Force Two. 'Look at all those shows on television – and then there's Murphy Brown.'

Dan Quayle had never seen *Murphy Brown*, a situation comedy watched by thirty-eight million Americans, in which a fictional TV anchorwoman, Murphy Brown, played by Candice Bergen, had become pregnant by her ex-husband and opted to have the baby. The Vice-President was quickly brought up to date and found an early opportunity to make the point. In a speech in Los Angeles about the riots he said: 'It doesn't help matters when prime-time TV has Murphy Brown ... mocking the importance of fathers by bearing a child alone and calling it just another life-style choice.'

The remark propelled Quayle, as had been intended, into the forefront of national debate. In a survey of 3,500 Americans a few days later, 65 percent were able to identify *Murphy Brown* as the show Dan Quayle criticised; only 21 percent answered Yugoslavia when asked what former communist country had been torn by civil war. But like so many schemes the hapless Vice-President tried, it went wrong. Quayle was not only picking on the second most popular woman in America after Barbara Bush; he was attacking a mother for having a baby rather than an abortion, which as a pro-life campaigner he should have applauded. He was also ignoring dozens of shockingly violent TV shows in which overgrown kids used guns to blow each other away, mocking the importance of fathers in bringing them into the world in the first place.

The show's producer, Diane English, led the counter-attack, saying: 'If the Vice-President thinks it's disgraceful for an unmarried woman to bear a child ... then he'd better make sure abortion remains safe and legal.' Quayle replied lamely: 'Hollywood thinks it's cute to glamorise illegitimacy, Hollywood just doesn't get it.'

Back in Washington there was panic in the White House as the public took the side of the fictitious Murphy Brown. Bush campaign official, Bob Teeter, rang Quayle's chief of staff, William Kristol, in Los Angeles and called for a reversal of the Vice-President's policy on Murphy Brown. 'I think the Vice-President should praise her decision to have the baby,' he said. Quayle was told of the concern in Washington and telephoned the White House chief of staff, Sam Skinner.

'Hey, this is a winner, believe me,' said the Vice-President.

'That's a minority view around here,' came the reply. Happily for the Vice-President the minority included Bush.

Though he enjoyed the loyalty of his patron, White House officials began plotting to have Quayle removed from the Republican ticket. The Republicans were also using focus groups and dial groups to test public opinion and their conclusions were that, without Quayle, the President would gain four to six points in opinion polls. This could mean the difference between success and failure in November.

As the first rumours began to seep out in Washington about Quayle's future, the Vice-President showed a shrewd instinct for self-survival. He went on CNN's *Larry King Live* to say he was prepared to stand down right away if he thought it would help the Republican ticket. Next day the press was dominated by stories about his imminent departure, as the Vice-President had anticipated. Quayle demanded of Bush that he do something to stop the speculation. The President said he could leak the fact that they had talked and that the case was closed – he would be on the ticket. The story was duly fed to the media and the speculation ended. The 'deer in the headlights' Vice-President had shown political cunning by opening the door a crack so it could be slammed shut.

With Quayle firmly on the ticket, the Bush campaign worked out a programme to make him look popular and dynamic, while keeping him out of harm's way. They sent him to the most conservative Republican strongholds where he would be assured of a rousing reception. The party handlers did the rest.

I discovered how it worked at a rally for Quayle at Auburn University in Alabama, the most conservative college in the Bible Belt. Long before the Vice-President arrived, the turnstiles of the baseball stadium where he was to appear were taken over by campus police in black uniforms and sunglasses. Everyone was allowed in, but a couple of Democrats had Clinton placards torn up on the spot. Inside the tiny stadium, Republican Party officials opened 18 inch by 30 inch cardboard boxes and distributed dozens of hand-written posters of various sizes, deliberately made to look amateurish as if they had been written by passionate supporters in their garage, and passed them out over the heads of the crowd. The young people cheerfully grabbed them. They carried such slogans as: 'WE LOVE YOU, DAN!' Television crews were directed to a platform facing the podium. No other camera angles were allowed so that the pictures would include the posters held high in front of the podium and on a high terrace of supporters behind. On this terrace sat about sixty band members, dozens of local Republican dignitaries in dark suits and a line of sun-tanned, strawberry-blond majorettes in plunging, sequined bathing suits. Their role was not clear, as they took no part in the proceedings from beginning to end.

As they waited for Quayle to appear, basketball coach, Tommy Joe Eagles, read a prayer. 'Most gracious heavenly Father, we acknowledge your truly awesome and omnipotent power. We're thankful for our Vice-President, Dan Quayle. Bless him, Lord.' A man with a guitar sang: 'I'm proud to be an American, where at least I know I'm free. And I won't forget the men who died to give that right to me.'

After what seemed an eternity, the band suddenly jumped up and blasted out 'Where's That Tiger', and three parachutists descended into the baseball field, trailing coloured smoke. Then the

Vice-President appeared, an hour late, and jumped onto the podium in shirt sleeves as if ready for a long, tough speech. He made a pistol with his thumb and finger and fired, as if greeting a top supporter. Quayle did this everywhere in front of cameras, even if it was only to the backside of a Secret Service agent.

He took a cue card from his pocket. 'Do you want a president who's going to raise taxes?' ('No!') 'Do you want a president who has trouble telling the truth?' ('No!') 'Do you want a president with the integrity to make the tough decisions?' ('Yes!') And that was more or less it. The Vice-President and Marilyn tossed some frisbees and orange-coloured balls into the crowd and suddenly they were gone. A few minutes for hand-shakes on the way out and they were off in the black reinforced-steel limousine to Air Force Two. On television that evening, the national news showed a picture of a resolute Dan Quayle, shirt sleeves rolled up for action, against a tableau of cheering supporters as he delivered what looked like the high point of a lengthy political speech. It was what he came to Auburn for and what he got.

It is expected in American presidential elections that the mid-summer party Convention in election year will give a candidate a boost of several points in the polls. Clinton had emerged triumphant from the Democratic Party Convention in New York and surged ahead of the Bush-Quayle ticket by seventeen points. Bush now expected it would be his turn when the Republican National Convention was held in Houston, Texas, in mid-August. Clinton's huge lead was thought to be as puffed up as a soufflé. Things would settle down when the Republicans presented their candidate in a triumphal, rousing, flag-waving celebration of patriotism.

The venue for the Republican Convention in 1992 was the famous Astrodome, the world's first full-size, indoor, air-conditioned stadium. The fifteen-storey arena had been fitted out with over 100,000 square feet of red carpet and seating for 40,000 delegates and supporters. A semi-circle of television and radio cabins lit with neon signs like giant ice-cream booths looked down on a stage even more awesome than in Madison Square Garden and resembling a mammoth juke box. Some 225,000 balloons, over a hundred for each delegate, were suspended in string bags ready to fall for the climax of four days of celebration, the nomination of George Bush and Dan Quayle as 1992 Republican candidates for president and vice-president. The triumphal acclamation would be magnified by 576 speakers, 221 microphones and 400 amplifiers to create a roar of triumph of 140 decibels, as noisy as a 747 on take-off.

But the noise and razzmatazz could not disguise the fact that the President's men had ceded control of the event to the hardliners on the right. The capture of the Convention had been achieved through the 107-member Republican platform committee which drew up the party's policy document. It included twenty members and eight allies of the Rev. Pat Robertson's Christian Coalition which had been working assiduously at grass-roots level to have its own delegates sent to Houston. Several other committee members were openly sympathetic to Buchanan. The Christian Coalition raised $13 million in contributions for the election campaign and could therefore call some of the shots. Robertson's members secured the removal from the text of the party platform, and from all Bush's future speeches, of the President's favourite (though fast becoming outdated) phrase, the 'new world order'. Robertson had co-opted the words for the title of his 1991 book on morality, *The New World Order*, and arrogantly regarded the phrase as his copyright. Robertson was a key figure of the religious right. He brought to the platform his personal war against the 'feminist agenda' which he defined as a 'socialist, anti-family political movement that encourages women to leave their husbands, kill their children, practise witchcraft, destroy capitalism and become lesbians.' At his urging, the committee wrote into the official platform an outright condemnation of abortion, stating: 'We believe the unborn child has a fundamental right to life which cannot be infringed.' The party document also rejected the 'notion' that clean needles and condoms were a solution to the spread of AIDS. It opposed school programmes which provided birth control counselling and criticised welfare payments as 'anti-work and anti-marriage'. The programme called for a halt to illegal immigration by equipping border patrols with the 'tools, technologies and structures necessary to secure the border'. This was a concession to the keep-the-immigrants-out rhetoric of Pat Buchanan and another personal affront to Bush, who had negotiated a Free Trade Agreement with Mexico.

Buchanan supporters were naturally delighted with the platform. 'We couldn't have written most of this ourselves in a stronger fashion,' said his sister and campaign manager, Bay Buchanan.

The fact was that a deal had been struck with Buchanan on the basis, as one Republican organiser put it, that it was better to have the acerbic, right-wing television commentator inside the tent pissing out rather than on the outside pissing in – a phrase coined by President Lyndon Johnson. He would be the key-note speaker on the first day of the Convention; in return he would throw his support behind Bush. Buchanan readily agreed, on the grounds that his differences with the President 'are not remotely as sweeping as they are with that crowd' (meaning the Democrats).

The deal was a miscalculation which drove many middle-of-the-road voters into the arms of the Democrats. The Convention, watched by the nation on TV, opened with Buchanan declaring a jihad, a holy war, against those who did not hold fundamentalist Christian views. 'There is a religious war going on in our country for the soul of America,' Buchanan said. 'It is a cultural war, as critical to the kind of nation we will one day be as was the Cold War itself. And in that struggle for the soul of America, Clinton & Clinton are on the other side, and George Bush is on our side, and so we have to come home and stand beside him.' In this war, they must 'block by block ... take back our cities and take back our culture and take back our country.' The Clintons would bring homosexual rights and abortion on demand to the US and a bill allowing gay and lesbian marriages, he said. They would make abortion on demand a litmus test for the Supreme Court. Clinton and Gore were the 'most pro-lesbian and pro-gay ticket in history'. They would allow gay counsellors for boy scouts and admission to the US for foreigners infected with AIDS.

Buchanan reserved his special venom for Hillary Clinton. He had been sharpening his knife for her since she worked for the committee to impeach his mentor, Richard Nixon. Hillary, he told delegates, helped channel aid to FMLN communist guerrillas in El Salvador. Hillary was a 'certifiable leftist'.

'What does Hillary believe?' he cried. 'Hillary believes that twelve-year-olds should have a right to sue their parents, and Hillary has compared marriage as an institution to slavery and life on an Indian reservation. Well, speak for yourself, Hillary.'

Delegates wearing 'Say No to Slick Willie' badges hooted and hollered, though in the VIP area Barbara Bush looked distinctly uneasy. Bashing Hillary Clinton was the blood sport of the right. The night before, many delegates had taken part in a 'Rally to Stomp Out Hillary Clinton', organised outside the Astrodome by the Committee for Decent Family Values, at which a live elephant – the symbol of the Republican Party – stamped on a doll representing Hillary Clinton's 'anti-family values'.

Buchanan's allegations were based on *Law Review* articles which Hillary Clinton wrote in the 1970s. In one she highlighted the difficulty of arguing that twelve-year-old children were as legally incompetent as new-born babies. In another she referred to past and present social arrangements, including 'marriage, slavery and the Indian reservation system' which society deemed in need of 'social institutions specifically designed to safeguard their position.' In context, neither view was considered extreme in the American legal world.

The Bushes tried to distance themselves from the intolerance and meanness of spirit which pervaded the Convention. They also attempted to manoeuvre around the Republican Party policy on abortion which polls showed was not popular with voters. In an orchestrated series of television appearances, the President declared: 'Of course, I'd stand by my child,' if his granddaughter wanted an abortion. Barbara Bush said that abortion was a 'personal decision'. Dan Quayle told Larry King on CNN that he would support his thirteen-year-old daughter, Connie, if she chose to have an abortion. On the Republican side, too, there was no reluctance to recruit children for political convenience. Any embarrassment Connie Quayle felt was compounded when her mother, Marilyn Quayle, refused to play the game, saying tartly: 'If she becomes pregnant, she'll take the child to term.' The opportunistic nature of the Republican exercise was made painfully obvious when Bill Clinton was asked what he would do if his daughter became pregnant. He replied: 'I wouldn't talk to the press about it.'

The icons of the conservative right flocked to Houston to be lionised. Prominent among them was the 21 stone, 6 pound figure of Rush Limbaugh, a forty-one-year-old right-wing populist who is the most listened-to radio talk-show host in America. Limbaugh is so popular that some roadside restaurants in the Deep South have 'Rush rooms' where people can listen uninterrupted to his talk-in programme. His $22 hardback book, *The Way Things Ought To Be*, topped the *New York Times* best-seller list from mid-1992 until well into 1993.

Limbaugh is a professional blowhard who is compulsive listening not just for conservatives but for many liberals because he is genuinely funny. As the patron saint of white male chauvinists, his message is simple: liberals are stupid and those who listen to Rush Limbaugh are clever. Syndicated to five hundred US radio stations and with 12.5 million listeners, Limbaugh captivates his audience with irreverent and biting attacks on such fearsome liberals as Anita Hill, Hillary Clinton, Edward Kennedy, Jesse Jackson and Mario Cuomo, and on a range of enemies which embraces 'commie libs', 'tree-hugging wackos' (environmentalists), 'feminazis' (liberal women who promote abortion), Hollywood liberals, advocates for the rights of the homeless and gay rights activists. In his reactionary bombast, Limbaugh touches upon all the issues which make middle-America mad, such as condoms being distributed at school. He rants against being made to feel sorry, as he put it in one memorable monologue, 'for this group and that group, for the downtrodden, for native Americans, for those who suffered because Columbus landed. What about feeling sorry for those that are living, who pay the taxes? Those are the people NO-ONE ever feels sorry for. The American middle class is just plain tired and worn-out. They get blamed for everything in this country. They are taxed more than ever and now they have to put up with lectures about how we have to ship billions of dollars to the former Soviet Union so they can eat this winter ... In schools we're teaching kids about tribal Africa instead of Aristotle ... We're told that cows are our biggest enemy. I say, pass the burgers ... I am weary and near my wits' end at having to listen to the complaint that the American safety net has holes in it and too many people are slipping through. Wrong. The problem is that too many people are using that safety net as a hammock ... I'm sick and tired of turning on my TV and being told that the AIDS crisis is my fault too because I don't care enough.'

Limbaugh once had callers jamming the telephone lines when he announced: 'It's time to get serious about raising taxes on the poor. It's time that the wealthiest poor in the world started paying their fair share ... Let's balance this budget on the backs of the poor ... What if they just can't pay? The poor in this country have an average of three television sets in their houses. Let's go and get two of them.' The callers, many of whom expressed approval for this Swiftian satire, failed to notice that the date was 1 April.

'On a roll here, Jimbo, on a roll, I'm in the Vice-President's box tonight,' cried Limbaugh as he passed me in the Wortham Centre, Dallas, on his way to a Convention party thrown to celebrate the triumph of the religious right in devising the party platform.

Opponents of the religious right used a variety of ruses at the Republican Convention to strike back, in sometimes unconventional ways. A southern belle, wearing a colourful hooped dress and carrying a dainty wicker basket, as homely looking as apple pie, presented former White House Chief of Staff Mike Deaver with two small packages. Only as he walked on did he realise that they contained condoms rather than cookies and that she was a pro-choice protestor from Planned Parenthood. (He kept them anyway.) When Dan Quayle tried to address two thousand Republicans at a 'God and Country' rally in a Houston hotel, he was heckled by AIDS activists who had infiltrated the gathering to protest that the religious right was helping to spread the disease by opposing safe-sex education. Burly police officers, some with plastic gloves, manhandled the protestors out as the young Republicans in their neat suits and haircuts visibly shied away from bodily contact. Demonstrators also infiltrated a gala luncheon for President Bush, heckling him several times.

Every day on the periphery of the vast car park around the Astrodome, groups of protestors gathered. On the first evening of the Convention hundreds of members of ACT UP, the AIDS Coalition to Unleash Power, clashed with police as they approached the Astrodome. Houston's KTRK-Channel 13 showed a protestor surrounded by officers falling to the ground while a voice said: 'Don't kick him when the lights are on.' The demonstrators were corralled in a field across from the Astrodome, a designated protest zone lit in the evenings by a searchlight from a helicopter and held in check by a line of baton-wielding police in visors and flak-jackets and two dozen mounted officers. As I walked past one evening an AIDS activist, Frances Summer, walked forward and lay down on the footpath in an act of civil disobedience, with a note on her chest asking 'What about AIDS?' An observer from the American Civil Liberties Union, a bearded merchant seaman called Gaynor Gibson, handed out leaflets with advice to anyone detained by police: 'Ask if you are under arrest.

If you are, you have a right to know. Do not "bad-mouth" the police officers or run away, even if you believe what is happening is unreasonable.'

As Frances Summer lay surrounded by reporters on the pavement, an elegant woman in evening attire was addressing delegates in the Astrodome. Mary Fisher, daughter of a multi-millionaire, was a picture-perfect Republican socialite, smartly-groomed, intelligent and well-connected. She was also HIV positive, having contracted the virus from a drug-abusing husband from whom she was now divorced. Her speech, on an evening devoted to family values, cut across the arguments of those who had been calling AIDS God's retribution on homosexuals. 'I am one with the lonely gay man sheltering a flickering candle from the cold wind of his family's rejection,' said Mary Fisher. These courageous words momentarily silenced the Convention where one of the most popular placards was: 'Family Rights Forever – Gay Rights Never'.

The appearance of Ronald Reagan at the Houston rally, for what amounted to the final curtain of his political life, symbolised more than anything else the end of the free-spending era he represented. The Old Gipper was at last showing his age. 'Tonight is a special night for me,' the eighty-one-year-old former actor said. 'At my age, every night is a special night for me.' He made his exit with the words: 'May every evening bring us closer to that shining city upon a hill.' The old cold warrior stumbled as he left the stage, but Nancy Reagan caught his arm firmly and led him away.

The Convention should have been a triumphal celebration of the end of what Reagan once called the 'evil empire'. Instead it was permeated with nostalgia for the good old days of political certainties when the Soviet Union was the enemy. In a hall adjoining the Astrodome, behind a life-size statue of George Bush striding into the wind, jacket slung over his shoulder, a political fair of 240 stalls was transformed into a post-Cold War flea-market. Chunks of the Berlin Wall were on sale, along with hammer and sickle badges, pictures of Gorbachev and Yeltsin and other political mementoes from the former Soviet Union. A specialist in political memorabilia offered one-rouble notes at five dollars each, an exchange rate which would have wiped out the Russian debt overnight.

It was as if they missed the old enemy. With the Cold War over,

Republicans could not rally patriotic Americans by claiming to be hard on communists where the Democrats were soft. They were deprived of an ideological foreign foe to unify them in their fight with the enemy – within the media, the liberals, the Hollywood elite, the pro-choice movements, gay-rights groups and, of course, Bill and Hillary Clinton. One of the hottest items on sale was a mock poster for a movie called 'Slick Willie – One man's story of saying whatever it is to get elected,' starring Hillary Clinton as Tammy Wynette, Gennifer Flowers as the bimbo, Ted Kennedy as his chaperone and Mario Cuomo as the Godfather.

On the Convention floor Bush supporters tried to make the most of the President's 'victory' in the Cold War. Senator Phil Gramm of Texas declared that 'in any hut in any village on the planet, one world leader is honoured and loved above all others; spoken in a thousand dialects, his name is still George Bush.'

Such bombast missed the point. The American people were worried about the future, not the past. They wanted a president who could fix the economy. They sensed that with Bush they were on the wrong track. Running through the Convention was an undercurrent of defeat which began to affect the candidate. 'This is going to be the worst two months of my life,' Bush remarked to friends as he contemplated the struggle between then and the 3 November election.

Bush's acceptance speech was completely out of touch with the serious mood of the electorate. It was a last-minute scissors and paste job lacking poetry or commitment. It dwelt on grievances about a Democratic Congress and an unfair opponent, rather than on the future. It was an apology rather than a vision of hope. 'Two years ago I made a bad call on the Democrats' tax increase,' said Bush. 'With my back to the wall I agreed to a hard bargain. Well, it was a mistake to go along with the Democratic tax increase and I admit it.' Hard-line conservatives in the Astrodome smirked in satisfaction.

The triumph of the right provoked a crisis within the party. Its dominance at the Convention and on the television screens discouraged many moderate Republicans. The 'Limbaugh-land' Convention was seen as a festival of darkness by those who feared a resurgence of nativism and bigotry in modern America. Fully one-third of Republican Congress members found a reason not to come to

Houston, and all ten Republican Congresswomen, of whom seven supported abortion rights, stayed away. Months later, the party chairman, Rich Bond, admitted that the Convention for which he was responsible had been a disaster, and he blamed Buchanan's speech, which was 'tragically placed at the top of the agenda,' for projecting an image of mean-spirited exclusivity. Too late, he urged Republicans not to cling to 'zealotry masquerading as principle'.

The big mistake the Republican Party made was to fail to address the issue of the economy, which was at the root of the dissatisfaction throughout the country, concentrating instead on moral questions like abortion. This issues not only divided the Republican Party; it was to be a significant factor, as events were to prove, in bringing about the defeat of George Bush in the presidential election ten weeks later.

Chapter 6

BEHIND THE BARRICADES

Abstract liberty, like other mere abstractions,
is not to be found.

EDMUND BURKE

BILL CLINTON HAD GOOD REASON to fear that the 'pro-life' movement would target him and divert attention from his economic message. Anti-abortion protests, many of them violent, had become a feature of American life in the late 1980s and early 1990s, and it was inevitable that the Democratic candidate would be singled out for special attention.

As Governor of Arkansas, Clinton had at first been a moderate on abortion, as were most southern Democrats. He said in 1989 that he was personally opposed to abortion but that he would allow it in the case of rape and incest and to save the mother's life. In the two years before his presidential bid he moved rapidly towards a strong pro-choice position, which polls showed was favoured by a majority of voters nationwide. In 1991 Clinton told the National Women's Political Caucus in Washington, whose endorsement he needed, that he was strongly in favour of a woman's right to choose, and made no mention of his previous support for restrictions such as parental notice for teenagers and a ban on the use of public money to fund abortion clinics.

Soon after he took to the road, pro-life hecklers began appearing at Clinton's rallies. Some got close enough to embarrass him. The most unpleasant incident happened in New York on 14 July 1992, when he was leaving the Intercontinental Hotel to attend the Democratic Party Convention in Madison Square Garden. A pro-life activist, Harley David Belew, approached Clinton as the candidate walked out of the lobby and asked for his autograph. As Clinton reached for his pen Belew removed a newspaper to reveal a nineteen-weeks-old male foetus in his hand. He put his face up to Clinton's and shouted: 'What about the babies, Governor?'

Clinton was shaken by the incident and his security was stepped up in anticipation of further harassment. In September he travelled to address students at the Catholic University of Notre Dame at South Bend, Indiana. The Catholic Church in the United States is adamantly opposed to abortion and Clinton, a southern Baptist, expected a hostile reception. He could have declined the invitation to speak at Notre Dame, which was automatically extended to all presidential candidates each election year, yet he did not want to cold-shoulder the main educational institution of Roman Catholics, who form the biggest single religious denomination in the United States. It was as important for him to visit Notre Dame to recruit Catholic support as it had been for John F. Kennedy, the first Catholic candidate for the presidency, to stay away thirty-two years earlier, when he wanted to play down his religious allegiance.

The Catholic Church had done little to disguise the fact that it favoured Bush in the election. On the day of Clinton's visit to Notre Dame, I found in the porch of the Basilica of the Sacred Heart, the main college church, a special election issue of the *National Right to Life News* displayed prominently among the religious pamphlets. It said that returning Bush to the White House was a key strategical goal in the fight against abortion.

There was also a discarded copy of *Christian American*, a publication of Pat Robertson's right-wing Christian Coalition, based in Virginia, which waged a war against abortion, homosexuality and pornography and sought support from all denominations, though it drew most of its backing from southern white followers of fundamentalist TV evangelists. The *Christian American* displayed with approval an interview with Bush in which the President said he was appalled by the 1.3 million abortions in the US each year and would veto any Freedom of Choice Bill submitted by a Democrat-controlled Congress.

When Clinton's motorcade arrived in Notre Dame, a few dozen noisy anti-abortion protestors were waiting. An earnest-looking student with glasses pressed a leaflet into my hands as I stood among the crowd. It asked: 'Would it be a sin for a Catholic to vote for Clinton?' The answer it supplied was that, as the Democratic candidate was 'adamantly pro-abortion', any Catholic who voted for him was guilty of 'an objectively grave immoral action'. Clinton's pro-choice policy did not seem to be of much concern to the majority of the Catholic students at the university. The Democratic candidate was given a standing ovation by a crowd of two thousand at the Stepan Center. Many of the undergraduates there told me they were more concerned to get rid of George Bush and replace him with a leader with new and fresh ideas on how to revive the economy than about his attitude on choice.

However, the anti-abortion protestors made their presence felt from the back of the hall. 'What about the babies, Bill?' came the familiar cry.

Clinton responded by pointing to Mayor Raymond Flynn of Boston, seated beside him on the platform, to make the point that the Democratic Party had room for both points of view. Mayor Flynn, an outspoken opponent of abortion with his roots in the traditional Catholic Irish stronghold of South Boston, was an old ally of Clinton's and co-chairman of 'Irish-Americans for Clinton-Gore'. A few days before, Clinton had telephoned Flynn, who was also chairman of the US conference of mayors, to ask him to come to Notre Dame to defuse by his presence opposition from anti-abortion demonstrators. The heckling eventually died away and Clinton received a standing ovation when he told of a conversation he had with a white woman in a crowd in Iowa. She was holding a black baby with AIDS whom she had adopted, he said. The woman told him: 'Governor, I respect this debate which is going on about "life" but how I hope we would all reach out to try to help the children who are living.' On the platform the unsmiling grey-haired university president, the Rev. Edward Malloy, alone remained seated during the outburst of cheering, with his hands firmly gripping his knees. I later heard Clinton repeat this tale several times in different cities when confronted by anti-abortion protestors, though he dropped the words 'white' and 'black' so as not to offend African-Americans.

Clinton had first experienced militant anti-abortion protestors in Atlanta, Georgia, during the Democratic Party National Convention in 1988. A mass picket had been placed on family planning clinics in Atlanta to coincide with the Convention and, in skirmishes with police, 134 protestors were arrested.

The use of human barriers physically to stop women using abortion clinics became a widely-used tactic in the late 1980s. It was a new departure in a bitter fight, waged for nearly twenty years, against a

Supreme Court decision legalising abortion. Altogether, 138 of the country's 4,500 family planning clinics were temporarily blockaded in 1988 alone, and 12,368 arrests were made by police trying to ensure free movement of people in and out of the clinics.

The Atlanta pickets had been organised by a militant pro-life organisation called Operation Rescue, founded in 1986 by a twenty-seven-year-old former second-hand car salesman from Binghamton, New York, called Randall Terry. It was Terry who was behind the ambush of Bill Clinton with the nineteen-weeks-old foetus at his New York Hotel. Terry was the product of an unplanned pregnancy at a time when abortion was banned.

'I was conceived out of wedlock,' he once said. 'I could've been aborted. I hope and I think that my parents wouldn't have, but I'm just real glad they didn't have the choice.'

A high-school drop-out, Terry was 'saved' by a minister from the Elim Bible Institute whom he heard preaching in the street when he was working as an ice-cream salesman. He developed the idea of Operation Rescue after anti-abortion activists began turning up in large numbers to support a picket he and his wife, Cindy, had mounted on the Binghamton family planning clinic close to where they lived. In January 1986, Terry and a group of six supporters locked themselves in a room in the clinic to invite arrest and publicity for their cause. As more anti-abortion activists joined their group, new tactics were developed to stop pregnant women going in to what they called the 'abortion mill'. Terry once went inside himself and repeatedly shouted the name of a woman patient to intimidate her into leaving. His supporters sprayed the locks of the clinic with glue. On one occasion they stormed the building and smashed furniture and pulled out telephone wires. The movement spread to several major US cities, attracting support from the religious right and from conservative Americans unhappy about the development of a 'guilt-free' society which suspended moral judgement on everything from abortion, divorce and homosexual activity to child misbehaviour and overeating.

The aggressive tactics of Operation Rescue put the abortion rights movement on the defensive. Pro-choice organisations found themselves unprepared for street warfare. In the summer of 1991, however, when Operation Rescue staged its most ambitious offensive, a forty-two-day 'Summer of Mercy' blockade of clinics in Wichita,

Kansas, pro-choice defenders finally came out in strength to oppose them.

During confrontations on the normally quiet streets of the Midwest city, 2,600 people were arrested and federal marshals were called in to help keep the clinics open. In a reversal of popular stereotypes, pro-abortion groups who usually identify with liberal causes found themselves singing the American national anthem and applauding US marshals, while, at a nearby gathering of pro-lifers, people wearing shorts and carrying kids on their shoulders clapped and boogied to a black group from Chicago called Cause and Effect.

The federal marshals who played a key role in keeping the clinics open were called out by Wichita District Judge Patrick Kelly, appointed to the federal bench by President Jimmy Carter. Judge Kelly used the Ku Klux Klan Act of 1871 to justify his action. The Act barred conspiracies to deprive any person 'of the equal protection of the law'. His ruling angered the anti-abortion Bush administration and the US Department of Justice began a long legal battle which they won in January 1993 to overturn it on the grounds that women seeking abortions should not be protected under old civil rights laws.

Judge Kelly, a tall, lean lawyer with white hair and eyebrows, descended from Irish immigrants and Cherokee Indians, received many death threats after he began giving three-month sentences to protestors who obstructed the marshals. He was forced to stop attending his local Catholic church because of anger among believers at his legal decisions. 'People ask: How can a Catholic Judge sit in this kind of case?' he said. 'It's simple. I have a duty to carry out the law and Roe [Roe v Wade] is the law.'

Roe v Wade was the landmark 1973 US Supreme Court decision which decriminalised abortion throughout the United States and declared a woman's constitutional right to choose. The anniversary of the ruling, 22 January, was marked every year by anti-abortion protestors with mass pickets at abortion clinics in the US capital. One of the sites selected for battle in 1992 was the five-storey brick building housing the Capitol Women's Center on the corner of 22nd and O Street, ten blocks from the White House. What happened there was typical of scenes all over the city.

Before dawn about sixty people gathered on the pavements beneath a couple of scrawny, leafless maple trees. They included students in anoraks, men in baseball hats and a few elderly women in tailored coats. They were members of the Washington Area Clinic Defence Task Force, an ad hoc organisation set up to ensure the city's abortion clinics stayed open for business. Their job, they explained to me, would be to accompany patients through any picket lines formed by anti-abortion protestors. Rubbing their hands together in the cold, they peered up and down the street as a young woman marshalled them into a line and issued instructions. 'You stay here, OK?' she called out to everyone. 'Hold hands if they push you. Avoid physical contact. Let the cops move them if they lie down. OK? Got that?'

Two men and two women were given orange jackets marked 'CLINIC ESCORT'. 'Remember,' she said, 'anyone else wearing orange is a fraud. OK?'

As daylight came the opposition arrived, about eighty Operation Rescue volunteers, many of them middle-aged, some carrying rosary beads and prayerbooks. They were dressed in accordance with instructions issued by Randall Terry: 'Operation Rescue is a grassroots organisation of respectable, upright, moral citizens and we should dress like it. When bystanders, police, newspaper reporters, cameramen and anchorpersons arrive on the scene, we want them to perceive us as Middle America, not some lunatic fringe demonstrating for their own rights. Weather permitting, jeans or comfortable slacks and a nice shirt are ideal. Wear an old pair of tennis shoes since they're likely to get scuffed up on the sidewalk. Avoid wearing T-shirts or hats that display advertising. Hopefully you will be blocking the entrance to an abortion clinic for several hours. To make the hard concrete sidewalk more bearable, you may want to bring a stadium cushion, a towel, some newspapers wrapped in plastic or some suitable pad to sit on.' They began their well-rehearsed tactics of passive protest borrowed from the Civil Rights movement of the 1960s. Several of the anti-abortion demonstrators went up to the clinic as if they were planning to go in, then suddenly went limp and lay down in front of the clinic door. One old man lay on his back, his stomach bulging upwards, and closed his eyes as if unconscious. The rest sang hymns and recited the rosary.

The Washington DC police, who had been through all this before, brought up two buses. Police officers lifted the protestors from the ground and heaved and shoved the limp bodies through the bus doors.

Once inside, the demonstrators, many of whom had also been through it all before, stopped their passive resistance and took their seats for the ride to police headquarters. Teenage girls among the defenders, who had grown in number, began chanting: 'Keep your rosaries off our ovaries,' and 'Right-to-life is a lie, you don't care if women die.'

The four orange-coated escorts had meanwhile staked out a position a block away at the corner of N Street. When two young women, one black, one white, came along to attend the clinic, which also advises on birth control, smear-testing and post-natal care, they were taken in hand by the pro-choice escorts and guided firmly through the crowd. A young woman in an orange jacket also emblazoned with the letters 'CLINIC ESCORT' suddenly ran out from the pro-life lines and thrust a brochure at the black woman.

'We love you, don't harm your baby,' she shouted.

'Fake! Fake!' shrieked pro-choice activists as they rushed forward and blocked her path.

The brochure had a lurid picture of an aborted foetus. The foetus, it said, is a baby which 'can make a tiny fist, get hiccups, suck her thumb, feel pain, yet can be legally put to death by abortion at any time until the day she is born.'

The confrontation ended when the Operation Rescue volunteers set off in mid-morning to join the annual anti-abortion march to Capitol Hill. Despite the location of the clinic – a short stroll from the major Washington media bureaus in M Street – only a couple of other reporters were at the scene. By then, such skirmishes had taken place so many thousands of times in so many cities in the United States that they were no longer important news.

In April 1992 Operation Rescue staged another major offensive, a month of protests outside the two abortion clinics in Buffalo, a mainly Catholic city of 328,000 near Niagara Falls in New York State. This time they were outnumbered by even better-organised groups from the National Organisation for Women and dozens of other pro-choice bodies. Operation Rescue's campaign attracted up to six thousand supporters but failed to close either clinic.

Buffalo is remembered for one particularly gruesome scene, when the Rev. Robert Schenck carried a seven-inch long foetus in his cupped hands towards a crowd of pro-choice demonstrators guarding the clinic in Buffalo's High Street. 'I want you to meet my friend Tia, a beautiful little girl who was aborted,' he said. People shouted, 'It's a fake.' There was a scuffle and the foetus fell to the ground amid screams and shouts. A flap of skin fell over its face. Schenck was arrested for disorderly conduct and a coroner later judged the foetus to be still-born, about twenty weeks old.

Pro-choice demonstrators carried equally gruesome pictures of bloodied women, the victims of botched abortions, in a defence line outside Dr. Parviz Taefi's obstetrics and gynaecology office in Buffalo. They brandished wire coat-hangers with the slogan: 'Warning, this is not a surgical instrument. Keep abortion safe and legal.' Before Roe v Wade, Dr. Taefi worked for six months at a hospital in a poor neighbourhood in New York. 'Not a night went by when I didn't see someone in the emergency room dying from a botched abortion,' the fifty-seven-year-old doctor told a *Life* magazine reporter. 'I saw X-rays taken during autopsies that showed coat-hangers in the uterus. And the instruments women used weren't sterilized, so they'd go into septic shock. Once that happens there's nothing you can do to save them.' His home was picketed by people with a ten-foot long banner reading 'Taefi kills children' and he got some ten calls a day from people asking for 'Dr. Death'.

After Buffalo, Terry set up the American Anti-Persecution League to establish a 'legal offence fund' to pay for rising legal costs. 'I've had enough of brutal police, homosexual thugs, savage radical feminists and cold-blooded abortion-mill guards who harm my brothers and sisters in the pro-life movement,' he said in a solicitation for funds which was accompanied by a picture with a powerful racist appeal to white fundamentalists – it showed a black police officer holding a white anti-abortion protestor by the throat. 'Every year thousands of pro-life activists are ... beaten by police, bitten and spit on by AIDS-infected sodomites, kicked and punched by radical feminists,' he wrote. 'Our bones are broken, our noses bloodied,' but now they would 'play legal hardball' against anyone who interfered with pro-life demonstrators.

The offensive against clinics was not limited to picketing. A wave of arson and bombing attacks by anti-abortion extremists, which began in the early 1980s, escalated in the second half of the decade and into the 1990s. From 1 January 1986 to 17 November 1992, thirty-two family planning clinics went up in flames, fires were started at twenty more, and three clinics were bombed, according to Gina Shaw of the National Abortion Federation in Washington, who said these were conservative estimates. In the same period there were 199 cases of vandalism, ninety-two invasions of clinics and three hundred instances of harassing calls, including twenty-four death threats made against individual clinic workers. Among the clinics to suffer in 1992 were the Women's Community Health Center in Beaumont, Texas, where a fire caused damage estimated at $300,000; the Intermountain Planned Parenthood facility in Montana, which sustained $75,000 worth of damage; the Redding Feminist Women's Health Center at Redding, California, where fire-damage repairs cost $70,000 and the Richmond Medical Center for Women in Richmond, Virginia, at which damage was estimated at $40,000. Several clinics had noxious chemicals sprayed through letter-boxes, the most serious of these attacks being on the Memphis Area Medical Center for Women in Memphis, Tennessee, in May 1992, where the clean-up cost was put at $225,000. From 1985 to 1988 intimidation contributed to a fall from 2,680 to 2,582 in the number of clinics providing abortions throughout the US. While this was going on, sham counselling centres, as many as two thousand according to a 1992 congressional committee report, were being set up at which unsuspecting young women were traumatised by being shown gory film of aborted foetuses.

Despite their setbacks on the streets, anti-abortion demonstrators had reason to feel they were winning the war against abortion in the early months of 1992 and that their real victory would come not at the barricades but in the Supreme Court. Their long-term goal was to get the Supreme Court to turn back the clock and reverse its 1973 Roe v Wade decision.

This was one of the most controversial rulings in US legal history. Wade was a Texas official whose duty was to enforce the law. Roe was a pseudonym for Norma McCorvey, a waifish twenty-five-year-old divorced drifter with a five-year-old daughter. She became pregnant in August 1969 when working with a circus in Georgia. She returned to her home town of Dallas where she tried, but failed, to get an abortion. Her case was taken up by two pro-choice lawyers, Linda Coffee and Sarah Weddington. Norma McCorvey told them she had been raped by a crowd of men who came to the circus and she did not want to have the baby. (Fifteen years later she would admit that she had not been raped but had become pregnant through consensual intercourse and had lied to avoid getting into trouble.) The lawyers were looking for a volunteer to challenge a 1857 law in Texas which made it a crime to procure an abortion except when the mother's life was in danger. Norma McCorvey agreed, though the process would take so long that she would have to carry her baby to term.

Anti-abortion laws had been introduced by most American states during the late nineteenth century, initiated more by concern about the butchery to women as a result of primitive medical techniques than about the morality of abortion itself. But illegal abortions, or legal abortions performed for 'therapeutic' or 'psychiatric' reasons, had become common in the United States by the 1950s. The issue became a subject for national debate in the 1960s because of two events which helped convince medical opinion that a change in the law was needed.

The first occurred in 1962 when Sherri Finkbine, an Arizona woman, discovered that the tranquilliser her husband had obtained for her in Europe was thalidomide, which had caused terrible birth defects in women in Britain and Germany. Unable to obtain a legal abortion, Mrs. Finkbine had to travel to Sweden where the embryo was aborted and found to be horribly deformed.

The second event was an outbreak of rubella, commonly known as German measles, in the early 1960s. The epidemic in the United States caused the birth of an estimated fifteen thousand damaged babies, with defects ranging from blindness to severe mental retardation.

Following the outcry over these cases, which encouraged many doctors to believe that abortion was in some instances preferable to childbirth, the American Medical Association for the first time recognised the legitimacy of abortion and called for liberalisation of state laws. It was also a matter of bowing to the inevitable. By that time the total of women seeking abortions each year had risen to an estimated 1.2 million.

The Roe v Wade case took more than two years to make its way through the lower courts. On 22 January 1973, the nine-member US Supreme Court issued its verdict in Washington. By a majority of seven to two, the Court declared that abortion was a right which could not be prohibited by individual states. They noted that when most criminal abortion laws were first enacted, the procedure had been a hazardous one for women – three out of ten abortions resulted in death in New York at the turn of the century – but that medical techniques had improved dramatically since then. They further noted that, although the US Constitution did not mention any right of privacy, a right of personal privacy had been established in previous Supreme Court rulings and this could be interpreted to give a woman the fundamental right to have an abortion in the first trimester of a pregnancy if she so wished. After the first three months, other considerations concerned with the quickening foetus would come into play; in the second trimester, the state had an interest in the life of the foetus and could regulate abortion, but only to protect the woman's health. In the third trimester, the state could forbid abortion, except where the life or health of the mother were threatened.

The decision was written by Justice Harry Blackmun, a liberal Republican appointed to the Supreme Court by President Richard Nixon. One of the two dissenting judges was forty-eight-year-old William Rehnquist, a right-wing conservative and also a Nixon appointee, who was sometimes called the 'Lone Dissenter' by his staff for his frequent differences with the more liberal Court majority. Rehnquist argued that a 'right of privacy' did not exist under the Constitution and that the ruling was without constitutional foundation.

The effect of the Roe v Wade judgement was to strike down total bans on abortion then in effect in thirty-three of the fifty states and the District of Columbia. The Catholic Church, whose world-wide opposition to abortion had grown steadily during the twentieth century, saw the ruling as a major setback. Cardinal Terence Cooke of New York called the decision 'horrifying'. There were calls for the excommunication of Justice William Brennan, the Court's only Catholic member. The opponents of abortion prepared for a war of attrition. Catholic pro-life committees were formed in every parish. Opposition to abortion became a vehicle for the rise of Protestant fundamentalism. Pro-life organisations came to the conclusion that their only recourse was to change the membership of the Court and get the decision reversed. The only person who could change the composition of the Court was the US president, who alone nominated a new member when another retired or died. If the president was pro-choice, then the president had to be changed.

In 1980, abortion opponents helped bring this about when they elected Ronald Reagan, an outspoken opponent of abortion, to the White House. For eight years Reagan, and after him George Bush, nominated only those judges to the Supreme Court who were thought certain to oppose Roe v Wade. Reagan appointed three judges – Sandra Day O'Connor, fifty-one, the first woman to be appointed to the bench, Antonin Scalia, fifty, and Anthony Kennedy, fifty-one. He also elevated Rehnquist, the long-time critic of Roe v Wade, to Chief Justice.

The first major test of Roe v Wade came in 1989, when the Court was asked to rule, in a case known as Webster v Reproductive Health Services, whether an anti-abortion law passed by the State of Missouri was constitutional. It prohibited abortion in public hospitals and clinics and required tests for foetal viability on the grounds that 'the life of each human being begins at conception.' Anti-abortion forces were very active in Missouri. In one public hospital, the Missouri Truman Medical Center in Kansas City, the number of terminations of pregnancies had fallen from 484 in 1986 to forty-nine in 1988, mainly because one of the two doctors performing abortions had been so harassed that he moved to California and the other lost the lease to his house after constant picketing. In this case the Supreme Court justices had to decide, in the light of the Roe v Wade ruling, whether to knock down the law.

Two of the nine judges – William Brennan, son of an Irish immigrant who had become police commissioner of Newark, New Jersey, and Thurgood Marshall, the giant figure of the Civil Rights struggle of the 1950s and 1960s – were opposed to any ruling which would weaken Roe v Wade.

Chief Justice Rehnquist argued that Missouri could interfere with abortion rights, on the grounds that the government had an interest in protecting human life throughout pregnancy.

Judge O'Connor suggested a compromise, stating that, while Roe v Wade still stood, it was unconstitutional to impose a regulation on a lawful abortion if it placed an undue burden on the woman's decision.

In a muddle of split opinions and arguments, the Court decided by five to four to uphold the Missouri regulations, without addressing the bigger question of the future of Roe v Wade. This could clearly wait for a more sweeping challenge from a pro-life state. In effect the

Missouri decision was an open invitation to other states to come up with new anti-abortion laws to challenge Roe v Wade. 'Darkness is approaching and a chill wind blows,' warned Justice Blackmun, author of Roe v Wade.

Two years later, when Justices Brennan and Marshall had retired, the critical challenge finally came. It was provided by Pennsylvania, a mountainous eastern state with a heavily rural, church-going population and a strong anti-abortion record. Its mining, farming and industrial small-town communities were deeply conservative and religious, and traditionally suspicious of the more liberal urban elite in Pittsburgh and Philadelphia. In 1982 it had been among the first states to attempt to bring in abortion restrictions in defiance of Roe v Wade but had been repulsed by Justice Harry Blackmun, who, in a majority opinion, told the Pennsylvania administration that it was not free 'to intimidate women into continuing pregnancies.'

The anti-abortion movement had an ally in Governor Casey, a Catholic who considered abortion as the taking of human life. It was aware, however, that Governor Casey had a high regard for the US Constitution and would not sign any law which ran explicitly counter to Roe v Wade, as it would be unconstitutional to do so while Roe v Wade still stood. They had to find a way to frame an anti-abortion law which would make the Supreme Court look afresh at Roe v Wade.

Anti-abortion groups met in the Holiday Inn in Pennsylvania's capital, Harrisburg, in September 1989 to map out a strategy. They ended up drafting an anti-abortion bill which Casey would feel comfortable signing. Called the Pennsylvania Abortion Control Act, it would require twenty-four-hour delays and compulsory pro-life counselling in all abortions and parental consent for under-eighteens.

The law would erect real barriers to many, mainly poor, women seeking abortions. A seventeen-year-old girl living in Wayne County, for example, who could get a four-hour car-ride to a clinic in Allentown for a $285 abortion and drive back the same day, would now have to get the consent of a parent or find a lawyer to obtain a judge's approval and plead her case to the judge, before even going to the clinic for counselling. She would then have to stay overnight in a hotel to allow twenty-four hours to elapse after her first visit to the clinic before the actual abortion took place.

The bill went through the Pennsylvania legislature and Casey signed it. The Southern Pennsylvania division of Planned Parenthood, the biggest of dozens of organisations which provide abortion facilities in the US, saw the bill for what it was – an attempt to further weaken Roe v Wade. The Bill had to be challenged by referring it to the Supreme Court. The case could precipitate the total overthrow of Roe v Wade but, at the same time, that it might be the least of a number of evils. For coming up behind the Pennsylvania case were fresh challenges, in the form of laws criminalising abortion outright, instigated by anti-abortion forces in Louisiana and Utah.

The decision to appeal to the Supreme Court was taken at a meeting in Philadelphia organised by Kathryn Kolbert, lawyer to the American Civil Liberties Union, and attended by several pro-choice groups. In their submission, they asked bluntly: 'Has the Supreme Court overruled Roe v Wade, 410 US 113 (1973), holding that a woman's right to choose abortion is a fundamental right protected by the United States Constitution?'

Both sides held their breath as the Supreme Court prepared to issue its decision in the summer of 1992. Cardinal John O'Connor of New York sent a dramatic reminder to the Court of Catholic opposition to abortion by personally leading an anti-abortion march against the Eastern Women's Center Abortion Clinic in Manhattan's East 38th Street on 13 June, two weeks before the ruling. Organised by a Brooklyn group, the Helpers of God's Precious Infants, the march was joined by Randall Terry, who called the Cardinal a hero. However, Frances Kissling, president of a small but influential dissident organisation known as Catholics for a Free Choice, told a reporter that the demonstration in fact betrayed frustration at the failure of Operation Rescue and the slow pace of judicial efforts to combat abortion.

The answer to Planned Parenthood's question came on 29 June. It was a qualified 'No'. By five votes to four, the Supreme Court decided not to overrule Roe v Wade. But it upheld most of the Pennsylvania restrictions, while leaving no doubt that laws prohibiting abortions – such as those in Louisiana and Utah – would still be considered unconstitutional.

To the dismay of anti-abortion fundamentalists, three Reagan-Bush appointees – Justices Sandra Day O'Connor, Anthony Kennedy and David Souter – joined their two more liberal colleagues, Harry

Blackmun and John Paul Stevens in securing Roe v Wade as the basis for abortion law. Despite their appointment by anti-abortion presidents, and despite a direct appeal from the Bush administration for them to do so, they said they were not prepared to strike down 'a liberty we cannot renounce', and they re-affirmed the 'essential holding' of Roe v Wade.

To many pro-choice activists, however, Roe was 'dead, despite the flimsy stay of execution', as Patricia Ireland, president of the National Organisation for Women, put it. Anti-abortion groups felt betrayed too. 'This is a loss for unborn children,' said Wanda Franz, president of the National Right to Life Committee, the largest pro-life group in the US. Randall Terry, never one to mince his words, said: 'Three Reagan-Bush appointees stabbed the pro-life movement in the back.' Bill Clinton said that the constitutional right to choose was 'hanging by a thread' and only his election would save it.

George Bush, the president who could do nothing right, had a chance before he left office to appoint one more judge to the Supreme Court. With America split over conflicts of moral absolutes, not just over abortion but also over capital punishment, religion in schools, gay rights, women's rights, children's rights, even the right to die, and divided over the concept of individual liberty, George Bush nominated a right-wing black conservative, Clarence Thomas, to fill the last Supreme Court vacancy of his four-year presidency.

In doing so, he opened the gates to a furious nationwide debate which was to contribute to his defeat, set back the cause he was trying to advance and made a modern-day heroine of an obscure Oklahoma law professor called Anita Hill.

Chapter 7

WOMEN AGAINST THE SYSTEM

If I have to I can do anything,
I am strong, I am invincible, I am a woman

HELEN REDDY, 1972

THE EVENT WHICH PRECIPITATED the nomination of Clarence Thomas to the Supreme Court was the sudden resignation of Justice Thurgood Marshall on 27 June 1991, five days before his eighty-third birthday. Marshall had been perhaps the greatest civil rights lawyer in American history, winning many celebrated Supreme Court cases to advance the black cause, including the 1954 Brown v Board of Education case which made school segregation unconstitutional. He had become the first black judge in the history of the Supreme Court and was now the last of the great liberal justices who, during a quarter of a century, had participated in a major reform of American law. During his time, civil rights and liberties had been expanded, equal protection guaranteed under due process of the law and abortion rights established.

That era had come to an end when Ronald Reagan was elected US president in 1980 and began filling Supreme Court vacancies with judges who shared his right-wing ideology. Reagan's goal was to create a conservative Supreme Court whose life members would be a bulwark against liberalism, no matter who controlled the White House and Senate. By 1991 the process was well under way and the Court had become predominantly conservative. Marshall, grey-haired and cantankerous, nearly blind and in failing health, was feeling increasingly isolated and frustrated.

The ruling which broke his spirit was Payne v Tennessee. Pervis Payne had brutally murdered twenty-eight-year-old Charisse Christopher and her two-year-old daughter, Lacie, with a butcher's knife in Millington, Tennessee, in 1987. Payne had been convicted but, before sentence was passed, his mother, father and girlfriend had testified to his normally caring character and a psychologist gave evidence that he was, in fact, mentally handicapped. The judge then allowed the victim's mother to testify, with great emotion, about the distress suffered by Christopher's other child, Nicholas, over losing his mother and sister. Following this heart-rending scene, the jury imposed a sentence of death. Payne appealed to the Supreme Court that the death sentence should not be carried out, as the same Court had already ruled in an earlier case that juries should not be subjected to emotional statements from victims before deciding the sentence.

The issue provoked a furious row among the nine justices. When the smoke cleared, six of the judges ruled that the precedent should be overturned and three, led by Marshall, that it should not. To Thurgood Marshall the court was trampling over the principle of *stare stasis* – that is, that its rulings once made should remain in force – in pursuit of a tough, right-wing law and order agenda. Marshall, who once declared he would never retire until a Democrat was back in the White House, decided to quit. With Bush the most popular president in history in the wake of the Gulf War and looking a certainty for re-election in 1992, a tired and dispirited Marshall felt his ability to influence events had ended.

'This truncation of the Court's duty to stand by its own precedents is astonishing,' he said. It was a 'clear signal that all the decisions implementing the personal liberties protected by the Bill of Rights and the Fourteenth Amendment are open to re-examination.' Such rulings, he warned, would 'squander the authority and the legitimacy of the Court as a protector of the powerless.'

At his farewell press conference that day, Marshall expressed his fear that President Bush would nominate a black conservative to replace him – that he would pick, as he put it, 'the wrong Negro. I'm opposed to that,' he said. 'My dad told me way back ... that there's no difference between a white snake and a black snake.'

Three days later President Bush nominated a black judge, Clarence Thomas, to take Marshall's place. Introducing the bespectacled forty-three-year-old African-American to the press at his holiday home in Kennebunkport, Maine, Bush described Thomas's appointment as an affirmation of the American Dream, the achievement of the pinnacle of success for a person who struggled to great heights from childhood poverty. The President denied that race was a factor in his decision, though White House officials had told journalists that it had been felt appropriate to replace one black judge with another.

'What I did is look for the best man,' said Bush. 'The fact that he is black and a minority is nothing to do with this, in the sense that he is the best qualified at this time.'

As with all Supreme Court nominations, Thomas had to be confirmed by the Judicial Committee of the US Senate, and then by the full one hundred-member Senate, which had a Democratic Party majority. A small army of liberal congressional aides and researchers immediately began following the paper trail of Thomas's writings and speeches to establish his ideological leanings and to find out whether in their opinion he was fit to fill Marshall's seat—or if he was 'the wrong Negro'.

An early discovery set the alarm bells ringing. It was a speech Thomas made to the conservative Heritage Foundation. In it, he appeared to praise an anti-abortion article written in 1987 by Lewis Lehrman, in which Lehrman described abortions as a 'holocaust' and called the Supreme Court's historic 1973 Roe v Wade ruling making abortion legal a 'coup against the Constitution'. Thomas had never stated his views openly on abortion but this, along with other evidence that he was most comfortable in the company of hard-line conservatives from the Republican Party, indicated he would throw in his lot with the anti-abortion judges on the Supreme Court.

Thomas's career was a rags to riches story. Born in 1948 in the poor village of Pin Point in the southern state of Georgia, he had been placed by his grandfather, a man of some influence in the Civil Rights movement, in a private school for blacks run by Irish Franciscan nuns. At sixteen, his grandfather enrolled him in an all-white Catholic boarding school, from which he graduated at the age of twenty and was offered a place in Holy Cross College in Worcester, Massachusetts. The mainly-white college was anxious to enroll black students as a surge of white guilt swept over the country after the assassination of Martin Luther King. At Holy Cross, Thomas went through a radical period and joined anti-Vietnam war protests. After graduating with honours in 1971, he was admitted to Yale Law School which had set a goal of having 10 percent of each class composed of blacks. Thomas never knew if he was the beneficiary of his own talents or of the affirmative action programme to promote minorities – an idea which he came to resent strongly. 'You had to prove yourself every day because the presumption was that you were dumb, and you didn't deserve to be there on merit,' he once said. He is remembered by fellow students at the time for two things: a steady move to the right away from his teenage activism and a fondness for attending pornographic movies in nearby New Haven.

On graduation, Thomas took a job in the office of John Danforth, Missouri's Republican attorney general and an ordained episcopal priest. By 1980 Thomas had sufficiently established his conservative credentials to be invited to a meeting of a hundred leading black conservatives in San Francisco. There he demonstrated how far he had travelled from his humble Pin Point origins. To illustrate the point that welfare payments made poor people over-dependent, he told his colleagues how his only sister, Emma Mae Martin, still living in Pin Point, 'gets mad when the mailman is late with her welfare cheque – that's how dependent she is.' It was a cruel remark. His sister, a deserted mother of three children, had once taken two part-time jobs, paying the minimum wage, to get off welfare, which she was drawing to care for an elderly aunt after a stroke. Since then Emma Mae Martin has taken a low-paying seven-days-a-week job as a cook in a Savannah hospital. Thomas was mortified when the remark was published and apologised to his sister.

With his increasingly conservative views, it was inevitable that Thomas would begin to advance rapidly after the Republicans came back to power in 1980. Right-wing blacks were not very numerous on the ground. He was first given an executive post in the Office of Civil Rights in the US Department of Education. From there in 1982 President Reagan appointed him chairman of the Equal Employment Opportunities Commission (EEOC), making him one of the most important black members of the administration.

The EEOC had been set up to monitor government policy of using affirmative action and setting racial quotas as a means of righting past wrongs and ensuring fair job opportunities for blacks and other minorities. It initiated litigation in cases of discrimination based on race, colour, religion, sex or national origin. The free-market Reagan White House, however, opposed affirmative action and racial quotas which required companies to reserve jobs for members of ethnic groups with high unemployment rates. Thomas dutifully scaled back the commission's activities. In his first six years, the number of cases in which the EEOC found discrimination in work fell from 73 percent to 43 percent of complaints submitted. In 1987 a General Accounting Office study found that 40 percent to 80 percent of alleged discrimination cases were closed without proper investigation.

The liberal investigators on Capitol Hill chronicled all this with increasing uneasiness. They also found that Thomas had once publicly voiced praise for Colonel Oliver North, the hero of the far right, whose secret negotiations to trade arms for hostages and channel the profits to right-wing Nicaraguan rebels were at the heart of the Iran-Contra scandal. He professed admiration for North's zeal for country, freedom and the limiting of government power. Thomas had also allowed his name to appear on the masthead of the ultra-right *Lincoln Review*, a journal which favoured the white South African government. Spiritually Thomas had also moved to the right, becoming a member of a fundamentalist anti-abortion Episcopalian church in the Washington suburbs. Socially he followed the same trajectory, marrying in 1987 Virginia Lamp, a white woman who had the same attitude to her sex as Thomas had to his race. Virginia Lamp lobbied Congress against increasing women's pay or rights in a battle against the liberal feminist agenda.

Thomas was further rewarded for his work on behalf of the Republican administration when in 1989 Bush made him a federal appellate judge. By the time the President nominated him for the Supreme Court, at the urging of his eccentric right-wing legal adviser, Boyden Gray, as 'the best qualified at this time', Thomas had been a judge for a mere fifteen months. Bush's view of Thomas's qualifications was not shared by the American Bar Association. It rated Thomas as only 'qualified' to sit on the Supreme Court, a reluctant 'pass' from a body which had almost invariably rated previous nominees as 'well-qualified'.

The blatantly political nature of the appointment created opposition to Thomas among liberal Democrats, those identified with the interests of civil rights and women's organisations, trade unions, environmental groups, professional and consumer bodies and with minorities. They were especially concerned by Judge Thomas's youth; if Thomas lived as long as Thurgood Marshall he would be decisive in shaping the ideology of America for four decades.

But there were difficulties for the all-white senators of the Judicial Committee in opposing a black nominee, whatever their feelings that

Bush's appointment was a cynical act of tokenism. It could appear racist and could be seen as running counter to the affirmative action policy supported by senators like Edward Kennedy, a member of the Judicial Committee, who believed that such bodies as the Supreme Court should have minority representation.

The black population was also divided by the nomination of a right-wing African-American judge. On the one hand, Thomas's advancement was a matter of black pride. On the other, he was identified with forces traditionally hostile to black development. The judge even had the backing of Senator Strom Thurmond, who ran for president in 1948 as a white supremacist, and of the racist Louisiana candidate for governor, David Duke. Notwithstanding this, 60 percent of blacks supported Thomas in opinion polls, many on the grounds that, if he was rejected by the Senate, Bush could easily appoint a white conservative in his place. The congressional Black Caucus, comprising all black members of Congress, opposed the nomination because of Thomas's opposition to the Civil Rights movement, as did the board of the National Association for the Advancement of Coloured People. But he was endorsed by the Southern Christian Leadership Conference, which had been founded by Martin Luther King.

Democratic senators had already once succeeded in blocking a white right-wing Supreme Court nominee, Justice Robert H. Bork, who had been proposed by President Reagan in 1987. On that occasion, Senator Kennedy marshalled the opposition to Bork because of his openly conservative views, saying his confirmation would mean 'women would be forced into back alley abortions, blacks would sit at segregated lunch counters, rogue police would break down citizens' doors ...' Republicans had bitter memories of that fight. They had been caught off guard. Things were different this time, especially as the nominee was black, which sowed dissension among the opposition. The right geared up for a battle they felt they could win. Weekly meetings to co-ordinate strategy were organised by New Right groups in the office of the conservative Family Research Council in Washington. The Christian Coalition, the religio-political movement run by television evangelist, Pat Robertson, who gave prime-time homilies on his Family Channel justifying such right-wing causes as the death penalty, spent more than $1 million on television commercials showing Thomas in patriotic colours.

Some days before the Senate nomination hearing was due to begin, a member of the Alliance for Justice, a liberal pressure group, heard that Professor Anita Hill, a Yale Law School graduate, had worked with Thomas at the EEOC and had complained to friends that he had sexually harassed her. The Alliance for Justice passed this information to the offices of the two most liberal senators on the fourteen-member Senate Judicial Committee, Edward Kennedy and Howard Metzenbaum. Telephone calls were made to Anita Hill at her law faculty at Oklahoma State University by Gail Laster, a lawyer on Metzenbaum's staff, and Ricki Seidman of Senator Kennedy's staff. They asked if the stories were true and if Anita Hill was willing to submit an account of her experiences to the Senate Committee. She did not deny the rumours but said she was not willing to come forward.

The Senate Judicial Committee met in public to consider the nomination of Judge Clarence Thomas in the Senate Caucus Room on 10 September 1991. Its eight Democrat and six Republican members seated themselves behind a long, raised table equipped with microphones. Thomas, sitting alone and facing them at a table covered with a green cloth, was greeted with the customary elaborate courtesy of these occasions. Committee chairman, Senator Joseph Biden, set the ball rolling. 'Now, Judge,' he said, 'in your view does the liberty clause of the Fourteenth Amendment protect the right of women to decide for themselves, in certain instances, whether or not to terminate pregnancy?' It was a transparent attempt to test Thomas's view on abortion but the judge refused to reply directly. Despite repeated questioning he would not be drawn on his views on abortion. He even assured a sceptical Senator Pat Leahy that he had never publicly nor even privately debated the merits of Roe v Wade, one of the most important US Supreme Court decisions of the century, which had made abortion legal. As the interrogation moved on to other areas of law, Thomas gave hesitant and unimpressive responses. His knowledge of the law was flawed but Democratic senators hesitated to ridicule a black nominee for lack of qualifications.

Watching the televised hearings, Anita Hill decided she had a duty after all to respond to the calls from Washington. She telephoned Ricki Seidman in Senator Kennedy's office and was passed on to a Senate staff member, Jim Brudney, to whom she poured out her story.

Professor Hill believed that the Senate Judicial Committee should privately investigate her charges before any vote on the nominee. Brudney gave this dramatic information to Senator Metzenbaum, who passed it like a hot potato to the office of Senator Biden, the committee chairman.

This placed Biden – a once ambitious Democrat from Delaware who had run for president in 1988 until he was caught plagiarising a speech by British Labour leader Neil Kinnock – in a difficult position. He was now faced with the prospect of alienating conservatives and blacks if he became involved in promoting a sensational allegation, which might be impossible to prove, against a black Supreme Court nominee. Biden decided to bide his time, leaving it up to Anita Hill to come forward and initiate a formal complaint of her own accord.

Three days later she did, this time naming a friend, Judge Susan Hoerchner in California, as someone who could confirm that she had complained to her about Thomas's behaviour at the time it happened. On the last scheduled day for the public hearings, Senator Biden proposed asking the FBI to interview both Thomas and Hill. Anita Hill agreed. In the meantime she faxed a four-page account of her allegations to Senator Biden's office. It described how Clarence Thomas had frequently and against her wishes made lewd remarks to her about sex, and given her graphic accounts of pornographic films involving orgies and sexual acts with animals. Still Biden delayed using this piece of dynamite.

It wasn't until seven days later, on Friday, 25 September, a week after the public hearings and just an hour before the Judiciary Committee was due to vote on Thomas's nomination, that other committee members were privately supplied with a copy of Professor Hill's shocking allegations. By then the senators had made up their minds. They voted seven to seven, with one Democrat joining the Republicans. The tie meant the nomination survived. Everything now depended on a vote by the full Senate in two weeks.

Nothing was yet known to the public about Hill's allegations, but a persistent reporter on Capitol Hill, Timothy Phelps of the New York newspaper *Newsday*, got wind that something was up. By some assiduous questioning of his sources he soon found out. On 6 October, the last day before the full Senate vote, Phelps published the story of the charges made by Anita Hill against Clarence Thomas and how senators had sat on it for a week.

His article created a sensation. Crowds of reporters and camera crews arrived at the University of Oklahoma to locate this black woman who had dared challenge the black choice of the white establishment.

They found a modest and respectable law professor who had been elected faculty leader and scholar-in-residence at the provost's office of the university. She was poised, articulate and well-groomed, and somewhat conservative in her views. Anita Hill also came from poor black beginnings. The youngest of thirteen children raised on an Oklahoma farm, she had graduated with honours from Oklahoma State University in 1977 and gone on to earn a law degree at Yale University in 1980. She had worked as an assistant to Clarence Thomas in the Office of Civil Rights in the US Department of Education and then followed Thomas to the EEOC before leaving suddenly in 1983 to return to the academic world. Her colleagues spoke of her as a woman of great integrity.

The first glimpse the American public had of Anita Hill was when she arrived to speak to reporters at a press conference in a packed university room that Monday evening. As she entered, her colleagues gave her a standing ovation. Anita Hill denied she was involved in any political ploy. 'There is no way that I would do something like this for political purposes,' she said. 'I responded to the committee's approach ... I resent the idea that people would blame the messenger for the message rather than look at the content of the message.' She had been afraid to speak out before, she said, because of Thomas's powerful position in the legal world.

The first reaction of many senators was outrage. Senator Orrin Hatch of Utah, a Republican member of the Judicial Committee with a record of opposition to civil rights legislation, fumed to Phelps over the telephone: 'This is a fine young man [Thomas] that they're smearing in the most reprehensible, dirty way possible, and that's because they're losing.' The White House issued a statement saying that the FBI investigation had concluded that the allegation was unfounded (which it hadn't). Right-wing Democratic Senator Alan Simpson of Wyoming forecast Hill would be 'destroyed, belittled, hounded and harassed' and claimed to have faxes and letters questioning her credibility 'hanging out of my pocket'.

Senator John Danforth, the fifty-five-year-old anti-abortion, anti-gun control Republican Senator from Missouri who had helped Thomas's early career, warned of what was to come, saying: 'I don't know anything about these charges except that Clarence Thomas is my friend and I've asked him about them and he says they're not true.' He told reporters he had obtained the telephone logs of Clarence Thomas's office which showed that his secretary had taken eleven calls from Professor Hill since she had left the EEOC in 1983 because of alleged sexual harassment. One of the entries dated 30 January 1984 said: 'Just called to say "Hello".' Another, on 9 May 1984, said: 'Sorry she didn't see you this week.' On that same day and again on 8 October 1986, the log had noted her message: 'Please call.' Another said: 'Please call tonight' and left the number of a Washington hotel. The recitation of calls damaged Anita Hill's story. Why would she remain in friendly contact with someone who had sexually harassed her?

At the same time, Capitol Hill was inundated with telephone calls from outraged women who had watched Anita Hill's press conference and were demanding that she be heard. On the floor of the House, Congresswoman Barbara Mikulski of Maryland voiced the feelings of anger and helplessness of women who were subjected to sexual abuse and who remained convinced that the victim would always be victimised.

'To anybody out there who wants to be a whistle-blower, the message is,' she said, 'you'll be left out there by yourself ... nobody's going to take you seriously, not even the United States Senate.'

The polls seemed to bear her out. Despite the fury of the women callers, public opinion surveys showed two out of three Americans still felt that Thomas should be confirmed. In a *New York Times* poll only one in five people said they believed Anita Hill. Many factors made them sceptical. The alleged events had taken place some years previously. There had been no physical abuse. The charges, some said, were not serious enough to wreck a career. There was resentment among blacks at the betrayal of one of their number by another in a white man's forum.

Support for an acutely embarrassed Thomas was nevertheless fast eroding in the Senate. As senators dithered about reconvening the Judicial Committee, Judge Thomas resolved their dilemma by announcing that he wanted the Committee to meet again to clear his name.

Thus began one of the most bizarre nomination hearings in the history of Capitol Hill. On Friday, 12 October, the fourteen senators arrayed themselves once more along the raised dais in the Senate Caucus Room. Before them was the table covered with green cloth. Beyond it dozens of legal advisers, relatives, friends, lobbyists, members of Congress and journalists had crowded into the room. Among them, almost unnoticed, was Rosa Parks, the heroine of the Civil Rights movement in the 1950s. The corridors of the Senate building emptied as staff gathered round their television monitors. Across America millions stopped work to tune in.

From the start the proceedings were weighted against Anita Hill. The chairman, Senator Biden, allowed Judge Thomas to speak first and have his denial on record before the allegations were formally made.

'I have not said or done the things that Anita Hill has alleged,' said Judge Thomas. 'From the very beginning, charges were levelled against me from the shadows, charges of drug abuse, anti-semitism, wife beating ... And now this.' This was not American, he said, but Kafkaesque. 'No job is worth what I have been through. No job. No horror in my life has been so debilitating. Confirm me if you want. Don't confirm me if you are so led, but let this process end.' He would not discuss the allegations, he said. 'I will not provide the rope for my own lynching or for further humilitation.'

The senators bowed to Thomas's refusal to discuss the charges – and to be cross-examined on them – and called Anita Hill. Wearing a demure, turquoise suit and speaking in a calm and confident monotone, she described how at the Department of Education Thomas had repeatedly made her uncomfortable by talking about sexual matters. He eventually stopped. When he was made chairman of the EEOC and asked her to take a post there, she accepted. The work was more interesting and she hoped the offensive behaviour had ended, she said. However he soon started pestering her at her new job.

'One of the oddest episodes I remember was an occasion in which Thomas was drinking a Coke in his office,' said Professor Hill as an audience of millions watched spellbound. 'He got up from the table at which we were working, went over to his desk to get the Coke, looked at the can and asked: "Who has put pubic hair on my Coke?" On other occasions,' she said, 'he referred to the size of his own penis as being larger than normal and he also spoke on some occasions of the pleasures he had given to women with oral sex.' The Oklahoma law professor said that this behaviour was largely responsible for her decision to leave the EEOC and pursue a career in teaching.

She then addressed the question that had been troubling her supporters – if he had treated her so badly, why did she telephone him eleven times in the following seven years? Once, she said, she returned a call. Three times she was acting as a conduit for others. On other occasions she had telephoned to talk to his secretary, whom she knew, and simply passed on some casual comment. A number of calls were on behalf of a Civil Rights group in Tulsa asking her to help persuade Judge Thomas to attend their conference as a speaker. The last call was at the request of her law faculty which mandated her to invite Thomas to speak at Oklahoma University.

Senator Biden began the questioning for the Committee. Were there any other bizarre incidents, he asked?

'There was a reference to an individual who had a very large penis and he used the name that he had been referred to in the pornographic material,' Hill replied.

Did she remember the name?

'Yes, I do. The name that was referred to was Long Dong Silver.'

Having helped to immortalise an obscure pornographic star, Biden pressed on. What was the most embarrassing incident she had endured?

'His discussion of pornography involving those women with large breasts and engaged in a variety of sex with different people or animals,' replied Professor Hill. 'This was the thing that embarrassed me the most and made me feel the most humiliated.' These conversations, she said, were 'very dirty and they were disgusting' and she believed they amounted to implicit pressure to have sex with him.

Senator Biden asked her to describe what Thomas had said about his own sexual capabilities.

'Well, I can tell you that he compared his penis size, he measured his penis in terms of length, those kind of comments,' she said.

Horror was written all over the faces of the senators. The nomination of a black Supreme Court judge was now turning on a discussion about the size of his penis. As corroboration of her story, Professor Hill named three people to whom she had complained at the time. Thomas's supporters in turn produced a black Texan lawyer, John Doggett, who testified that she was prone to sexual fantasies and that she had imagined he was attracted to her. His theory would later be demolished under cross-examination but to television viewers it raised new questions about Anita Hill's credibility. A number of senators questioned her gruffly, as if she herself was on trial.

'Are you a scorned woman?' barked Democratic Senator Howell Heflin of Alabama. 'Do you have a martyr complex? Are you interested in writing a book?'

'No,' she replied to each question.

The hearings dragged on into the evening. At 9 p.m. Judge Thomas returned, his face a study in fury. He denied the specific allegations and accused the senators of allowing a travesty of justice.

'This is a circus,' he said. 'It's a national disgrace. And from my standpoint as a black American, as far as I'm concerned, it's high-tech lynching for uppity blacks who in any way deign to think for themselves, to do for themselves, to have different ideas, and it is a message that unless you kowtow to an old order, that is what will happen to you. You will be lynched, destroyed, caricatured, by a Committee of the US Senate, rather than hung from a tree.'

Faced with the pitiable image of the victimised black man, liberal senators held back from pressing Thomas about the allegations. The fourteen white members of the Judicial Committee did not relish being portrayed as a lynch mob, though no black man had ever been lynched on the word of a wronged black woman.

When the hearing resumed after a break, Thomas's supporters continued their quest to discredit Hill. Senator Orrin Hatch raised the possibility that Hill had borrowed her allegations from published material. He cited the 1988 case of Carter versus Sedgwick County, Kansas, in which a black woman claimed she had been sexually harassed and sacked by her white boss, named Brand, due to her race. Hatch read from an account of the case: 'Plaintiff further testified that on one occasion defendant Brand presented her with a picture of Long Dong Silver, a photo of a black man with an elongated penis.' He then produced and read from a copy of *The Exorcist* which had a character called Sharon who claimed that a man remarked to her that there was 'an alien pubic hair floating around in my gin'.

'What do you think about that, Judge?' asked Senator Hatch.

'Senator, I think this whole affair is sick,' replied Thomas.
'I think it's sick, too,' said Hatch.

Senator Arlen Specter took over the questioning. A moderate pro-choice Republican who had a good relationship with women's groups, Specter was facing a tough Republican primary re-election test in Pennsylvania. Seizing a chance to prove his conservative credentials, he accused Anita Hill of perjury.

At the end of that long, exhausting day, many in the crowded Caucus Room felt that Anita Hill had been smeared by tactics similar to those used by Senator Joe McCarthy in rooting out suspected communists in the 1950s.

Only at the close of the third and final day of the reconvened hearing did Senator Edward Kennedy break his silence and intervene. The character assassination of Professor Hill was unworthy, he said. 'The fact is that these points of sexual harassment are made by an Afro-American against an Afro-American. The issue isn't discrimination and racism; it's about sexual harassment. And I hope we can keep our eye on that particular issue.' In a powerful speech on the floor of the Senate when the nomination came to a vote the following week, he asked: 'Are we an old boy's club, insensitive at best and perhaps something worse ... to tolerate any unsubstantiated attack on a woman in order to rationalise a vote for this nomination?' There was no proof, he said, that Anita Hill had perjured herself and 'shame on anyone who suggests that she has.'

The bitterness of the hearings oozed out in Senator Hatch's retort to Kennedy. For anyone who believed Kennedy, there was 'a bridge up in Massachusetts' that he'd be happy to sell to them, he said – a clear reference to the Senator's controversial accident at Chappaquiddick in 1969.

Senator Kennedy's intervention came too late. Thomas was confirmed by the Senate by fifty-two votes to forty-eight, though it was the smallest ever margin for a Supreme Court nominee. Ten Democratic senators, including Senator Alan Dixon of Illinois, voted for Thomas. Senator Dixon argued that as both parties were credible the balance of the doubt must go to the accused.

The repercussions of the Senate hearings began to be felt immediately. Anita Hill's defiant stand raised the nation's consciousness of the issue of sexual harassment. Instead of leaving women more fearful of making allegations of sexual harassment, more women were emboldened to lodge complaints: the numbers increased from 6,883 in 1991 to 10,522 in 1992. In a *Newsweek* poll on Anita Hill at the end of 1992, 66 percent of women said bosses had become more sensitive to the problem of sexual harassment during 1992, though 47 percent felt they were worse off in terms of job opportunities and pay and only 12 percent thought they were materially better off.

The hearings defined the age in the same way Watergate shaped the early 1970s. They redefined the perception of women's role in American society. They created an atmosphere in which other women were prepared to go public in the fight for equality.

Naval Lieutenant Paula Coughlin, for example, told the press in June 1992 a horrifying story of institutionalised sexual harassment in the Navy. She had been violently assaulted by naval pilots at a Tailhook Association convention at the Las Vegas Hilton on 7 September 1991 which she was attending as a helicopter pilot. The association, whose members include past and present naval flyers, is named after the hook on a plane that catches landing cables on an aircraft carrier. It had gained notoriety for holding wild parties, and on this occasion some of the 1,600 pilots in attendance had organised a gauntlet on the hotel's third floor corridor along which women were groped and pinched and had their clothes pulled off. Many women came along for the fun; there were strippers in some of the rooms. But others were unwitting victims. Lt. Coughlin came to the third floor to meet friends. As she stepped out of the elevator, a man grabbed her by the bottom and lifted her off the floor. Others clutched at her breast and buttocks as she screamed: 'What the fuck do you think you are doing?' A hand reached into her skirt and tried to pull off her panties. She fell to the floor but eventually managed to break free and escape. When Paula Coughlin made a formal complaint, it was passed from department to department for a month before the Naval Investigative Service was asked to investigate. The pilots closed ranks and the investigators ran into a wall of silence. It was at that point that she went public.

What might once have been dismissed as over-enthusiasm by the boys with the 'right stuff' became the cause of a major scandal in the atmosphere of heated debate in the wake of the Anita Hill case. Two days after Coughlin spoke out, US Navy Secretary Lawrence Garrett resigned. Other commanders were demoted or removed. Investigations were launched to find out who was responsible for the gauntlet.

In his first judgements, Clarence Thomas confirmed the worst fears of the liberals that he was 'the wrong Negro' by aligning himself with the most conservative justices and taking a hard line against abortion. In one dissenting opinion he stated that it was not unconstitutional to beat a prisoner, earning him the *New York Times* headline: 'The Youngest, Cruellest Justice.'

One of the ironies of the affair was that Judge Thurgood Marshall did, after all, live to see a Democratic president in office again. He was still alive when Bill Clinton was inaugurated president on 20 January 1992. If he had hung on until the Republicans had left the White House, as he once intended, so that a liberal could be named to replace him, Thurgood Marshall would have made it by five days. The old Civil Rights warrior died on 25 January 1992.

The other accident of fate which helped determine the outcome of the Clarence Thomas hearing was the fact that Senator Kennedy, the one liberal member of the Judicial Committee who could have led a powerful assault on the nomination of Clarence Thomas, was in no position to do so.

Kennedy was uncomfortable at the idea of pulling down a member of a minority. For the most part, the Senator from Massachusetts sat through the proceedings in untypical silence; he had refused to get involved when Anita Hill rang Ricki Seidman at his office, passing her on to the Senate staff instead, and once, at a crucial moment during the hearings, he had declined an opportunity to question Thomas.

Kennedy had been rendered politically impotent by the embarrassment of the impending trial in Florida in which his nephew, William Kennedy Smith, was accused of rape after drinking with the Senator in a nightspot called the Au Bar on Palm Beach, Florida. During the Senate hearings, television advertisements produced by hard-line Republican activist, Floyd Brown, highlighted his behaviour at Palm Beach, taunting him with a picture of a tabloid headline saying: 'Teddy's Sexy Romp.' The public debate on the treatment of women was only just beginning and Kennedy was a part of it.

Chapter 8

SCHOOL FOR SCANDAL

To create a public scandal is what's wicked;
to sin in private is not a sin.

MOLIÈRE, *TARTUFFE*, ACT 1V, SCENE 5

AU BAR IS DECORATED INSIDE like a large drawing room. It has chintz-covered couches and little tables with matching high-backed chairs around the walls. A curved marble-topped bar counter protrudes into the room and a tiny space is left clear for dancing. The clientele is usually made up of middle-aged men in blazers, silk shirts and ascots, younger men with gold medallions round their necks, wealthy, tanned, forty-something women in Armani dresses, and bare-armed young women in tight-fitting skirts from Scaasi or Roehm. Au Bar is an expensive pick-up joint. A shot of whisky there, purchased in the interests of research, cost me $10. It is one of the trendiest nightclubs on Palm Beach, which is a seven-mile long island of high palms, jacarandas and begonias off the Florida coast.

Palm Beach is a warm-weather, make-believe haven for the rich and famous in America. Connected to the mainland by three bridges, it is the largest community in the US without a mortician or a cemetery. Strangers are not encouraged to linger on the narrow roads, no parking is allowed on residential avenues and tour buses are forbidden. Every day servants and gardeners stream across the bridges from the mainland to service the kitchens and gardens of the island's 10,859 mansions and villas, whose owners included at least twenty-four of the *Forbes* four hundred richest Americans. Among these were casino developer Donald Trump, who had a 128-room castle called Mar-a-Lago; Ronald Perelman, the Revlon owner who was worth $2.75 billion; Estée Lauder of the cosmetics empire and many less well-known residents distinguished by little other than vast wealth, like Carl Icahn, a corporate raider worth $1.2 billion.

The Palm Beach season gets under way at Christmas and lasts until the northern winter lets up at Easter. It is a non-stop round of parties, charity balls and card games; contract bridge was invented here by

Harold Vanderbilt in 1923. For the fast crowd, the action on Palm Beach is on Royal Poinciana Way, a tree-lined avenue where socialites hand the keys of their Rolls Royces and Cadillacs to parking-valets in shorts and white shirts, so they can drop into night spots like the Au Bar for a flute of champagne or a Brandy Alexander and a glimpse of celebrities, like Ivana Trump or Roxanne Pulitzer, among the regular customers.

The Kennedy family, also on the *Forbes* list with a fortune estimated at $850 million, has a holiday home on North Ocean Boulevard, facing the Atlantic at the northern end of the island. Joseph P. Kennedy, patriarch of the Kennedy clan, bought the compound with 126 feet of ocean front for $120,000 in 1933, marking the family's final transition from Boston-Irish immigrants to the millionaire world of wealth and privilege. Many world leaders came to know well this mansion by the sea, called La Guerida, when it was the winter White House for President John F. Kennedy from 1960 to 1963. During the Easter holiday in 1991, Senator Edward Kennedy came for a short holiday to the Kennedy mansion with his twenty-four-year-old son Patrick, his sister Jean Kennedy Smith, her son William and some close family friends, making up a party of eleven.

On Wednesday, 27 March, the fifty-nine-year-old Senator, unattached since he divorced his first wife, Joan, went to the Au Bar, a ten-minute drive away, at about 11 p.m., accompanied by his son Patrick. Ivana Trump was in her usual place and they exchanged brief greetings. The two Kennedys stayed for about an hour, then left with two young women.

Two days later, on Good Friday, they returned, this time accompanied by thirty-one-year-old William Kennedy Smith. Senator Kennedy had retired to bed earlier that evening but found he could not sleep because, he said, of a 'draining' conversation he had had with family members about Steve Smith, Jean Kennedy Smith's husband and William's father, who had died the previous August and whose loss was deeply felt – it was Steve Smith who always managed the family finances and its crises. The Senator woke up Patrick and William, who were sharing a bedroom, and asked them to accompany him to the Au Bar for a beer. Later he would say: 'I wish I'd gone for a long walk on the beach instead.'

In the crowded nightspot the small group brushed up against some of the women drinking there. William, a quiet fourth-year medical student at Georgetown University Hospital in Washington with a crooked smile and unkempt brown hair, got talking to Patricia Bowman, the twenty-nine-year-old step-daughter of a retired Republican industrialist, a single mother with a two-year-old daughter who lived in the nearby town of Jupiter. Patricia Bowman introduced her friend, a former model, Anne Mercer, to the Kennedy party. The Senator had what he called a 'brief exchange and not a pleasant one' with Mercer. When he introduced his son, who is a member of the Rhode Island Assembly, as 'Representative Patrick Kennedy', Anne Mercer replied: 'Am I supposed to be impressed?' Patrick got up and went to the bar where he got chatting to Michelle Cassone, a waitress from Testa's Restaurant. After a short time, he and Michelle joined the Senator and the three left, leaving William behind.

When they arrived at the compound the trio drank some wine on a veranda by the ocean before the Senator retired to bed. Shortly afterwards he came to Patrick's room in his night-shirt to say goodnight. Patrick and Michelle were embracing in the room. Michelle was startled by Kennedy's appearance and the couple grabbed a blanket and retired to the beach instead.

Meanwhile, William Kennedy Smith and Patricia were dancing the night away in Au Bar and when it closed she drove him in her car to the Kennedy mansion. It was about 3 a.m. but the night air was warm. The couple also went to the beach, where William swam naked in the sea, and they returned to the garden, where they had sex on the lawn.

That much was never disputed. Smith would say later that intercourse was consensual, Bowman that it was rape. Whatever happened, she used the house telephone, in some agitation, to call Anne Mercer, who arrived with her boyfriend Chuck Desiderio and escorted her away, taking some small items from the house, supposedly to prove they had been there. Next day Miss Bowman went to the sheriff's office on West Palm Beach and brought charges of sexual battery – the Florida equivalent of rape – against William Kennedy Smith.

The trial of William Kennedy Smith, 'Willie' to his family but introduced as 'Will' in court, began on 2 December in Room 411 of the West Palm Beach courthouse under Judge Mary Lupo. Because of the Palm Beach location and the Kennedy connection the trial was treated as one of the most sensational in US legal history. Less than two months after the Clarence Thomas hearings, people in the United States were presented with another morality play on their television screens, this time involving America's equivalent of a royal family. CNN Television and a new US cable channel, Court Television, carried the graphic testimony live into millions of homes.

'He slammed me to the ground, then he pushed my dress up and then he raped me,' claimed Bowman.

'She put me inside her on the lawn. I was not quite ready. She was helping me,' said Smith in rebuttal.

Hours were spent debating every aspect of the sexual encounter, down to the approximate number of grains of sand found in the underwear Bowman had bought in a store called Victoria's Secret. Experts were called on architecture, weather and lingerie.

Senator Kennedy himself was summoned to the witness stand by the prosecution. An awe-inspiring and dignified figure, the jowly silver-haired Senator dominated the courtroom, evoking the family's tragic past to explain why he asked Patrick and William to accompany him to the Au Bar so he could talk with them.

'Steve Smith, Will's father, was very special to me, a brother. We lost a brother, Joseph, in the war. When Jean married Steve we found another brother,' he said, 'and when Steve was gone, something left all of us – when we buried him. I found at the end of the conversation I was not able to think about sleeping. It was a very draining conversation, a whole range of memories came as an overwhelming wave in terms of emotion and I thought I can't possibly sleep.' It was a masterly performance.

The trial went on until 11 December when Smith was acquitted. Both he and his accuser had given conflicting testimony but the jury gave the accused the benefit of the doubt. Patricia Bowman's story had several inconsistencies, and in the circumstances she was not destined, like Anita Hill, to become a heroine for women. Nor did her friend Anne Mercer do her case any good: a key prosecution witness, she admitted in court to accepting $40,000 for two interviews on a tabloid television show called A Current Affair.

The hearing highlighted the fact that when a man was accused of rape, the woman also went on trial, just as when Supreme Court nominee Clarence Thomas was accused in a Senate committee hearing of sexual harassment, the woman who accused him was put in the dock. The affair also provoked new questions about the nation's moral values concerning sexual harassment, date rape and the private lives of public figures. And it impinged on the national debate between liberals and conservatives by damaging Senator Kennedy at a time when the cause he championed needed him most in the Clarence Thomas hearings.

It was an excruciating experience for Senator Kennedy, who was put on trial before the nation for taking his son and nephew to a pick-up bar. Early in the trial, when Smith's defence counsel, Roy Black, anxious to weed out hostile jurors, questioned prospective jurors on which member of the Kennedy family they respected least, the name 'Ted' was given in reply time after time. 'My God, we're paying this guy,' Kennedy complained, only half-jokingly, to an adviser, after watching the process on television. One prospective juror, an earthy, outspoken woman named Florence Orbach, said: 'The worst thing I ever heard about the Kennedys is that they are very smart but when they get horny their penis takes over and their brain closes.' The right-wing radio talk-show host, Rush Limbaugh, regularly played on his programme a parody of the 1960s hit, 'The Wanderer', renamed 'The Philanderer', which went:

> I'm the type of guy who likes to roam around,
> I'm never in one place, I roam from town to town,
> And when I find myself falling for some girl,
> I walk right to that car of mine, I take her for a whirl,
> 'Cos I'm a Kennedy, yes I'm Ted Kennedy,
> I sleep around, around, around, around, around.

In the circumstances Senator Kennedy could hardly have taken an aggressive role on the Senate Judicial Committee when it was presented with evidence by Anita Hill of sexual harassment. During these crucial hearings Kennedy sat 'with a bag over his head', in the words of the popular Miami-based humourist, Dave Barry.

Even before the trial began, the Senator had felt compelled to apologise publicly for his private behaviour. In an address at the John F. Kennedy School of Government at Harvard, Boston, he conceded that there were 'faults in the conduct of my private life,' and 'I realise that I alone am responsible for them and I am the one who must confront them.'

Senator Kennedy had reason for concern. In his constituency of Massachusetts, he would face re-election in 1994. The consequences of Kennedy's invitation to his son and nephew to go drinking at midnight were splashed across the pages of Boston's two daily newspapers, the *Boston Globe* and the *Boston Herald*. The *Globe*, a broadsheet which was usually loyal to Kennedy, sent only two reporters to the trial, but the *Herald*, a tabloid owned by Rupert Murdoch – who bitterly resented Kennedy's role in denying him a television franchise in Boston – assigned two reporters, two columnists, three lawyers, a photographer and a sketch writer. It came as a shock to Kennedy when the *Globe* turned on him in a scathing editorial which said that the periodic reports of reckless behaviour had diminished his moral authority and damaged his effectiveness as a public official.

Kennedy's Harvard apologia, which noted the 'disappointment of friends', was not enough for some Kennedy supporters in the Massachusetts legislature, the golden-domed State House on Boston Common where President Kennedy is commemorated by a statue near the entrance. A Boston-Irish Senator told me drily in his office: 'What's really damaging Kennedy now is the idea that he might not be a good parent. Before this my mother would never hear a word against him, but now the image conjured up is of Kennedy leading the next generation into a pick-up bar – on a Good Friday!'

'An illusion has been destroyed,' said another Massachusetts Senator, 'the illusion that the days of important sinning were behind him.' Opinion polls reflected similar public disapproval. After a series of successful Senate elections in which he averaged 66 percent support in Massachusetts, Kennedy had fallen to less than 50 percent approval in public esteem. Kennedy had been treated protectively by the media, which had been unwilling to expose the private excesses of one of the most effective US lawmakers of the century. Now journals openly probed his personal life to unravel the paradox of a champion of righteous causes whose morals were perpetually under fire – though the unfavourable coverage diminished when in 1992 Kennedy married Victoria Reggie, a thirty-eight-year-old Washington lawyer and long-time family friend, also divorced and the mother of two children. The ceremony was held in the Senator's house at McLean, a suburb of Washington in July. The surrogate father to twenty-one nephews and nieces was judged to be settling down at last.

Kennedy had been burdened with his role as the sole male survivor of his generation in a family dedicated to public achievement. For half a century, he had been haunted by family tragedy. His sister Rosemary was severely retarded as a result of a prefrontal lobotomy carried out in 1941 to correct behavioural disorders. His brother Joe was killed in World War II when his bomber exploded over the English Channel. His sister Kathleen died in a plane crash in France in 1948. His brother, President Kennedy, was shot in 1963. His brother Robert was assassinated in Los Angeles in 1968. When his car plunged into the dark waters off Chappaquiddick Island in 1969, his companion, twenty-nine-year-old Mary Jo Kopechne, perished. Edward Kennedy's son, Edward Jr., lost a leg to cancer, aged twelve. His nephew, David, who at the age of twelve was watching television alone in a hotel bedroom and saw his father Robert Kennedy being shot, died from a cocaine overdose in a Palm Beach hotel not far from Au Bar, aged twenty-eight.

What set this Boston-Irish family apart was a sense of being destined to serve and to suffer on a grand scale, as well as to enjoy the privileges attaching to a glamorous political dynasty with a unique appeal to the poor and oppressed. There was an abiding decency in the Kennedy political philosophy which made Ted Kennedy the champion of the underprivileged. Driven to match the legendary stature of his brothers, Kennedy assembled a staff of over a hundred aides in his Senate office and carved out for himself a role as an innovative and successful legislator. For more than two decades he was the legislative hero of the liberal left. For a generation he has personified liberalism in America as William Gladstone did for British politics in the eighteenth century. His collegiate instincts helped Kennedy forge alliances with political enemies to reach compromise on contested bills. As chairman of the Labour and Human Resources Committee in the Senate he passed fifty-four bills in the 1990-91 session, the best performance of the committee for half a century.

For many he was the re-embodiment of the hopes which died in Dallas in 1963. Kennedy was a potential candidate in every presidential election since 1972, and made a serious challenge for the Democratic Party nomination in 1980 but, haunted by Chappaquiddick and marginalised by his liberalism in Reagan's

America, he finally gave up his aspirations to the White House in the mid-1980s. His vision of America's future was no longer acceptable to a majority in the Democratic Party. In the 1992 presidential election campaign, Kennedy worked quietly for Bill Clinton, who campaigned on a centrist Democratic platform, and they avoided appearing together. Kennedy-style liberalism no longer drove the Democratic Party because it could not triumph on its own in an increasingly middle-class America, and because its champion was seriously flawed.

While the William Kennedy Smith case focussed the nation's attention again on sexual harassment and the line to be drawn between consensual sex and rape, it also raised acute questions about the responsibilities of the media. The names of alleged rape victims are not normally published in the United States, out of respect for their privacy and because of the stigma associated with being violated. In April, eight months before the trial, NBC television broke the unwritten rule and named Patricia Bowman as the alleged victim: the next day the editors of the *New York Times*, the daily newspaper which sets the standards for news coverage in the US, took this as sufficient reason to abandon the convention. It published Bowman's name along with an unflattering profile in which anonymous friends described her 'little wild streak', her speeding tickets, her out-of-wedlock daughter and even the books on her child's bookshelf, glimpsed through a window blind.

Over three hundred *New York Times* staff members, angry at the intrusion into the privacy of an alleged victim, held an impassioned confrontation with their editors in an auditorium at the *Times's* West 43rd Street headquarters. One woman said: 'They don't get it. They don't understand they set it up to look like the slut asked for it.' Executive editor Max Frankel admitted that 'we did not sufficiently guard against the imputation that "she deserved it".' National editor Soma Golden declared, to some jeers, that negative judgements on Bowman were in the mind of the readers. 'I can't account for every weird mind that reads *The New York Times*,' she said.

Many journalists were infuriated by Bowman's treatment compared to the paper's coverage of a Central Park rape by black youths of a well-connected white woman whom the newspaper had not named. *Times* columnist, Anna Quindlen, wrote a stinging rebuke of her own paper's standards, saying: 'The obvious conclusion was that women who graduate from Wellesley, have prestigious jobs and are raped by a gang of black teenagers will be treated fairly by the press. And women who have below average high school grades, are well-known at bars and dance clubs and say that they have been raped by an acquaintance from an influential family after a night of drinking will not.'

Patricia Bowman herself went public in an ABC television interview on 18 December, after the trial verdict had been given. During the court proceedings, her face had been hidden by a large grey dot or by electronic distortion, turning her into a hidden accuser. Many journalists felt that only by coming forward publicly would the shame attached to rape be lessened. 'I wish she had done it earlier,' Edward Sears, editor of the *Palm Beach Post*, said. 'The only way the stigma's going to be erased is for courageous women to identify themselves in rape cases.'

Date rape, once a taboo subject, became a focus for national debate, a manifestation of a changing society which a few years earlier would not have taken such an issue seriously and where many men's attitudes towards women had been moulded by Hollywood movies like *Gone With the Wind*. Meg Nugent, a former assistant director of the Women's Center at Towson State University in Maryland and a victim of acquaintance rape, told a reporter: 'The incredibly sexy Clarke Gable picks up the kicking and screaming Scarlett O'Hara and carries her off and rapes her. The next morning she wakes up humming and singing and happy. The message is if you just keep going they'll come round and dig it.' According to the FBI, the number of reported forcible rapes in the United States is rising steadily: from 92,490 in 1989 to 94,500 in 1990, 106,590 in 1991 and 112,000 in 1992. The majority were committed by acquaintances of the victim – they were, in effect, mostly date rapes.

The Kennedy phenomenon in American political life also became a topic for renewed national debate in the wake of the Kennedy Smith affair. Numerous new volumes about the Kennedys appeared in the bookstores, underlining the ambivalence of people in the United States towards the Kennedy brothers, whose failings were mercilessly exposed, but who had come to represent for many – Ted, as well as Bobby and Jack – the American Dream.

There was a national ambivalence towards the Kennedys, who were perceived as something between a liberal political dynasty with a divine right to power and a family of wealthy and ruthless careerists. This explains why, despite the scandals connected with the Kennedy name, of which Palm Beach was but the latest in a long list, President John F. Kennedy remains a compelling symbol of unfulfilled hopes and dreams to millions of Americans.

The seven-storey Dallas School Book Depository, from where he was shot on 22 November 1963, has been turned into a shrine to his memory. Over the years so many tourists, sightseers, convention delegates, journalists, writers and pilgrims had come to Dealey Plaza in downtown Dallas to visit the site that a quarter of a century later, in 1989, the Dallas County Historical Foundation opened the whole of the sixth floor to the public.

The red-brick structure, built in 1901 as a warehouse, served for a time as the Texas School Book Depository and is now the Dallas County Administration Headquarters. The sixth floor has become a memorial of atonement, dedicated 'not to the pain and sorrow of death but as a permanent tribute to the joy and excitement of one man's life – John Fitzgerald Kennedy.' Every day over a thousand people crowd into the special visitors' centre at the back, built on as part of a $3.5 million project organised by the Foundation. It contains a shop selling souvenir pencils and rulers marked 'The Sixth Floor' and books on Kennedy's life. A $5 ride in a special non-stop lift brings visitors to the sixth floor which has been partitioned into a maze of exhibitions with photographs, documents and film and video clips recalling Kennedy's life and death. Recordings of his voice fill the room: 'The new future of which I speak is not a set of promises but a set of challenges'; 'Ask not what your country can do for you but what you can do for your country.' The corner from which the shots were fired is enclosed behind glass walls, with book cartons marked 'Scott Foresman, Chicago' piled up beside it as they were on the day of the assassination. The recorded sound of shots rings out as people gaze through the adjacent windows at the roadway below. The rest of the exhibit is cluttered with the memorabilia of that dramatic day, like the famous Associated Press bulletin, typed out with frantic haste: '(Dallas)1 — an unknown sniper fired three shots at PTUU ... FLASH ... Kennedy seriously wounded ... stay off all of you, stay off and keep off, get off—BULLETIN (Dallas)—A sniper seriously wounded LOJUMUENT

Kennedy in Downtown Dallas today ... perhaps fatally.'

At the exit visitors are asked to write their comments in books with blank pages for the benefit of future historians interested in how contemporary America views the death of John F. Kennedy. Some were irreverent scribbles, such as: 'Why pay tribute to an adulterer who nourished enemy soldiers against Americans in Vietnam?'; 'JFK needed to be shot' and 'Elvis killed Kennedy to avenge Marilyn.' But many had written plaintive appeals for the truth to be told about the assassination and the majority of comments, some printed inside heart shapes, testified to a continuing love-affair with John F. Kennedy and the deep sense of loss which most Americans still feel.

'All I know is nothing – save that he's gone and something very wrong has been done,' said one. 'I wish he was alive today,' wrote another in childish handwriting. 'JFK always will be the best. Not Bush! We love you,' wrote a visitor. 'I was 13, I miss JFK deeply. I was robbed of his leadership,' said another. One simple message, signed Andrew Christian, in neat script, stated: 'I still wonder what the world would be like if Kennedy lived.'

Three decades after the shots were fired from the sixth floor, 73 percent of Americans remain convinced there was a conspiracy to kill their President, according to a 1992 *Time* magazine poll, and that Lee Harvey Oswald, if he was the killer, did not act alone. President Lyndon Johnson expressed this view in 1973; so too did a congressional select committee which concluded in 1979 that there was a conspiracy by unidentified individuals. Many people believe that Kennedy was a victim of the Cold War, shot down by extremists when he showed a willingness to come to terms with the communist rulers of Vietnam and Cuba. The Dallas County Historical Foundation lists the suspects in a sixty-two page pamphlet called *The Sixth Floor*. They include the KGB, Cuban leader Fidel Castro, anti-Castro Cuban exiles, the Mafia, the FBI, the CIA or some other government agency, the far right, or a New Orleans-based group comprised of former CIA employees, the Mafia and local businessmen.

The final suggestion was picked up by film-maker Oliver Stone for his December 1991 movie *JFK* which suggested that Kennedy was killed as the result of a complex right-wing plot amounting to a *coup d'état* aimed at removing a leader prepared to deal with Castro and Ho Chi-Min. The ensuing debate about who killed Kennedy dominated the media and the bookstores for months afterwards. It still matters to Americans. The writers in the museum comment books expressed longing for a lost leader and what they perceived to be a golden age of elegance and style and idealism, and clearly felt a deep sense of unease about a possible abuse of power which had denied the country a better future.

This disquiet contributed to a feeling of distrust in government among people who were young at the time. These members of the Vietnam war generation felt alienated and betrayed by their leaders in the conduct of national affairs. For many it is tempting to believe that if John F. Kennedy had lived, there would have been no Vietnam, no Richard Nixon, no Watergate, perhaps even an earlier end of the Cold War, and that America would in some way have been a better place in which to live.

The main beneficiary of this phenomenon was Bill Clinton, with his good looks and vigour and imagination, who held out hope that he might lift America again and bring back some of the lost magic. Clinton assiduously cultivated the Kennedy image, trying to adopt the same rhythms of speech and rewriting some of Kennedy's best-known rhetoric. If people voted for him, he seemed to be saying, Camelot might return.

Chapter 9

A PLACE CALLED DESPAIR

Anarchy, anarchy! Show me a greater evil!
This is why cities tumble and the great houses rain down,
This is what scatters armies!

SOPHOCLES, *ANTIGONE*, 442 B.C.

'I HAVE GOOD NEWS AND BAD NEWS,' the captain said over the intercom on United Airlines Flight 57 from Washington to Los Angeles. 'The good news is that if you want to go to Los Angeles you are on the right plane. The bad news is that we have been told we may be delayed going into Los Angeles or diverted as gunfire is being directed at incoming aircraft.'

In the middle of a presidential election campaign which had little relevance for inner cities, the United States was jolted into the realisation that its political and social system had broken down in its second-largest city. On Thursday, 29 April 1992, Los Angeles erupted in the worst explosion of urban violence in the United States this century, following the acquittal of four Los Angeles police officers on charges of beating a black motorist, Rodney King.

The fact that a major American metropolis had suddenly been transformed into a war zone was brought home to us on the flight to Los Angeles by the laconic commentary of the captain, who occasionally interrupted the in-flight movie *Star Trek VI* to give a running commentary on the developing situation in California. As we flew over Arizona he finally told us that Los Angeles airport had indeed closed and we banked to the north and made for Las Vegas, Nevada. Dozens of other Los Angeles-bound flights were doing the same and when we landed our plane was forced to wait on the tarmac in what the captain called the 'penalty spot' for an hour for a place to disembark.

To keep us entertained, the crew beamed a Las Vegas television channel onto the in-flight movie screens. The *Cosby Show* was on, a situation comedy about a middle-class African-American family with typical middle-class problems which always ended happily. Then the programme was interrupted by a news flash – crowds were rioting and looting shops in Las Vegas, only a short distance from the airport where we waited. A child and a police officer had been shot, the announcer said. Stay away from the area.

Nowhere was safe that evening, it appeared. In the airport terminal I joined passengers besieging the car-hire desks and, with a British colleague, Andrew Stephen of the *Observer*, managed to hire virtually the last car available. With little prospect of the flight resuming that day, the only way to get to Los Angeles was to drive the three hundred miles across Nevada and California. Smoke and flames were rising in the air from a poor district of north Las Vegas as we headed out into the desert along Route 15, leaving behind the neon lights of the hotels and gambling casinos.

On the car radio, local stations carried news of looting and arson spreading across California, from Los Angeles to Beverly Hills, Hollywood, Sunset Boulevard, Santa Monica, San Francisco, Pasadena and Sacramento, and further afield to Las Vegas and Atlanta, Georgia. Throughout the night a steady stream of headlights appeared out of the darkness, heading away from Los Angeles. Many cars shot by at high speed. There was no sign of traffic police. We stopped at an all-night Safeways and exchanged news with a couple at the coffee dispenser. They lived near Sunset Boulevard, they said, but had decided to get out of southern California and stay the weekend with friends in Las Vegas after they saw a crowd of looters carrying television sets from a local store. I told them about the scenes in Las Vegas. 'God, no,' said the woman.

Entering Los Angeles at dawn, we encountered little traffic on the palm-lined freeway, which is usually snarled up in the morning rush hour. A single large plume of white smoke rose over the city, spiralling lazily upwards for a few hundred feet until it hit a cold air layer, and then trailing across the valley to the north to merge with a smoky haze. In the outer suburbs cars queued in long lines at petrol stations. Stores which would normally be open were shuttered.

The first sign of trouble was at a parking lot where a black plume of smoke was rising into the sky from burning petrol which had spilled from an overturned car. Nearby was a yellow-painted Mexican restaurant, the black scorch marks over the windows and wisps of smoke showing that it had been gutted by fire. There was a curious, lazy, ominous atmosphere there; the few people standing around ignored the fire except for one man who walked up and threw a bucket of water at the flames.

I began to list in my notebook the names of burned-out shops as we drove down Western Avenue, a long palm-lined thoroughfare stretching for miles through south-central Los Angeles. Park Furniture was gone, as was Savron Drugs, Kinny Shoes, J. Kim Store, Cosmos Appliance.

It became a hopeless task as the rows of destroyed shops stretched into the distance, block after block, and down every side street. Everywhere there was chaos. It was like entering the city of *Blade Runner*, the futuristic film which portrays Los Angeles in the grip of anarchy. At Ace Glass, at Western and Slauson Avenues, sheets of cracked and broken glass lay blackened in the interior. The huge car park of the corner mall at Western and 17th Street was strewn with boxes, wrapping paper, cartons and spilt liquids taken from Savron Drugs Liquor and Pharmacy Store, Pioneer Chicken and Payless Shoes. Flames were leaping from the window of the Chinatown Express Restaurant near the Korean Community Center.

In the middle of the devastation was an untouched Sizzler steakhouse, inside which we glimpsed several people, black, white and Latino, having breakfast, chatting with the waitress and reading newspapers. Not far away from this island of surrealism, a Wendy's Café framed by red azalia bushes had been reduced to a smoke-blackened shell.

We drove further down Western Avenue. A shop on which 'BLACK-OWNED' had been painted with dripping distemper stood undamaged beside the smoking shell of a jewellery store. A couple of black vigilantes stood guard. Little shopping malls, corner business centres with semi-tropical vegetation and ornamental flowerbeds typical of California, were still being looted casually by blacks, Latinos and whites. Contrary to media reports of racial violence, a multi-ethnic stream of people flowed along footpaths on Western Avenue and in narrow side streets. Cars cruised by, some with frightened Asian faces peering out, others with white sightseers, a few with Latino or black youths.

This was a city where the law-enforcement agencies had lost control. In some streets there were no police; in others male and female cops stood in desultory groups beside patrol cars, doing little. In one avenue police were rounding up looters and two officers had their guns trained on fourteen black men standing spreadeagled against the wall, while two other suspects lay on the ground with their hands cuffed behing them with white plastic straps which protruded like hospital identity tags. But just round the corner, a little single-storey clothes shop was burning fiercely, coughing grey-black smoke through the broken glass of the window, as three overweight women snatched clothes from hangers inside the door.

On some blocks order had been re-established by armed civilians. At one point on Western Avenue, a Korean businessman in a neat suit was muttering into a cellular telephone which he used as a walkie-talkie to monitor the movement of looters. Nearby were other Koreans with 9mm semi-automatics. The Koreans had been singled out by the rioters in a festival of looting. 'Everyone was doing it,' said a Honduran who lived on Third Avenue and who undertook to guide us through the most dangerous parts of the area where strangers could run into trouble. He had spent the night guarding his apartment block with his neighbours, afraid it would be torched in the mayhem. 'I saw Anglos, blacks, Hispanic, Chinese, all going crazy, stealing and burning all last night,' he said.

The Los Angeles riots had their origin in an incident which happened more than a year earlier, at 12.40 p.m. on Sunday morning, 3 March 1991. A California Highway Patrol car with husband and wife team of Melanie and Timothy Singer was overtaken on Interstate 210 by a white 1988 Hyundai being driven at high speed. At the wheel of the Korean car was a twenty-five-year-old black man, Rodney King, a high school drop-out and part-time Dodger Stadium groundkeeper. Two black companions, Bryant Allen and Freddie Helms, had come along with him for a night of drinking and driving around.

The driver of the patrol car switched on its siren and flashing lights and drove up behind the Hyundai. Rodney King did not stop. At the time he was on parole for a robbery he committed in 1989 during which he used a two-foot tyre iron as a weapon to steal $200 from a Korean-owned store. He had been released after twelve months of a two-year prison sentence and would be sent back to prison if convicted of another offence. He speeded up instead, left the freeway, continued through a stop sign at fifty miles an hour and eventually came to a halt, after a chase of 7.8 miles, at the corner of Osborne Street and Foothill Boulevard.

By this time the Singers had sounded the alert and eleven other LA Police Department patrols were screaming along the freeways towards the scene, carrying a total of twenty-one officers. Among them was Laurence Powell, aged twenty-eight, who came in the primary pursuit car and Sergeant Stacey Koon, aged forty, who arrived a few seconds later as King was getting out of his car. Sergeant Koon took charge of the situation. He was an experienced police officer with a Master's degree in criminal justice.

King was big and muscular, 6 foot 3 inches tall and 16 stone. An officer ordered him to lie flat on the ground and King slowly got down on all fours. Powell tried to force him to lie down. King resisted, according to the police report, and nearly knocked Powell off his feet. Koon reached into his squad car and brought out a Thomas A. Swift Electric Rifle, known by its initials as a TASER gun. This was an electronic stun-gun that fired two cassette cartridge darts and was capable of jolting a suspect with 50,000 volts through wires that connect with hooks to the clothes or skin. King was now dancing about, wiggling his bottom at the cops. Four police tried again to overpower him but failed, so Sergeant Koon came forward with the TASER and fired it twice. The big black motorist shook and cried out for five seconds as the hooks caught his clothes and the low amperage electricity convulsed his body. Several officers approached with batons drawn.

At that point George Holliday, a plumber who had come out onto his balcony in an apartment block at Lakeview Terrace 150 feet away to see what was happening, switched on his new hand-held camcorder and captured the subsequent action. At the start of his footage King was on the ground, with the TASER wires visible coming from his body. King rose and moved forward and Powell struck him with his baton on his head. King went down immediately. Powell hit him several more times with his metal PR 42 baton. Officer Theodore Briseno, aged thirty-eight, moved in to restrain Powell who then backed away. King then tried once more to rise to his feet. Officers Powell and his patrol car partner Timothy Wind, aged thirty, on the orders of Koon, began striking King blow after blow with what Koon would later describe as 'bursts of power strokes', then backed off once more. The tape showed King still trying to get up. Koon ordered the officers: 'Hit his joints! Hit his wrists! Hit his elbows! Hit his ankles! Hit his knees!' After a total of fifty-six baton swipes and six kicks, half a dozen officers swarmed over King, handcuffed him and dragged him on his stomach to the side of the road to wait for an ambulance. While this was going on, the other two passengers were lying face down on the far side of the car as ordered. Freddie Helms lifted his head once to get it out of the dirt, but was kicked in the side and hit with a baton. When the beating was over, the police called an ambulance and Rodney King was taken to Pacifica hospital. There he was treated by Dr. Edmund Chein, who said the baton blows had been so violent they had knocked the fillings out of King's teeth. His cheekbone was fractured, his ankle was broken, he was concussed and his body was covered with bruises. There was painful nerve damage to his face. King was booked for trying to evade arrest.

Next day George Holliday, shocked by what he had captured on videotape, tried to register a complaint with the police at Foothill Station. The desk officer showed no interest. Holliday contacted instead the Los Angeles televison station KTLA-TV Channel 5. They agreed to pay him $500 for the twelve-minute video tape. That night Channel 5 broadcast eighty-two seconds of it on its 10 p.m. news. The following day it was shown nationwide on Cable News Network. Soon that cameo of the LA Police in action would become one of the most watched videos in television history, ranking with the explosion of the *Challenger* space shuttle.

After it appeared on the news bulletins, a sense of deep outrage swept over Los Angeles and the country. Television played over and over the scene of a prone and pleading man being brutally beaten by police as several other officers stood by. The police violence struck a chord in other American cities where blacks felt themselves at the mercy of police officers. Police chiefs from ten major cities convened and admitted 'the problem of excessive force in American policing is real.' Los Angeles Mayor Tom Bradley, an African-American and former police officer, said he was 'shocked and outraged' and promised a swift prosecution of the officers involved. But the damage to the reputation of the LAPD seemed irreparable. The American Civil Liberties Union in Southern California ran a full-page advertisement in the *Los Angeles Times* asking: 'WHO DO YOU CALL WHEN THE GANG

WEARS BLUE UNIFORMS?' There were signs of what lay ahead. The first weekend after the beating, hundreds of youths rioted outside a cinema showing a film about a Harlem drug czar.

In this atmosphere quick action was necessary and justice had to be seen to be done for the police to maintain any credibility. The four officers most clearly identified in the video, Koon, Powell, Wind and Briseno, were booked and charged, then freed on bail. The mayor, Tom Bradley, asked a prominent Los Angeles lawyer, Warren Christopher, later to become Secretary of State in the Clinton administration, to conduct an independent investigation. Behind the scenes Bradley tried to organise the firing of the Los Angeles police chief, Daryl Gates. The city council refused to go along with that, arguing that it did not have the power to sack Gates, a popular chief among the rank and file. The police commission, appointed by Bradley, put Gates on leave, but the council reinstated him the next day. At a time when united civic action was most needed, all communications between the city's mayor and police chief broke down. From then until the city went up in flames more than a year later, they did not speak to each other once.

The Christopher report, published four months later, on 9 July 1991 (on which the above reconstruction of the incident is based), was a predictable indictment of the Los Angeles Police. The LA Police Department was accused of failing to control crime in a fast-growing metropolis of 3.4 million people. Partly this was due to undermanning: Los Angeles sprawled over 465 square miles and had the lowest number of officers per resident and the fewest officers per square mile of any big American city. The LAPD had a staff of 8,450 officers, of whom 68.7 percent were white, 16.5 percent Latino and 12.4 percent African-American, drawn from a population which was 37 percent white, 40 percent Latino, 13 percent African-American and 10 percent Asian and others. There were special difficulties. Los Angeles was subdivided into a patchwork of communities, neighbourhoods, barrios, ghettos and enclaves. Yet the LAPD logged more arrests per officer than any other US city, heightening resentment of the police.

Unlike their European counterparts, US police are quick to handcuff and subdue suspects, fearing armed resistance; 740 police officers were killed on duty in the US in the period 1982-1992. Even people who are non-violent and have not committed serious crimes are often overpowered by officers and subjected to humiliating physical treatment when being detained. The high number of arrests had made little difference. Crime in Los Angeles had increased sevenfold in the previous thirty years, more than twice the national average but still less than New York. The Christopher Commission found that over a five-year period allegations of excessive use of force had been made against 1,800 police officers, while disciplinary action was rare. Probing deeper into police practices, the commission trawled through countless computerised police radio messages and found many instances where officers talked and joked about beating suspects. It listed examples:

'Capture him, beat him and treat him like dirt.'

'A full moon and a full gin makes for a night of fun.'

'Take one handcuff off and slap him around.'

'Sounds like a job for the dynamic duo ... after I beat him what do I book him for?'

'Don't seat-belt him in and slam on the brakes a couple of times on the way to the station.'

The commission also identified allegedly racial remarks such as:

'Sounds like monkey-slapping time.'

'I would love to drive down Slauson with a flame thrower, we could have a barbecue.'

'I almost got me a Mexican last night but he dropped the damn gun too quick.'

Sergeant Stacey Koon, in a book he later wrote about the Rodney King incident, *Presumed Guilty*, said that 'monkey-slapping time' was police slang for relaxation and originally meant masturbation. But he confirmed what everyone knew. 'Racism in the LAPD?' he wrote. 'You'd better believe it!' Koon had a tough-guy reputation but had once given mouth-to-mouth resuscitation to a black transvestite prostitute who had the AIDS virus. He described how his name was sometimes used by his colleagues to have fun with blacks. One would shout 'Hey, Koon,' then say with feigned innocence, as the black squared up: 'Hey, I was only talking to my partner, look at his badge.' Koon also volunteered one racist acronym of his own – NWOB – often used by officers on patrol. It stood for 'Nigger West of Balboa', meaning 'a black person wasn't where he or she was supposed to be.'

One exchange between officers using the computer keyboards in the patrol cars suggested a policy of randomly stopping automobiles with black people inside.

'U can C the colour of the interior ... dig.'

'Ya stop cars with BLK interior.'

'Bees they naugahyde?'

'Negrohide.'

'Self-tanning no doubt.'

Police messages at the time of the King beating also suggest a pattern of police abuse. Shortly before King came to the attention of the police, Powell and Wind had transmitted a call from their patrol car about a domestic dispute between an black couple which, the message said, was 'right out of *Gorillas in the Mist*'.

The initial report of the beating of King was greeted by the watch commander at Foothill Station with the words: 'Oh, well, I'm sure the lizard didn't deserve it. Ha! Ha!' When a police officer called the LA Fire Department for an ambulance the exchange went as follows:

Officer: '... like he got beat up.'

Fire Department: '(laugh) Wait (laugh).'

Officer: '... he pissed us off so I guess he needs an ambulance now.'

Fire Department: 'A little "attitude adjustment"?'

Officer: 'Yea, we had to chase him ... that kind of irritated us a little.'

Fire Department: 'Why would you want to do that for? (laugh).'

Officer: (laughter) 'Should know better than run, they are going to pay a price when they do that.'

Fire Department: 'What type of incident would you say this is?'

Officer: 'It's a ... it's a ... battery, he got beat up.'

The King beating was not the only cause of heightened tension in Los Angeles. The recession was wiping out jobs at every level and reducing the revenue from taxes available to Mayor Bradley and California Governor Pete Wilson, forcing them to cut back many community services from teachers to after-school child care at campuses. General Motors had just closed its Van Nuys complex, paying off 2,600 people. Military-industrial plants had dismissed thousands more as defence spending was trimmed in response to the collapse of the Soviet Union. At the same time the city was paying huge sums – $13 million in 1991 – in compensation for police brutality.

The situation was similar to that in Los Angeles in 1965 when black people in the Watts district vented their frustration over years of neglect and abuse from the police in six days of burning and looting which left thirty-two people dead and two hundred buildings destroyed. At the time, Los Angeles had experienced a huge inflow of poor blacks, attracted to a city which was described by the *Los Angeles Times* as 'Valhalla with orange groves ... glamorous and sophisticated ... the capital of the American Dream.' The black population had doubled to 461,000 people in the 1950s, and then doubled again in the early sixties. But blacks who had come seeking a better life had been kept in their place. The best jobs, houses and shops were off limits to 'people of colour'. Black schools were under-funded and crowded. Many houses had no plumbing. Police routinely stopped blacks, shouted at them, pushed them around and sometimes killed them. The arrest by police patrolman Lee Minikus on 11 August 1965 of Marquette Frye, aged twenty-one, on suspicion of drunk driving became the incident which touched off the explosion. Rodney King was simply history repeating itself. A presidential commission established in 1965 to determine the cause of black unrest concluded that America had become two nations, separate and unequal, black and white. By 1992 little had changed.

In recent years, blacks in Los Angeles have, in turn, been overtaken by waves of Latino and Asian immigrants. Unemployment in the inner city is still widespread but drugs have devastated familes and guns have become the accepted means of resolving teenage feuds, mainly between two city gangs, the 'Crips' and the 'Bloods'. Because of the violence, most big department chain stores have refused to move into south-central Los Angeles, leaving whole communities exploited by the high-price corner shops. The poverty rate among urban blacks rose from 21.2 percent in 1969 to 33.8 percent in 1990. Cut off from the mainstream economy, inner city blacks slipped further into despair.

Other racial time bombs had started ticking around the same time as the beating of Rodney King. Towards the end of March 1991, in the Empire Liquor Market Deli on South Figueroa Street in south-central Los Angeles, a Korean storekeeper, Soon Ja Du, had an argument with a black teenage girl, Latasha Harlins, over a bottle of orange juice, which he accused her of trying to steal. The girl put the bottle on the counter and turned to leave. Du pulled a gun and shot her in the back of the head. Once again a video-recorder, this time a security camera, filmed everything. On 15 November 1991, Soon Ja Du was brought for trial. The judge in Los Angeles Superior Court found the storekeeper guilty of the homicide of Latasha, and promptly released him with five years' probation and no time behind bars, while at the same time making a plea for racial harmony. It was an astonishing judgement and the plea fell on deaf ears. Another court case five days later convinced blacks that they could not expect justice under the Los Angeles court system. It concerned the ill-treatment of a cocker spaniel puppy called Baby, whose twenty-six-year-old owner, Brendan Sheen, kicked and stomped her, breaking the dog's rib and pelvis. He was arrested and given thirty days in jail. Word quickly spread: beating a dog was a worse offence than killing a black. In a further incident, a black man called Lee Mitchell tried to rob Chung's Liquor Market on Western Avenue and 79th Street by pretending he had a gun. The Chinese proprieter, Tae Sam Park, pulled a real gun and shot him dead. There were also four disputed police shootings in August and September with black men the victims. The police, too, were edgy and resentful. In the two weeks before the Rodney King beating, a female officer had been shot dead through the window of her patrol car. With the arrest of the four officers involved in the beating of Rodney King, many patrol car units felt that Police Chief Daryl Gates had abandoned the street cops who had been looking out for their lives in a dangerous situation.

Los Angeles judge Stanley Weisberg set in motion the final act of the tragedy. He ordered the trial of the four officers to be held in Simi Valley in Ventura County, forty-three miles outside the city limits. This was a mostly white, middle-class suburb where residents were normally sympathetic to the police. The six men and six women picked for the jury were white, except for one Latino and one Filipino. Three had worked as security guards or served in the US military. Three others were members of the right-wing National Rifle Association. One was a brother of a retired LA Police Department officer. The failure of the prosecution to challenge such jury members was the first indication that the trial would be handled badly.

Day after day the video was played in the court with the defence seeking to justify every blow on the grounds of King's aggressiveness. It was examined frame by frame. Incredibly, Rodney King was not called to testify. By the time the trial ended the four officers had been transformed in the jury's eyes into courageous and much-maligned defenders of the peace, frightened for their lives, unable to control a maniacal, possibly drug-crazed, black brute, who might well have had a gun.

(In a second trial of the officers in a Los Angeles federal court in March 1993 on a charge of depriving King of his civil rights, Rodney King was called to the witness stand and presented a much less threatening figure. He testified in a sing-song voice that he had offered no resistance and was just trying to stay alive. He never got a chance to lie still after police ordered him to the ground, he said. They shouted at him either: 'What's up, nigger?', or: 'What's up, killer?'; and he said that one officer called out: 'We're going to kill you, nigger.')

On Wednesday, 29 April 1992, the jury gave its verdict to a city which fully expected all four officers would and should be found guilty. There were ten charges in all against Stacey Koon, Theodore Briseno, Timothy Wind and Lawrence Powell. The verdicts were read out one by one in Courtroom No. 3. 'Not guilty, not guilty, not guilty, not guilty ...' The jury unanimously voted to acquit all four of every charge, except for one count of assault against Powell, on which the jury was deadlocked.

The feeling of disbelief was widespread across America. No-one who had seen the video, played over and over and over on television, could believe that the police officers were not guilty of brutality. Bill Clinton said: 'I can't understand the verdict' – one of the more moderate reactions. President Bush remarked: 'Viewed from outside the trial it was hard to understand how the verdict could possibly square with the video.' He was stunned,' he said, 'and so was Barbara and so were the kids.' The Rev. Cecil Murray, the black pastor of the eight thousand-member First AME Church, cried as he heard the verdict on radio. 'To see them whitewashing something that the whole world witnessed – that is a brutalisation of truth,' he said. Mayor Bradley said he was shocked and outraged. 'Today this jury told the world that what we all saw with our own eyes was not a crime,' he said. 'The jury's verdict will never blind the world to what we saw.' The Ku Klux Klan announced that it had given honorary membership to the Simi Valley jury.

The television pictures had supplied the oxygen for the fire that would follow. During the trial, reports of the proceedings had been accompanied by constant replays of the beating on TV screens, rather than by the more mundane legal arguments presented by the defendants in court which tended to show it was not an open-and-shut case. Night after night for a whole year, television viewers had seen nothing about the affair other than a black man being beaten by white police. Now the people of Los Angeles were being asked to accept that the four officers had done nothing punishable in law.

As news of the acquittal spread, a crowd gathered outside police headquarters in downtown Los Angeles, shocked, disbelieving and getting angrier by the minute. Stanley Sheinbaum, president of the city police commission, arrived at the building and found his way blocked by blacks and whites demonstrating together. Round the back he met Police Chief Daryl Gates. Unbelievably, Gates, a taut, highly-strung man who believed in tough measures to preserve law and order and who constantly complained of an unfair press, was on his way to a cocktail party in the suburb of Brentwood, held to raise funds to fight against police reform.

As the police chief drove off, the streets behind him went out of control. At 6.30 p.m. an eighteen-wheel truck carrying 27 tons of sand to a cement-mixing plant came to the intersection of 71st Street and Normandie Avenue in south Los Angeles. People were milling about and bits of masonry and bottles were flying through the air. The police were nowhere to be seen, officers of the 77th Street Division having retreated to a bus terminal thirty blocks away. Several black men surrounded the lorry. One opened the door and pulled out the driver, Reginald Denny. Two others beat him on the head and kicked him. A fourth took a fire extinguisher from the truck and smashed it against his head. All of this was also filmed, this time by a TV camera crew in a helicopter overhead, and relayed live to the television screens of the city. The horrifying scene was to become, like the King beating, a symbol of the tragedy of Los Angeles. At the police station Detective Lieutenant Bruce Hagerty saw Denny being beaten. He ordered an undercover car with four officers to rescue him but they had to turn back when they came under sniper fire.

An hour later the first store was set ablaze at the corner of Florence and Normandie. Soon whole streets were filled with smoke and flames. Latinos and blacks and whites poured onto the streets to loot liquor shops, discount clothing outlets and convenience stores in what quickly became a poverty riot. The first person to die in the conflagration, three and a half hours after the Simi Valley verdict, was Louis Watson Fleming, a young black man who had moved school several times to avoid recruitment into the Los Angeles gangs. He was shot dead at a bus stop. Crowds broke every ground floor window of the *Los Angeles Times* offices and spilled onto freeways where drivers panicked and drove back the wrong way through traffic. At Los Angeles airport landing patterns were changed after police reported a helicopter was fired upon; then, as smoke billowed across the runways, the airport was closed.

This was a war with no front line, where a quiet street could become a scene of mob fury in seconds. Kirk McKoy, a black *Los Angeles Times* photographer was confronted by a man with a bottle of whisky in one hand and a Beretta in the other who screamed 'motherfucker' and shot at him six times. The looter was so drunk all the shots missed. John Lichfield of the London *Independent* was told to get out of his car by a teenager with a gun who smashed the driver's window as he waited at traffic lights at the corner of Century Boulevard and Manchester Avenue. Lichfield jammed down the accelerator, banged his car into others in the queue to make space, and managed to drive off. Jeff Kramer, working for the *Boston Globe*, was surrounded when he drove off Martin Luther King Boulevard and onto Normandie Avenue. The mob punched and kicked him through the door of the car. He pretended to be unconscious but was shot three times in the leg. Kramer managed to drive off but another bullet hit his shoulder blade. He stopped a few streets away where two blacks risked their lives to get him to safety. Some looters even posed for the camera. Tina Griego of the *Los Angeles Times* drove past the Compton mini-mall where people were emptying shops, drinking and laughing. 'Someone pulled back the security gate of a liquor store,' she said, 'and while one man crawled under it another came up to me and said: "Take a photo of me, I'm the one who did that."'

All night victims of gunshots, mostly innocent people, were brought in to the city mortuary. One was Arturo Miranda who had been driving home from soccer practice with his family when a bullet tore into his car and killed him. Another was Ira McCurry, a forty-five-year-old white man shot on Avalon Boulevard. At Long Beach another white man, Matt Haines, set out with Scott Coleman on a motorcycle to help a friend, a black woman, move out of the riot area. A mob of black men surrounded them. 'Hey, we're on your side,' said McCurry, but they were knocked to the ground and beaten. One man inserted a gun under Haines's helmet and shot him in the head. When he turned the gun on Coleman it ran out of bullets.

But it was the black community which suffered most of the fatalities. Of the twenty-seven bodies lying in the morgue after two days, twenty-one were black. They included young men like Dennis Jackson and Anthony Taylor who had been hanging out at a parking lot in Watts. Friends said that police had fired at an armed man wearing a hood who had run through the lot and hit them by mistake.

Next day it continued. The arsonists vented their fury on Korean-owned businesses, restaurants, dry-cleaners, service stations, liquor outlets and convenience stores built up in the previous twenty years. The Koreans formed a distinct community. Most were Presbyterian and driven by a merchant ethic to make good in their new country. Appeals were made on Korean-language radio stations for young men to mobilise in defence units. Carl Rhyu, one of the organisers, said: 'When our shops were burning we called the police every five minutes: no response.' On the rooftop of a Korean supermarket Jay Shin set a box of ammunition next to three rifles and watched his liquor store across the way. On the second day of rioting he and his companions engaged in several gun battles. On Friday they were still there with their guns and the store was still unscathed.

More often than not the arsonists did not discriminate. Any commercial building became a legitimate target. A black storekeeper, Art Washington, faced a crowd of looters with a hammer in 20th Street and was heard shouting hysterically: 'I worked for that, not you. Don't burn down none of my business. I worked too hard for this. It's not right what y'all do! I come from the ghetto too like you. You call this black power?'

Looting spread across the city, even to peaceful suburbs, as the police became overwhelmed. Women climbed over broken security gates into supermarkets and emerged laden down with baby food and nappies. Cars were backed up to shops and furniture tied to the roofs. A few middle-class people drove into districts where looting was going on and dashed from their Acuras and Camrys to grab merchandise from shop windows. All this was broadcast live on local television. In some places there was a carnival atmosphere as participants and onlookers raced from area to area to watch or join the fun. Looters appeared in Hollywood Boulevard where designer clothes were torn from models in Frederick's fashion store.

In the movie-world mansions nearby and in the affluent suburbs there was a sudden demand for hand guns. Gun sales soared that month in Los Angeles, rising to 14,125 compared to 8,594 in May 1991.

The crisis was made worse by incompetence in marshalling the police and the six thousand-strong National Guard which had been called out by Governor Wilson. The National Guard, part-time soldiers trained to deal with civil disturbance, had reached armouries in Los Angeles on the morning after the verdict but spent several hours waiting for ammunition and deployment orders. Police Chief Gates admitted at a press conference that his force had been overwhelmed, but he congratulated rioters for smashing windows at the *Los Angeles Times*, his long-time tormentor, adding hastily: 'Joke! joke! joke!' Gates, who had spent one and a half hours at the cocktail party, had completely failed to comprehend what the Court verdict meant. He had allowed most of the force's one thousand detectives to go home before the rioting started.

As the city waited for the madness to end, Rodney King, heavily sedated, emerged as an unexpected peacemaker. He had retired to his bedroom after the verdicts. Now, with his voice shaking, he faced a hundred reporters to say: 'Can't we get along. Can't we stop making it horrible for the older people and the kids ... It's just not right, it's not right and it's not going to change anything. We'll get our justice. They've won the battle but they haven't won the war ... please, we can get along here. We can all get along. We've just got to, just got to. We're all stuck here for a while ... Let's try to work it out. Let's try to work it out.'

At dawn on Saturday, the third day of violence, Governor Wilson and Mayor Bradley spoke with President Bush by telephone. At 7.15 a.m. the White House announced that a thousand US troops would be sent in, including two hundred of the US Marshals' special group that had gone to Panama in 1990 to kidnap Manuel Noriega. The National Guard had meanwhile received their ammunition and long lines of military convoys appeared on the freeways and everyone knew it was almost over.

Sixty people died in the four days of rioting, though the LA police said later fifteen of the deaths were not riot-related, and 2,383 were injured. Over a thousand buildings had been destroyed or damaged, 853 of them burned, and over ten thousand businesses wrecked. Eight thousand people had been arrested. Damage was estimated at one billion dollars.

In the aftermath, some brave people expressed the hope that they might come together to rise above their tragedy. In Koreatown on Western Avenue, seven thousand people attended a clean-up rally as loudspeakers broadcast messages of love and peace. Another thirty thousand people carrying brushes and plastic bags marched to Koreatown to remove debris from the streets.

But when I returned to Los Angeles six months later at the height of the presidential election campaign, the city appeared to be disintegrating rather than coming together. The atmosphere was full of pessimism for the future. The violence had left ugly physical and psychological scars. Some reconstruction was under way and of eleven thousand people who had applied for special federal loans to rebuild their businesses, 3,100 had received cheques, totalling $250 million. Half-rebuilt shops had sprouted brave signs saying: 'We are coming back!' But racial battle lines were more distinctly drawn than before, separating districts where fear, hatred and apathy predominated. Fights between blacks and Latinos had become more frequent in schools and prisons. A black-Korean alliance, formed to prevent conflict, had fallen apart. Only a few of the hundreds of Korean businesses damaged or destroyed had re-opened. Many south-central streets were still half-derelict and menacing, with groups of unemployed men and youths hanging around corners with bottles of liquor. There had been bitter struggles for supremacy in the umbrella organisation 'Rebuild LA', headed by Peter Ueberoth, a former baseball commissioner. In the suburbs where high rents kept out the minorities, whites had withdrawn in upon themselves.

The black-white alliance which had voted in Mayor Bradley was also losing its cohesion and there was a feeling that no-one was really in control of the city. The most significant change had been the departure of Police Chief Daryl Gates and his replacement by black Philadelphia Police Chief Willie Williams, who had reformed and restored trust in a police force long known for brutality and racism. In response to public outrage the four police officers involved in the

Rodney King case were put on trial again, this time in a federal court, and charged with depriving King of his civil rights. The gangs meanwhile were preparing for further confrontations with the police. As Bill Clinton was being inaugurated in Washington with a message of hope for the nation, leaflets were appearing in LA streets. They said: 'To all Crips and Bloods. Let's unite and don't gangbang. An eye for an eye and a tooth for a tooth. If LAPD hurts a black, we will kill too: pow, pow, pow.'

'We've been saying for years to the younger generation "Hold on, there's hope",' said Julius Butler, a sixty-year-old black Los Angeles lawyer involved in youth affairs to whom I spoke. 'I ask myself many times, have I been responsible by saying that? Have I been responsible by continuing to advocate Martin Luther King's dream? Is it a dream or is it a fantasy?'

Chapter 10

CHASING THE DREAM

Hope is a waking dream.

ARISTOTLE, *DIOGENES LAERTIUS*

WAS THE LOS ANGELES LAWYER, Julius Butler, right? Was Martin Luther King's dream a dream or a fantasy? To its poets and politicians, America has always been the land of dreams. To Ronald Reagan the dream was the Shining City on a Hill. To Bill Clinton it was a Place called Hope. Ross Perot, billionaire, boasted: 'I live the American Dream.' The writer Nicholas von Hoffman once declared: 'One of the things that makes America such an unusual place is that it is perhaps the only society in history in which a vast number of its members are living their private dream.' In America, he said, 'you have that intoxicating feeling that you can make your own history, that you really count.'

During the summer of the presidential election campaign, I travelled around America to visit some of the diverse communities which exist in out-of-the-way places and who make up parts of the extraordinary mosaic of the United States; people who still seek to make their own history according to their own version of the Dream, but who rarely come to the attention of the media. The great political debates of the election touched them hardly at all, I found, though all their futures would be affected in one way or another. The people I met, gamblers in Atlantic City, Indians in New York State, migrant workers in New Mexico, farmers in Iowa, country singers in Tennessee, shopkeepers in Missouri, diamond hunters in Arkansas, Amish folk in Pennsylvania, all had different versions of the Dream.

I began by making a pilgrimage to Memphis, Tennessee, the one place in America where the Dream is officially commemorated. In a black district of downtown Memphis stands the Lorraine Motel, where the Rev. Martin Luther King checked in one April day in 1968 to support a strike by black garbage men. He went to room 306 on the second floor, stepped out onto the balcony with the Rev. Jesse Jackson and was shot dead from Bessie Brewer's boarding house across the road. After his killing the motel became a metaphor for the death of his dream. It degenerated into a haven for prostitutes and drug-pushers. But in 1981 a local black group bought the building, evicted the last inhabitants, including the receptionist, Jacqueline Smith who had stayed on to show pilgrims the blood-stained concrete where King fell, and re-opened it in September 1991 as America's first National Civil Rights Museum. Room 306 was restored and a series of exhibition rooms opened in a separate modern building. Displayed prominently near the entrance is Martin Luther King's famous speech at the Civil Rights march on Washington on 28 August 1963, one of the most compelling passages of oratory in American history.

'I still have a dream,' he said. 'It is a dream deeply rooted in the American Dream. I have a dream that one day this nation will rise up and live out the true meaning of its creed "We hold these truths to be self-evident, that all men are created equal." I have a dream that one day on the red hills of Georgia, the sons of former slaves and the sons of former slave-owners will be able to sit down together at the table of brotherhood. I have a dream that one day even the State of Mississippi, a desert state sweltering with the heat of injustice and oppression, will be transformed into an oasis of freedom and justice. I have a dream that my four little children will one day live in a nation where they will not be judged by the colour of their skin but by the content of their character ... I have a dream today. I have a dream that one day every valley shall be exalted, every hill and mountain shall be made low ...'

Rosa Parks was at the museum's opening ceremony; she was the black woman who in 1955 refused to leave a whites-only seat on a city bus in Montgomery, Alabama, when ordered to do so. Her subsequent arrest led to a bus boycott by blacks organised by Dr. King, which in turn launched the struggle for civil rights in the Deep South. An old bus of the type used in Montgomery has been placed in the museum complete with plaster models of a driver and of Rosa Parks defying the recorded voice of the driver saying: 'Please move to the back of the bus. If you don't move out of that seat I'll have you arrested. I need that seat.'

The junk-strewn concrete lots and decaying buildings in the streets around the Lorraine Motel define the limitations of Martin Luther King's dream in today's America. But things have in fact changed considerably since 1968. Memphis, a 55 percent black city of nine hundred thousand people, where many blacks for years never bothered to vote even after winning the right to register, has just elected 'Willie' Harrington as its first black mayor. It has acquired its first black police chief. Blacks still do lower paid jobs but the garbage collectors get twice the minimum wage and middle-class blacks frequent the exclusive Peabody Hotel and the Beale Street nightspots.

Peace prevailed in Memphis when Los Angeles exploded, said Juanita Moore, the forty-year-old black museum director, because of new hope among blacks in the Deep South that things are on the move after years of stagnation. Judge D'Army Bailey, a Tennessee circuit court judge and chairman of the National Civil Rights Museum, said: 'Visitors probably will have a sense that the Civil Rights movement ended or slowed down drastically after Dr. King's assassination – not that it should have. But that movement did what it was supposed to do. It's time to measure our progress and start all over again.'

Jacqueline Smith, the motel receptionist who was evicted three years earlier, spends every day on a couch on the pavement outside the motel surrounded by hand-written placards protesting about its conversion to a museum. She said the dream had not been realised because of the failure to integrate fully. Sixty percent of Tennessee schoolchildren still go to segregated schools. The unemployment rate for blacks is twice as high as for whites. 'The last thing we need in a ghetto is a museum,' she said. 'It's a cheap tourist trap. Around here we need affordable housing, health-care centres and day-care centres. These people are playing with history in order to make a buck. It should have been converted into housing for the poor, the homeless or the elderly. Don't rob us of our dream.'

* * *

Memphis is also the home of another shrine which 'is woven into the fabric of our culture, representing all the joyful heights of the American Dream'. These words are taken from the official guidebook to Graceland, the mansion where Elvis Presley lived in a Memphis suburb. Elvis was the personification of the dream of the poor white boy from the south who finds fame and fortune through musical talent. He is buried in a 'Meditation Garden' at Graceland beneath a stone slab in a grotto embraced by a 10 foot high semi-circular wall with stained-glass windows and overlooked by a statue of the Sacred Heart of Jesus. On the tombstone are inscribed the words: 'Elvis Aaron Presley, January 8 1935 – August 16 1977 ... a living legend in his own time.' This hallowed spot is a place of pilgrimage for millions of Elvis fans every year. Some say they believe that Elvis, who would have been fifty-seven when his most prominent admirer, Bill Clinton, ran for president, is still alive. On his anniversary they hold a candle-lit vigil at the Meditation Garden and attend commemoration events in Memphis, including a 'Dead Elvis Ball'.

Across the busy roadway, named Elvis Presley Boulevard, is a reception centre where visitors pay a $2 parking fee and buy a $7.95 ticket for the 'Graceland Mansion Tour'. While waiting to be escorted to the mansion – there is always a long queue – they can buy a coke in the Hound Dog Café or take a $4.25 tour of Elvis's Hound Dog 11 Lockheed JetStar plane and his customised aircraft, *Lisa Marie*, or buy an $11.95 *Presley Family Cookbook* in the gift shop with recipes like 'Pig in the Sandwich' for breakfast. ('Take 6 Tennessee Pride sausages and 6 homemade biscuits, fry sausages and place into biscuits, warm in oven 3 to 5 minutes and serve with grape jelly and Mazola margarine'.)

The tour of Graceland is conducted at anything but a graceful pace. At every door there is a guide whose task is to move people on as quickly as possible. The bedroom where he died is off limits. 'No-one was ever allowed upstairs except by Elvis's express permission,' said a guide. 'Only if you have an invitation from Elvis you can go.' We were ushered in and out of the living room with a sensuous white couch as long as a stretch limousine, the games room with walls and ceiling draped in pleated cloth, the 'jungle room' with carpeted ceiling and the golden disc room which the guide told us was 'one of your most impressing stops'. Last was a museum room where Elvis's utterances were displayed in frames, such as: 'I learned very early in life that without a song the day would never end; without a song, a man ain't got a friend.'

* * *

Without a song, one cannot make dreams come true in Nashville, Tennessee, the home of country music, sometimes known as Music City, USA. Singers and guitarists still wear rhinestoned, polyester outfits, but country music is a multi-million dollar industry today and the buildings on Nashville's 'Music Row' are models of modern executive architecture. The world's country music celebrities, like Randy Travis, Minnie Pearl, Waylon Jennings and Dolly Parton, have homes in Nashville's plush suburbs of Magnolia Hill, Oak Hill and

Brentwood. Their mansions can be glimpsed through the smoked windows of little tour buses. Our driver and guide on one of these tours was Lee Johnson, a burly, tanned composer of country music in a large cowboy hat. He dreamed, he said, that he would one day make it to Magnolia Hill, but in the meantime he had to make a living showing people around; he sang one of his own country songs and assured us the company allowed him to accept gratuities, which he would use to make demonstration tapes to make his dream come true.

We passed the house of blind composer, Ronnie Milsap. 'Tour traffic doesn't bother Ronnie,' said Lee. 'He can't see us.' Next was the house of Little Jimmy Dickens which had wrought-iron music notes on the balcony railings and a post-box shaped like a guitar. Randy Travis's swimming pool was also guitar-shaped. The residence of singer Tammy Wynette, whose fading star sparkled when Hillary Clinton said: 'I'm not some little woman standing by her man like Tammy Wynette', was a plush bungalow with a 150-seat dining room. According to our driver, Tammy ignored her own advice and was now on her fifth husband. Further along we came to the residence of one of her ex-husbands, George Jones, who had a well-publicised drink problem. One day before they split up, said Lee, Tammy broke all the bottles and took the keys of his cars, but George managed to get a drink by driving into town on the power-driven lawnmower. The high point of the tour was the twenty-three-room, southern-style mansion of singer Dolly Parton, with its American flag and private chapel. Lee had us all call out: 'Well, hello, Dolly!', knowing that no sound emitted from the sealed, air-conditioned bus. She may not have been at home in any event, as Ms. Parton, owner of three hundred wigs made from human hair, also has residences in Hawaii, Los Angeles, Knoxville, Pidgeon Ford and New York. She was happily married to an asphalt contractor, Lee said, and they stayed happy because they never discussed country music with each other, nor asphalt.

Our journey ended in Opryland, a 120-acre musical theme park which contains the world shrine of country music, the Grand Ole Opry, with the biggest recording studio on earth. I found a tube of Fixadent on my seat when I went to a recording of *Nashville Now*, a ninety-minute evening television show presented by Ralph Emery, a veteran of the country scene. Emery, whose permanent smile is the result of several surgical face lifts, asked the thousand happy, noisy fans in the audience to wave the tubes of Fixadent in the air and to cheer for the cameras. He repeated the process with a remedy for flatulence, holding up a packet to the cameras during a commercial interlude and proclaiming solemnly: 'FASTGAS fights gas fast.' The country music world seemed fixated on bodily functions. The warm-up man joked that he was on a 'light diet' – 'As soon as it gets light I start eating.' His friend was on a seafood diet – 'When he sees food he eats.' The stars in the show that night were the Nitty Gritty Dirt Band and Faron Young, an ex-roadie with Elvis Presley, who sang 'When I Fall in Love' from large cue cards. We applauded wildly at all the right times, prompted by a red sign that flashed 'APPLAUSE'. An appearance on *Nashville Now* is a way of breaking into the big time and a ready platform for politicians. George Bush made a guest appearance that summer on the show which goes out on cable to fifty-five million subscribers. The white working class forms a huge country music constituency in the southern states. Country music, said George Day, the founder of Grand Ole Opry, in a message inscribed on a plaque inside the artistes' entrance, 'expresses the heart-beat of a large percentage of Americans who labour for a living.'

It was at the Grand Ole Opry, when I talked to country music fans about their American Dream, that I heard of the existence of a place in Arkansas known as the 'field of dreams'. 'There you'll sure find people looking for their dream!' said a man in check shirt and baggy shorts. 'That's where you can still be a prospector and strike it rich.'

* * *

The 'field of dreams' turned out to be an open-cast diamond mine near Murfreesboro, a one-street town on Highway 301 in Pike County in south-west Arkansas, consisting of a courthouse, a dozen motels, fourteen churches, mainly Baptist, Raymond's Thriftway store, the Jif-E-Mart and the 'Pizza and Games' parlour. Hundreds of people come to this remote town to hunt for gems in the only diamond mine in the United States. I asked for directions in a log-cabin restaurant not far from the town.

A leather-skinned old woman with inch-long painted fingernails told me how to get there, and offered some advice on finding the precious stones. 'You should ask that nigger who's always there,' she said. She beckoned to the waitress and demanded: 'What's that coloured man's name who finds all the diamonds?' 'James Archer,' replied the waitress. 'Ask him,' the old woman said. 'He's found mor'n anybody.'

The mine lies at the end of a paved road through a coniferous wood with a sign at the entrance saying: 'Crater of Diamonds State Park'. At the edge of the mining area is a large wooden visitors' centre with restaurant, audiovisual room, shop and restrooms. This was mining made easy. The mine itself is a 40-acre undulating ploughed field edged by distant pine trees. A few dozen people, tiny figures in the vast expanse of yellow-brown earth, were walking around in the baking hot sun or hunkering down to sift the earth through aluminium screens rented out in the visitors' centre.

The first diamond was found in Murfreesboro in 1906 and since then more than seven hundred thousand have been uncovered by people picking through the surface dirt. Hillary Clinton wore in her brooch a $20,000 diamond from the Crater of Diamonds State Park at Bill Clinton's first inauguration as governor of Arkansas in 1979. The park has always been open to all comers. The park authorities helpfully plough the land over every month to expose new earth. There are still many diamonds to be found; on average two turn up every day. The park is a 'mighty crater of dreams' said a sign in the visitors' centre, 'and many of the diamond-hunters are romantics, adventurers with backs bent and eyes fixed downward, seeking those precious gems carried by molten rock from the depth of the earth long ago.' Among the regular miners was Charles Rockhart, a tall, sun-tanned man in wide black hat, who had been coming to the 'crater of dreams' from Alabama several times a year since 1978. He had found many diamonds, he said, as he expertly sifted dirt through a series of screens at a wooden table which he shared with a black couple, Norman and Virginia Tate from Louisiana. His wife, Annashe, showed me one of their diamonds set in a gold ring on her finger. It was dull-looking and rounded, the colour and texture of fish scales, worn as a trophy rather than a jewel and worth, she said, about $400. There is great excitement when a siren hoots twice at the visitors' centre, signalling that a precious stone has been found. It is a precarious moment, however. The diamonds are so elusive and oily that many are lost when dropped by trembling finders back into the soil.

The anticipation of something for nothing lures people back every year. One woman with two children said as she brushed away a giant dragonfly: 'My husband lost his job, maybe here we'll get a few hundred dollars at least.' A few had struck it rich. James Archer, the 'coloured man', was one. A legendary figure among regulars and helpful to strangers, the sixty-eight-year-old amateur prospector said he had quit counting how many he had found. His biggest was 4.25 carats, which he picked up in 1983. Another veteran, Raymond Schall, a dignified old man known for his trademark cane and brown bag, had found two hundred gems by the end of the 1980s. One day his friends ran to his side as Schall, then seventy-four, appeared to suffer a heart attack. He lay trembling in the dirt with his fist clenched tightly. He recovered sufficiently to shout: 'If you found this you would have a heart attack too,' and opened his fingers to expose an ice-white stone, worth $25,000 uncut. Some of the biggest diamonds are found by first-timers in their initial few minutes' walking over the big rills of earth. The sun can catch a diamond and 'it shines at you like a flashlight,' said Charles Rockhart. After some minutes wandering around, shovel in hand, screen at the ready, with the sun behind my back, I saw a bright glittering object and hurried towards it. Alas, no siren was to sound – it was the twist-off cap from a Coca-Cola tin.

* * *

West of Arkansas, at the very far corner of Texas, is a place to which hundreds of thousands of people come who regard the United States itself as a field of dreams. It is the Texas city of El Paso, on the Mexican border. El Paso is a staging point for Hispanic migrants, whose dream is to work and earn dollars on the chilli farms of New Mexico. Many have got green cards and live in the city. At three o'clock in the morning I went to El Paso Street in the centre of El Paso to witness the hiring of day-labourers.

People were lying under plastic bags in the doorways of shops with names like La Supresa or standing under street lights talking softly in Spanish. They wore T-shirts and cowboy hats. A group of men squatted on the ground beneath a mural depicting a family at work with the legend in giant letters: 'Until this dream belongs to everyone, it won't belong to anyone.' Most come across the El Paso del Norte Bridge across the Rio Grande which links El Paso (population 600,000) with the Mexican city of Ciudad Juarez (population 1.5 million). On these streets America meets the Third World. On one side are the bright neon lights of El Paso; on the other the dim, bluish street lamps of Ciudad Juarez. The bridge is open to US citizens and American youngsters drive across at night to the cheap Ciudad Juarez bars. Some returning teenagers shout from their car: 'You bums, why don't you get some work?' It is a cruel taunt. The people are hard-working peasants, with thin faces and sad eyes. Among them are permanent residents of El Paso, Mexicans who sleep under flyovers or in shacks, and a few 'illegals' who wade across the shallow Rio Grande and who are called 'wetbacks' because of their wet clothes. US immigration vans crawl along the streets but those without green cards are more likely to be caught at US immigration checkpoints on roads out of El Paso through the semi-desert.

The workers are chosen by crew leaders, Mexicans contracted by US farmers to recruit work gangs. They own old buses and vans, many with bald tyres and rusting bodywork. When they arrive, people crowd around. Crew leaders pick their regulars, the least troublesome workers, shouting in Spanish: 'You, you and you.'

By chance I had come on the night when strike action was being organised. People gathered round a tall, dark man in glasses called Carlos Marentes, who said he was the leader of the Union de Trabajadores Agricolas, the Border Agricultural Workers' Union. Marentes was organising a stoppage on a farm as part of a long battle to end what he called 'a moral disgrace to the country'. The union had negotiated a contract with farmer Lloyd Anderson the previous year, under which the $4.35 hourly minimum wage would be paid to 150 workers. But the agreement had broken down. The farmer was paying 85 cents a bucket for jalapenos peppers and it took an hour to collect four bucketfuls. He said he simply could not pay more. A crew leader, thin and wiry in short-sleeved shirt and jeans, denounced Marentes shouting: 'Why go on strike? Others will get paid.' He made a sweeping gesture with his hand. 'These people will be losers.' Workers gathered around listening silently, afraid to offend the crew leader.

Among the crowd handing out business cards and urging people to call him was Mark Schneider, a Spanish-speaking Texas Rural Legal Aid lawyer, with greying hair tied back in a pony tail and a union T-shirt. He described to me the hardships suffered by the farm workers, most of whom could not read or write.

'Many walk here, wait for an hour for a bus, spend two hours travelling to the fields, wait for sun-up, work eight hours, wait another hour to get paid, and then start back again,' he said. 'They never know if they have a job. A thousand didn't get work last night. Tonight it will be the same.' In the fields they often had no lavatories or drinking water. They had to buy canned soda at exorbitant prices and they got no pay if it rained.

The $59 million US chilli industry is enjoing a phenomenal expansion, said Schneider. Mexican food is now an American food. Every US town has a 'Taco Bell' fast food restaurant. Salsa has overtaken ketchup. It is a success story for the State of New Mexico, where most of the chilli farms are located, thanks to close co-operation between the state and the farmers. By law, labourers should get $30 a day but many farmers, tied to contracts with big packaging corporations, pay less. Workers die at fifty, on average, sometimes with diseases linked to pesticides. One big farmer told an El Paso newspaper: 'Well, they're going to die of someting.' Young Hispanic workers, born and brought up in El Paso, are growing rebellious, according to Ed Kissam, a farm labourer policy consultant. 'They are desperate and often bitter. This is not the American Dream they heard about at school.'

* * *

The land has always attracted immigrants to America. Over a hundred years before the wave of Hispanic workers started coming across the Mexican border to find work on the farms, Irish, Scots-Irish and German immigrants came to settle in places like Iowa in the Midwest, in search of the American dream of land and sufficiency.

John O'Connor, a big, gentle farmer in his sixties, who lives on a gravel road near the 'city' of Cumming (population 139) in Madison County, Iowa, can trace his ancestry to settlers who arrived at the time of the famine in Ireland one and a half centuries ago. So too can most of his neighbours in this Catholic enclave where the official notepaper is headed 'Leprechaun City'. There are statues of the Virgin Mary on some of the lawns in Cumming, which has no grocery store but has a bar. Pope John Paul visited the tiny wood-framed St. Patrick's church at Irish Settlement beside Cumming during his tour of the United States in 1979. Then the little community was relatively prosperous. Since that day, commemorated by a colour photograph of the Pope and John O'Connor in the O'Connor's farmhouse, Madison County has been through bad times.

'It will take ten presidents to undo the work of Ronald Reagan,' said John O'Connor bitterly. They had a vested interest in the outcome of the election. In the mid-1980s it seemed every farmer faced foreclosure as interest rates soared to 15 percent. Prices for milk, cattle and hogs fell steadily. 'In 1940 you could buy a tractor for 350 bushels of corn. You now need twenty thousand bushels,' said O'Connor, who has six hundred acres in corn and two hundred beef cattle. Much of the corn ends up as gluten for export to Russia as cattle fodder – it is on such struggling American farms that the chain linking aid from the US to the former Soviet Union begins.

The farmers of Iowa sometimes despair of a better future. They are losing their land. Many have had to give up ownership of some or all of their property to meet huge debts and interest payments. Outside investors have bought up about a quarter of the acreage in Madison County and rented it back to the farmers. O'Connor's neighbour, Richard Hanrahan, loves the peaceful Iowa land and believes 'it's the only place to bring up kids,' but he shares in the disillusion with America's political leadership. 'You can't raise corn and beans and make money; overheads have got too high,' he said, taking a break from tractoring corn silage to cattle on his 885-acre farmstead. 'One bad crop and a whole generation will leave the land.' Iowa has major crop failures every ten years, and regular partial failures. The farmers are kept on the edge of bankruptcy by property tax of $10 an acre and expensive health insurance. For Richard Hanrahan's family of five, Blue Cross insurance cost $2,500 a year in 1989. By 1992 it was $5,000.

'When an older person dies or retires there is often no-one there to replace them and a lot of these families are now the last generation on the land,' he said. 'The government has a policy of cheap food. They don't want you to go broke but they want to keep the food cheap.'

John Wayne was born in the nearby town of Winterset in 1907. The son of a red-haired Irish mother and a father descended from Antrim Presbyterians, John Wayne's real name was Marion Michael Morrison; he had a brother called Robert Emmet Morrison, after the great Irish patriot. Winterset (population 4,100) is where the farmers of Madison County come to buy grain, get their tractors fixed and have a drink in the tavern or a hoagie delight in Kirk's Steakhouse.

The main street of Winterset used to be Highway 169. Three years ago it was changed to John Wayne Drive to honour the star of *The Green*

Berets and *The Quiet Man* who was born in a little wood-board house at 224 South Second Street. A glass jar stands on the counter of a nearby souvenir shop for contributions to help construct a carriage house for Wayne's favourite horse Dollor which has outlived its master and which will be stuffed and put on display when it dies. 'Hopefully, Dollor will live a while because right now I don't know where we'd put him,' said Mrs. Priscilla Steenhoek, who looks after the Wayne house. To her the slow-talking cowboy was an all-American hero. 'It's very hokey but I think John Wayne was a real man, with good Iowa upbringing. Nobody ever said anything bad about him,' she added. 'John Wayne to me represented the American dream of the good overcoming the bad to make a better life.' Mrs. Steenhoek is the mother of ten children, all working, and was brought up in a Dutch household so strict they were forbidden to watch John Wayne movies. They worked to create a better life for the next generation. Now people have grown worried about the future because of a slump in farming and other economic setbacks.

'Times are better than twenty years ago but the next generation will have to lower its sights,' said Priscilla Steenhoek. 'The young people drink pop now as if it was their right and they eat what they please, but we had birthday cakes only on our birthdays.'

* * *

There are many thousands of Americans also descended from nineteenth-century European immigrants whose dream is not to prosper materially, but to live a simple frugal life to ensure they do not lose the spiritual values they hold dear. These are the Amish people, who reside mainly in Pennsylvania in remote rural areas where the land rises towards the Appalachian mountains.

There are about 130,000 Amish in the United States. They take no part in presidential or any other elections. Their Swiss-German forefathers first came to America in the 1720s, fleeing from religious persecution in Europe. They were followers of Jacob Ammann who rebelled against the opulence and vanities of Roman Catholicism and preached pacifism and separation from the world. They shun modern ideas and inventions, refuse government aid, even pensions, and do not take oaths or hold public office. The typical Amish farmers wear black wide-brimmed hats or straw hats with a black band, black high-top shoes and collarless black coats that fasten with hooks instead of buttons, which are considered foolish ornamentation. The Amish strive to be plain and simple; they are sometimes called the 'plain people'. They do not trim their beards and they let their hair fall to shoulder length. The women wear high-necked dresses of home-spun material, long black coats and full black bonnets over white prayer caps. Unmarried women wear white aprons, married women black. They do not question their life-style, at least not with strangers.

'Why do you wear wide-brimmed hats?' I asked Moses Hostetler, a friendly, outgoing farmer who lived along a narrow country road in central Pennsylvania. 'Well, it's tradition I suppose,' he replied, adding with a trace of irony, 'and it's useful when the sun is shining.'

You can recognise an Amish home by the absence of any electricity or telephone wires. At night, lighting comes only from oil lamps, except in some homes which have little windmills to provide power. The houses do not have doorbells, mirrors, pictures, musical instruments, washing machines or refrigerators. The only book is the High German Bible. In Moses Hostetler's house there was a wooden pew instead of a couch. They did not have television or radio.

'How do you get news of what is happening in the world?' I asked him.

He took a few moments to answer. 'That's a pretty good question,' he said courteously. 'Perhaps we don't need to know – most things anyway.'

It is said the Amish were unaware of Pearl Harbour for several weeks after it happened and did not learn for some days of the nuclear accident at Three Mile Island in 1979 which caused panic in towns not far to the east. Now they had no interest in Bush or Clinton or Perot.

Most of the Amish travel in black horse-drawn buggies which clip along the roads at about eight miles an hour. Their only concession to modernity is red luminescent triangles on the back. With their lack of acceleration they sometimes have to wait a long time to cross a highway. The Amish do not regard the automobile as evil but rather as a device which would erode family values by giving people greater mobility. Some do travel in cars and not all reject twentieth-century technology. There are in fact several gradations of Amish, explained a young Amish called Noel, whose second name was also Hostetler. He was a member of the Beachy Church of the Amish Mennonites, founded in 1927. 'We can use the telephone and can drive cars and tractors, but we can't have television or radio,' said Noel. Even then their cars had to be black and they had to paint the chrome black as well. 'We have churches but the others have services in their homes,' he went on. 'And some Mennonites don't wear beards. We grow a beard only when we get married.' Noel had given up farming two years previously to became an excavator driver. 'There's more to life than getting up every morning at four o'clock to milk cows,' he said, grinning.

Whatever their differences, all Amish have one thing in common. In the last twenty-five years or so their dream of being left alone has been rudely disturbed. Tourist buses clog up the narrow roads, especially at weekends. Sightseers look at them like fish in a bowl and take pictures despite the religious objection to photography of the Amish. In Lancaster County, where most Pennsylvania Amish are concentrated, day-trippers cruise the narrow roads in cars clicking camera shutters as if on a wild-life preserve. The popular movie, *Witness*, in which actor Harrison Ford played a fugitive who hid among the Amish, was mainly to blame. It made people curious. Three million visitors came to Lancaster County at the height of the tourist madness in 1985 after the film was released. Many see the Amish as relics of the past rather than as a community which has chosen its own way to deal with the present and the future. An Amish museum has now been built and has sidetracked many of the curious, but the official Pennsylvanian tour guide still invites visitors to 'share country roads with the buggies of Amish and Mennonite farmers' and 'find reminders of a time long past.'

* * *

Just north of the Pennsylvania border, on the Seneca Indian reservation in the foothills of the Allegheny Mountains of New York State, the native Indians nourish the oldest American dream of all, that of repossessing the land which was taken from them by the first American settlers. And they are making their dream come true, not by clinging to an old style of life but by adopting the paleface ways.

The seventy-one-year-old leader of the Seneca Indians, Calvin John, is a bespectacled Presbyterian who wears a suit and tie. He calls himself 'President' rather than 'Chief'. Law books line the shelves of his spacious office where the Stars and Stripes and the red-coloured flag of the Seneca nation are displayed together.

The Seneca Indians were first assigned land for a reservation in the Allegheny mountains early in the last century, but the Great Western Railroad was driven through the reservation in 1853, despite the Indians' protests. With the railroad came settlers who built the town of Salamanca, the only 'settler' town on a reservation in the whole of the United States. In 1892 the elders of the Seneca Indians were plied with drink and persuaded by the settlers, who wanted to legalise their squat in Indian land, to sign a ninety-nine-year lease agreement. A derisory ground rent was set of less than $5 a year for each property.

'This was a sad, unfortunate period in our history,' said President John. 'Our ancestors were duped by white lessees who were bent on securing leases in Salamanca because it was becoming a booming railroad town.'

The Indians were allowed to keep a small measure of sovereignty on the reservation; they were exempt from federal taxes though not from military service or federal criminal law. They sank into poverty. Most of the 6,300 native Americans living on the reservation today dwell in trailers rather than houses because they could not get mortgages. That requires putting up land as collateral, but no Indian individual owns any land on the reservation as it belongs collectively to the Seneca nation.

But recently the Indians have begun to reassert themselves in their own land. Their new-found self-confidence springs from the fact that the ninety-nine-year leases their ancestors were tricked into signing expired in February 1991 and President John has laid claim on behalf of the Seneca nation to the title of all the three- and four-room frame houses and the tree-shaded little mansions of Salamanca where the burghers of the town now live in middle-class comfort.

They had the right to do so because, when the land reverted to the Seneca nation, so too, under New York State legal precedent, did all the improvements on the land – which meant the houses. President John has offered the home-owners new leases, at much higher ground rents, under which they can stay on for forty years, and then another forty in houses whose deeds would belong to the Seneca nation. Some angry home-owners formed a protest movement, the Salamanca Coalition of United Taxpayers, or SCOUT, to keep Indian hands off their properties, but the state courts and the US Supreme Court refused to interfere, saying that they had no jurisdiction in leasing matters over a sovereign Indian nation.

The Wetherbys were one of the 3,300 non-Indian families living on the reservation. They had been paying $2.50 ground rent a year for the land on which they had built a handsome ranch-style bungalow on a road outside town. It was typical of many wooden dwelling houses in the area, situated on a half-acre lot with a pick-up truck and a sedan car parked nearby. The Seneca Indian nation asked the Wetherbys to sign a new forty-year lease and pay $140 a year ground rent. 'Nothing doing,' said Gail Wetherby, a cheerful, plump thirty-four-year-old welfare worker. The Wetherbys had built their home by hand, hammering in every joist and board themselves. They were not going to give it to the Indians. They decided to move house, literally, and hired a giant flatbed hydraulic truck at a cost of $20,000.

In the space of a day the house was moved a mile up the road and deposited on another half-acre lot – outside the reservation. The operation was performed so delicately that the contents of the house were not disturbed. The pictures of wild life barely swayed on the wood-plank walls, the deer antlers above the bedroom corridor did not fall down, the rocking chair in the living room barely rocked. 'Even the ornaments stayed on the table,' Mrs. Wetherby told me as she heated tea in a microwave oven for two elderly neighbours.

It wasn't the higher ground rent that drove the Wetherbys to such extremes, she explained. In fact, Gail Wetherby felt the new assessment, based on modern valuations, was fair. Nor was it any problem with Indians. Some of the family had intermarried with native Americans. The Wetherbys simply could not bring themselves to sign away the house they had taken such pride in building. 'We pounded in every nail,' she said. 'We worked hard for what we have, but on the reservation we have no American rights.'

The moving of the house became a pivotal event in the historic land dispute in Salamanca. The Wetherbys were lucky: the border of the reservation was just along their road. Others could not move their houses because of underpasses and narrow roads. Few could afford the cost. And the Seneca nation threatened legal action. After all, by law the houses belonged to them.

'We lost one house, we let it go,' said President John. 'But no more.' He added, however: 'We don't want a mass exodus. We have to depend on each other for survival here.'

Townspeople tried other tactics. A Catholic priest said he would toll church bells if anyone was evicted. Some householders pledged to burn or tear down their homes rather than give them up. SCOUT tried to organise a tax strike but 96 percent of residents in the end signed the new leases rather than face eviction. On 19 December 1991, town mayor Antonio Carbone handed over a cheque for $706,675.37 for the new ground rents in the president's office, fourteen times the previous amount.

The Seneca Indians have just begun to discover the mechanism to make their own history again. To them, conventional politics mean little. Their political battles are fought through highly-paid lawyers. They are part of an unheralded revolution across the United States in which native Americans are regaining their dignity and tribal assets. Most Indians are still unemployed and demoralised, but the trend is upwards. Compensation for past wrongs has placed vast sums at the disposal of many tribes. The Seneca Indians in Salamanca have found legal ways to exploit their sovereignty rights – by claiming reservation properties and by selling cheap petrol and cigarettes at duty-free shops. The next step, many believe, will be to establish the one business which is guaranteed to bring wealth to the reservations – gambling casinos.

* * *

If gambling is the ultimate route to the American dream of get-rich-quick, Atlantic City is the ultimate dreamland for the gambler. It is the most-visited vacation spot in America. This city built beside the sands of the Atlantic shore of eastern New Jersey, 120 miles south of New York, draws more people every year than Las Vegas, Disneyland or New York. They pour in by car, train and aircraft from all over the Eastern United States, summer and winter, in search of the elusive dream. The city is an analogy for modern America: a strip of high-life surrounded by a ghetto, through which visitors pass on elevated highways.

The strip consists of a dozen mammoth casino-hotels – Shoboat, Resorts International, Sands, The Claridge, Bally's Park Place, Caesar's, Trump Plaza, The Taj Mahal, Trop World, Bally's Grand, Harrah's Marina and Trump Castle – all situated along a short stretch of the Atlantic City boardwalk, the 60 foot wide walkway which runs high along the edge of the sandy beach, safe from the ocean waves.

The Taj Mahal is the most glittering of them all. It is a Disney-land hotch-potch of oriental designs with seventy minarets and onion-shaped domes whose architectural style was borrowed freely from Moscow, Bangkok and Beijing. It houses the biggest casino in the world, a vast concourse of 120,000 square feet which can accommodate seventeen thousand people. Gamblers can commute from one hotel to another on rolling wicker chairs with parasols attached like rickshaws, relics of the days when Atlantic City was a great family holiday resort on the east coast and the watering place which popularised the picture postcard and the Miss America beauty contest.

It's only when you've been in Atlantic City for a while that you realise there are no children among the souvenir stalls, fudge shops and pizza parlours. They are not made to feel welcome. Atlantic City is a gambling mecca specifically designed to attract grown-ups with money or credit cards, with nothing to distract them from the tables or the one-armed bandits. Even the ghetto, I thought, peering into the inner-city darkness, served a purpose. It kept visitors confined, with nothing else to do. There aren't any clocks either, nor are there any windows in the casinos, so that time becomes meaningless. And watching over everything are the secret police. The Taj Mahal has 309 surveillance agents. You cannot see them but they can see you, through video cameras hidden in each of 534 brown glass bubbles among the twenty-five German crystal chandeliers hanging from the ceiling. The casino is like a totalitarian state. The decision of the management is final. Those who don't fit in are told to leave. Dissidents are not tolerated. Another 650 video cameras monitor the rest of the building so that every room and corridor and gambling machine can be constantly monitored on four-way split screens in 'KGB headquarters', fifteen stories above. They spy as much on the players as on the staff, the highly-paid dealers at the $1,000 maximum crap tables, or the $9 an hour slot attendants, who are exposed to round-the-clock temptation to cream off the biggest cash flow in the western world. They catch about four each day.

What I wasn't prepared for in the Atlantic City casinos was the noise. There is a permanent cacophony of sound in the gaming rooms; the frenetic clunking of quarters and half-dollars into plastic cups, the endless electronic squeals and toc-toc-tocking of three thousand slot machines being played at once, the computerised jangles of one-armed bandits as winning lines come up, like dozens of doorbells going off at once. Even in the roped-off, carpeted baccarat salons, the noise is inescapable. Donald Trump, who gave his name to three of the casinos in Atlantic City, compared the scene to that on Wall Street. 'The New York Stock Exchange happens to be the biggest casino in the world,' he said. 'The only thing that makes it different from the average casino is that the players dress in blue pinstripe suits and carry leather briefcases.'

Here the dream is the jackpot, and those who pursue it form a huge sector of America's population of middle-aged and elderly men and women, dressed in open-neck shirts with outsize shorts stretched tight over ample hips spilling over the edges of their stools. They make occasional human sounds, emitting brief whoops of joy when coins cascade forth from the machine, then revert to assembly-line motions, arms moving up and down, working the controls of the slot-machines and electronic poker and blackjack games, on screens which flash up electronic messages like 'Happy Days Are Here Again', 'Columbus Took a Chance' and 'Easy Come, Easy Go'. They sit for hours, concentrating intently, sometimes playing two or three machines at the same time, pausing only to take free soft drinks from voluptuous, scantily-clad waitresses at whom they scarcely glance. The dream in Atlantic City is not to lose. The reality is that slot machines are fixed to pay back only 83 percent of what they ingest.

* * *

Many decent, hard-working people in middle-America have come to feel in the past few years that in life, as in the Atlantic City casinos, the odds are stacked against them. I found this to be the case when I came across the town of Sedalia, which boasts the title 'Queen of the Prairies' and is situated on Route 50 between Kansas and St. Louis in central Missouri. Sedalia is the epitome of peaceful small-town America. Its population of twenty thousand is served by sixty-six Protestant and two Catholic Churches, a daily newspaper, forty-seven police officers, 250 stores, thirty-four manufacturing plants and forty-five restaurants, mostly fast-food joints like Eddie's Drive-in-Burgers, Ken's Pizza and the Dickie-Doo Bar-B-Que. It even has a 'Dream Factory', a civic centre which makes dreams come true for handicapped children.

Sedalia was always the sort of town where people knew each other. Parents were greeted by name when they went to C.W. Flowers drapery store for their children's back-to-school clothes. Philip and Ruth Hoffman, who ran the hardware store on Ohio Street, would give hand-written receipts to their customers. Such tradespeople formed the backbone of America's small towns, passing on and improving their business and their standard of living from generation to generation. Theirs was the core dream of Norman Rockwell's America. But one by one they are being forced out of business all across the United States. Four years ago C.W. Flowers drapery store closed down. Now the Hoffmans had a notice on the door declaring 'GOING OUT OF BUSINESS SALE'.

'It's very sad,' said Philip Hoffman as he wrapped in brown paper a carved wooden bread-box inscribed with the words 'Give us this day our daily bread'. Gesturing sadly towards rows of shelves with notices such as 'Enamel' and 'Nails', he told me: 'My grandfather started the store three generations ago. We're in our mid-seventies now. Young people today don't want to work the long hours. They can earn more in other jobs. So we have no choice but to close.'

The decline of the 'mom and pop' store is partly due to a drift to the suburbs, a phenomenon not limited to the cities. The character of Sedalia is changing because many townspeople are moving to the Walnut Hills Country Club neighbourhood, where the doctors and lawyers always lived, in search of a suburban lifestyle, said George Wimmer, vice-president of Sedalia's development corporation. It is also due to a revolution in America which has its origins in Arkansas and which goes by the name of Wal-Mart.

Wal-Mart is the ultimate discount chain. When it arrives in a small town it draws people away from the main street to its plastic-fronted retail warehouse, set amid acres of carpark asphalt. No-one can match it for rock-bottom prices and aggressive customer research. It swallows up family businesses and depersonalises small-town America. Wal-Mart's 2,200 stores in the US sell everything from garden tools to children's clothes. The organisation multiplies at the rate of one Wal-Mart every day. Its arrival is fiercely contested in many small towns but the chainstore's advance planners almost invariably overcome the resistance, which can take the form of candle-lit vigils and multiple planning objections. When Wal-Mart does establish itself, it declares war on Main Street. Its employees are taught to chant: 'Stack it deep, sell it cheap, stack it high and watch it fly! See those down-town merchants cry!'

Wal-Mart came to Sedalia in the middle of the 1980s. It went into competition with every downtown store, even the chemists' shops, opening its own pharmacy counter with offers of free blood pressure tests, free mailing and 'easy to swallow' prescription costs. 'Wal-Mart hurt a lot of downtown stores in the town,' said Catherine Cote, a business project manager for Missouri, who misses in particular the friendliness of C.W. Flowers drapery store. A middle-aged man from a nearby shop, who wandered into the Hoffman's hardware store while I was there to commiserate with the retiring owners, said: 'If everybody goes to shop at Wal-Mart, then the money goes out of the town, that's the real catch. The Hoffmans here make money, they spend it up the street. Now they are closing down, there's less to go around. That's the way it goes. We're all going broke round here, I guess.' George Wimmer, in the development office around the corner from the Hoffmans, was sympathetic, but pointed out: 'The Wal-Mart is here, that's good; it means cheaper prices. When I was a kid there was a greengrocer at every corner. Then the supermarkets came and we thought it was the end of the world. It's not the end of the world.'

Some say that the chainstore brought employment – 225 people work in Sedalia's Wal-Mart store – though the pay is often minimum wage and the jobs part-time. The day Wal-Mart came to Sedalia to recruit employees, many of the people queueing up for its $5 an hour jobs included skilled men and women who had been earning $8.50 an hour and more in factories which had closed down.

All across the United States I found this to be a recurring theme. For such people, living standards are falling, not rising. Workers in factories and plants which close through bankruptcy, corporate greed, movement of companies abroad or at the end of the industrial revolution, are losing well-paid jobs and being forced to settle for less.

For each person who slips down the ladder, the middle class is diminished, and so too is the dream of the ever-improving life which has been one of the most powerful driving forces in the making of modern America.

Chapter 11

IT'S THE ECONOMY, STUPID

If a free society cannot help the many who are poor,
it cannot save the few who are rich

JOHN F. KENNEDY, INAUGURAL ADDRESS, 1961

TO FIND OUT WHY MIDDLE-CLASS AMERICA is shrinking, and with it the hopes of millions of people who were brought up believing that each generation would have a better life than the last, one need go no further than Royersford in eastern Pennsylvania.

The story of Royersford is a familiar one to workers in countless towns where the local industry has closed. It is a story of heartbreak and disillusion. It explains more than any set of economic statistics or financial indicators why so many voters in the United States decided in 1992 that they could no longer tolerate the 'trickle-down' economics of the Reagan-Bush era.

Royersford is a little industrial town of about five thousand people roughly thirty-five miles from Philadelphia. For most people growing up in and around its narrow, hilly streets the dream was to get a job in the Diamond Glass Company plant, which made mainly high-quality bottles for liquor and pharmaceuticals.

Diamond Glass was a family-owned concern which started up in 1874. The plant is located on a stretch of land in the middle of the town between the river Schykill and the railway line carrying coal from Pottstown to Pennsylvania. The social and business life of Royersford always centred round the glass plant's little complex of buildings with its skyline of four furnace stacks and a sand silo like a look-out tower where sand, soda ash, cullet and other ingredients of the glass were mixed.

The plant worked three shifts around the clock and every weekend. To accommodate the night workers, the Royersford branch of Fidelity Bank opened at eight o'clock in the morning, the only bank in fifty miles to do so, but it was worth the bank's while. There was good money at Diamond Glass.

Larry Weikel was brought up in Spring City, a small town adjacent to Royersford. He got a start at the glass plant at the age of twenty-three after serving four years in the air force.

'When I went to work there I thought I had died and gone to heaven,' he said in the ranch-style home in which he lives in the countryside a few miles north of Royersford. 'The bosses were good. Everybody knew everybody else. Everybody had an uncle there. In fact, so many people were related you had to watch what you said! The supervisors were all very nice. They could be tough but – back then when I was drinking – we would go out together after work. When urgent work had to be done we would take the place apart, nuts and bolts, and put it together again. There was a good camaraderie there.

'I loved to go to work. I worked holidays and weekends. I spent Saturdays and Sundays down there. I didn't do anything with the kids. The owner, Frank Foster Junior, always talked to everybody when he came in. He knew everybody. He was an old man, stooped over, and he wore pants up to here.' He pointed to his chest. 'I remember him saying to a foreman: "Why are you sitting down?" And the foreman replying: "You ought to be glad I'm sitting down. It means you're making money."

'In the 1960s a person could work his way up the ranks and achieve the middle-class life. I started as an apprentice operator and went from operator to shift upkeep man to shift foreman. By the end of the 1980s, I was earning in the high forty thousands a year. The men under me were making $15 to $16 an hour for a forty-four-hour week. It was really good money. There was a credit union and a profit-sharing scheme as well. People bought their cars from the credit union. People got enough to buy a good house and a car. I had a Corvette and a Harley Davidson.'

Another employee at the plant was George Tobias, who was born in Phoenixville, five miles down the river. He started work in Diamond Glass in 1971 at the age of nineteen.

'The plant had such a good reputation that you couldn't get in unless you were related to someone – you couldn't buy a job there,' he told me. 'At first I worked as personal chauffeur for Frank Foster Junior. He was a great man to work for. He expected a lot from you but you were treated with respect. People loved him. I don't think you could find five people who disliked the old man. After he died in 1977 his son Frank Foster III took over. He and I had a personality conflict so I changed jobs and went to work in the mould shop. I actually got $2 an hour more there. The pay was $13.78 an hour for a forty- to sixty-hour week. That was very good money.

'But everything about Diamond Glass was outstanding. They even had a full-time gardener just to keep the grounds manicured. The pay scales were good. The benefits were good. You had to work hard – you got in trouble if you thought you were going on Easy Street. We tackled the more intricate bottles, high-quality bottles for whisky and cosmetics. Avon and Listerine used our bottles. Everybody was proud to work there because we had a name.'

In 1983 the plant went public and the atmosphere began to change as the pressure for profits increased.

'Frank Foster III brought in high-priced hatchet men,' said George Tobias. 'Morale began to decline steeply. They stopped caring about quality. They wanted us to make three hundred bottles a minute, they didn't see that the machines weren't capable of that. The plant began to tear itself apart.'

Under its new corporate management, the company began to expand, buying up other glass plants all over the United States. In 1987 it was purchased by the Anchor Glass Container Corporation of Tampa, Florida.

'When Anchor took over they were going to change our life, whether we wanted to or not,' said Larry Weikel. 'The newcomers had no family ties with the company. There were no promotions from within any more. They would get someone from elsewhere. They knew everything, we knew nothing. These were guys who would travel all over, glass gypsies. They'd get fired in one place and go to another. The message they sent down the line was – you just have to produce or we're getting rid of you.

'Every time I went to work I had a knot in my stomach. If things didn't go well, they humiliated you, they treated you like dirt. Things started getting nasty and out-of-hand. They didn't care what you did to get the numbers.'

Things got so bad that Weikel's wife, Linda, who had been working as a packer and quality control inspector at $11.02 an hour, quit in 1989, unwilling to take the abuse any more, and got a job in a sewing factory for $6 an hour.

Then in 1990 the Royersford glass company plant was closed down and the jobs of the five hundred workers were eliminated. Workers like Larry Weikel and George Tobias tried to figure out what had gone wrong. All they knew from the attitude of the management was that the plant was closed because they had somehow failed to match the performance required in the modern glass industry.

It wasn't like that, as they learned the following year when two journalists from the *Philadelphia Inquirer*, Donald Bartlett and James Steele, published an investigation into Anchor Glass and several other US companies which had closed down. They discovered that they had become victims of a process under which thousands of US businesses had shut because of a change in the economic rules in the Reagan-Bush period which yielded fabulous riches for a few investment bankers and corporate managers but which brought disaster to small communities like Royersford.

Put simply, new tax rules approved by Congress encouraged corporate restructuring by allowing big tax advantages on debt, while at the same time making it profitable to buy and dismantle companies rather than develop them.

With Diamond Glass the slide into disaster started with a management buy-out at the beginning of the 1980s, after which the company changed its name to Diamond-Bathurst Inc. In 1981 Diamond-Bathurst purchased a bankrupt glass plant in West Virginia. In 1985 it bought Container General Corporation, a glass company in Tennessee with twelve plants, and three months later it acquired most of the assets of Thatcher Glass Company in Connecticut. It assumed control of other plants in New Jersey, Ohio and Pennsylvania. Shareholders began to make huge profits as the stock rose from $6 a share to $29 and sales exceeded $400 million. The expansion enabled Frank Foster III, Diamond-Bathurst's president and chief executive officer, to say: 'We became in three short months one of the largest glass container manufacturers in the United States, with projected annualised sales of $550 million.'

To finance its empire-building, Diamond-Bathurst pushed its debt up from $13 million to $104 million within one year. But it overstretched itself. The year following its big acquisitions, Diamond-Bathurst recorded a loss of $6.2 million. It began to slim down by closing plants in several states but it was unable to stave off a takeover in 1987 by a competitor, Anchor Glass of Florida.

Anchor Glass was the product of a leveraged buy-out with borrowed money. It was formed by an investment banking firm. Anchor Glass borrowed $76 million. Of this $48 million was returned to the investment bankers, who used it to purchase the land, buildings and machinery of Anchor Glass – and lease it back to the plants. By 1988 the principal partners in the investment firm had sold their holdings and retired from the scene with profits and fees running into tens of millions of dollars.

In 1989, Anchor Glass was purchased by a glass-manufacturing Mexican Company, Vitro S.A. One of the first acts of this company, which exports products into the US to compete with American-made glass, was to close the plant at Royersford.

'On the day it closed it was very depressing,' said George Tobias. 'People were just going through the motions. The feeling between management and the men was one of animosity.'

'It was heartbreaking,' said Larry Weikel, a grey-haired man with a moustache who was forty-five when the plant closed. 'I looked around and thought, for twenty-three years I've been pounding this concrete, now I won't be here anymore. I said to myself – what am I going to do now? It was all I ever did in my life after I came out of the service. I never learned anything else except to make bottles. I was liked there. I loved it. Twenty-three years there, and an outfit comes in like this and destroys everything you lived for. That really hurts. It is as if I prostituted my whole life to that company. They gave us all one of the bottles from the last run. After twenty-five years they gave us a bottle.'

'An empty one!' said his wife Linda.

The closing of the old Diamond Glass Company had a devastating effect on the town. It was the last of a number of moderate-size companies in the area to shut. Firestone closed first in the 1970s. Then Goodrich in the mid-1980s. The only firms left today are small, like the Royersford Spring Company which makes seat springs, a company that washes radioactive clothes from the nearby nuclear power plant and a machine and tool company which assembles tools from parts made elsewhere.

The pipes and metal struts at the glass factory are now rusting. A waist-high heap of broken green glass near the old foundry is all that remains of the product of which the workers were so proud. The big carpark is empty. Despite rumours that someone would take over the plant, no-one did. There is a problem with polluted land because dumping of waste for over a century has made the site environmentally unattractive to potential new occupants.

It a familiar scene in Royersford where other industrial plants and factories lie empty. Right in the centre of the town, at the point where the railway line crosses the Main Street, a derelict three-storey red-brick factory, with most of its little square windows broken, stands as the most visible evidence of Royersford's decline. A notice set in stone declares it was the Roy Foundry & Machine Company. A poster on the wall says that 277,000 square feet of space is available. No-one has inquired about it for some time.

In Tom's Bar and Grille at the far end of Main Street, where the glass plant workers liked to drink and play pool, Mary Jo Kerchner works behind the counter. 'The result of the closure of the glass plant is that nobody works in town anymore,' she said. 'You had the fathers and brothers working there. Now everybody's working out of town. The life of Royersford has fallen apart. If there's a fire during the day the fire service can't get anyone, maybe just one or two men. They're all out of town.' She added: 'Whatever jobs are going they are only part-time and there are no health insurance benefits.'

The barman, Dennis Ross, just out of college, said: 'I would have started in the glass plant three years ago if they had been hiring. I'm looking for work as an aircraft maintenance engineer, which would pay about $9 an hour, but everywhere I go they are not taking anyone on. Here I get paid $5 an hour plus tips.'

George Tobias's wife, Sandra, is assistant manager of Fidelity Bank where many of the glass workers had accounts. In her office just inside the entrance door she said: 'At the bank our transactions are maybe a third of what they were. The effect on the town has been very depressing. Everywhere you look there are empty stores, empty gas stations, empty warehouses. Some of the workers made good money, $9 to $10 an hour. They are now working for $5 to $7 an hour. They work as receptionists, waitresses, file clerks, checkers in supermarkets, anything they can get. The bank still opens at 8 a.m. but there's no-one lining up outside at opening time any more. There's still some early-morning traffic but basically they've all gone.'

Larry Weikel had to refinance the mortgage on his house after the plant closed and spend his savings. He works part-time for his brother-in-law in Grubbs Marine in Spring City doing 'everything and anything' for $7 an hour. His income has been reduced to a quarter of what it was, and he has had to come to terms with the fact that jobs paying the type of money he was earning in the plant are not to be found. He worries about his company pension. 'They say it's guaranteed,' he said, 'but I've seen things change before.' They had also lost health insurance cover, something which most American firms once provided automatically for their employees.

'We had automatic health insurance,' said Larry Weikel. 'Before we went public, I'd go to a doctor and tell him I worked for Diamond Glass and that would be the end of it. The company paid the insurance and had a couple of doctors of its own. That was tradition in all companies. It's dying out now.'

George Tobias said: 'A lot of us could have transferred to another plant, but none of us could trust them anymore. You might pull up your roots and go somewhere else and then in six or eight months they'd close the plant there too.' He saw the end coming and began a part-time photographic agency, 'Tobias Photography', which is now his full-time business.

'Since the plant closed I have never ever in my life worked so many hours for so little money,' he said.

'I had a friend call by to see me the other day who worked in the glass plant,' added George Tobias. 'He's fifty-nine now. He's now doing three jobs and he's still making less than when he worked at the plant. He's an attendant on a school bus for handicapped children and he has two other jobs as a janitor. He thinks it will kill him.'

The story of Royersford's glass factory is common to thousands of towns throughout the United States. The takeovers and the rapacious demands of the profiteers on Wall Street have helped destroy a huge swathe of the middle class. The businesses whose workers were able to climb the ladder to make a good living for their families and who were looked after in exchange for dedicated service – the type of business like Diamond Glass where a good relationship between management and workers was matched by the quality of the product – are mostly gone. In the United States, at the end of the Reagan-Bush era, millions of workers are competing for fewer jobs at less pay. The number of people employed in manufacturing fell from 20.2 million in 1981 to 18.4 million in 1991 while at the same time the total workforce grew by almost 20 million.

Bill Clinton appealed directly to the victims of this phenomenon of modern America in his campaign to be elected president. 'We can never again allow the corrupt do-nothing values of the 1980s to mislead us,' he said in a statement of policy on US industry. 'Today the average chief executive at a major American corporation is paid a hundred times more than the average worker. Our government rewards that excess with a tax break for executive pay, no matter how high it is, no matter what performance it reflects. And then the government hands out tax deductions on corporations that shut down their plants here and ship our jobs overseas. This has to change.'

It was the realisation of the deep unhappiness about falling living standards, especially among the blue-collar and white-collar middle class, that prompted the slogan on the wall of the Clinton campaign headquarters in Little Rock: 'IT'S THE ECONOMY, STUPID' to remind everyone that this was the main issue. Larry Weikel's vote could not be taken for granted, however. Like many other religious people in Pennsylvania he had problems with Clinton's pro-choice stand on abortion. But 'I couldn't take a chance on another four years of Bush.' Ross Perot on the other hand 'opened a lot of eyes', he said.

The closures of the Royersford glass plant and thousands of industrial concerns like it are evidence that the problems of the American middle class go far beyond any recession and that it will be many years, if ever, before the infrastructural flaws in the economy are corrected so that a strong middle class emerges again as in the 1950s. The borrowing spree during the 1980s pushed up new corporate debt to $1.3 trillion, forcing the diversion of resources into interest payments and lowering the capacity of companies to invest in new equipment or conduct research and development. Millions of workers have been forced to move from jobs paying $10 to $20 an hour to jobs paying $5 to $10 an hour. At the same time workers have lost medical insurance benefits, pushing up the number of those without cover to thirty-seven million, proportionately the highest of any industrial nation.

For the first time the sons and daughters of a generation of middle-class workers are watching their parents' standard of living decline and do not anticipate that their life will be as good or better.

'For a growing number of individuals and families, the exploding difference in wages and salaries among the people at the top and everyone else means the end of the American Dream,' concluded Barlett and Steele, the *Philadelphia Inquirer* journalists.

Linda Weikel said: 'For me the American Dream is to be able to own a home and to be able to provide things for our kids which we can't give them, and and to have insurance to look after the kids if they get sick. But how can people do this now? My sister and her husband, they don't know which way to turn to send their kids to college.'

Said Larry Weikel: 'I don't see how any of my grandchildren will have the money to send their children to college. I don't see how the younger generation will ever be able to save money to buy a house. There's going to be rich folks and there's going to be poor folks. The American Dream is a paradigm – at least that's what it used to be. You came out of school. You worked or you went to service. You got married. You saved to buy a house. You had children. That's gone. The American Dream has been diminished.'

Chapter 12
OCTOBER SURPRISE

The leaves they were withering and sere:
It was night in the lonesome October
of my most immemorial year.

EDGAR ALLAN POE, *ULALUME*, 1847

THE SIGN 'IT'S THE ECONOMY, STUPID' was put up in a war room at Clinton's Little Rock campaign headquarters after the Democratic Convention. The war room, equipped with computers, TV sets and wire services and commanded by James Carville, had a strategic goal: to bring the fight to Bush by focussing relentlessly, to the exclusion of all else, on the country's economic problems while not painting too gloomy a picture, as hope was to be a crucial part of the message. The message was hammered home. Clinton would cut by half the budget deficit of $300 billion, which, thanks to Perot, voters were more and more convinced was the cause of many of their woes. The Clinton campaign embarked after the Convention on a triumphal road tour in luxury silver buses, drawing unexpectedly large crowds in Pennsylvania, West Virginia and Ohio. In five days the Clinton-Gore roadshow visited eight states. Democrats were haunted by the memory of 1988 when Michael Dukakis went home after the Convention and lost a seventeen-point lead. Bill Clinton was not going to make the same mistake.

From behind the two-way mirrors, Stan Greenberg's pollsters found that Clinton was being seen more and more as an average guy and the 'Slick Willie' image was fading. The tide began to turn Clinton's way in crucial places like Macomb County in Michigan, the industrial suburb of Detroit, which was the home of the American automobile and the heartland of the 'Reagan Democrats'. If Detroit was the combination lock which guarded the presidency, Macomb County was the key.

Here voters did not give their favours lightly. The remarks of a tool and die maker from Chrysler, with whom I talked in the Pampa Lanes Bowling Alley in Macomb County, were typical. His workmates discussed the election all the time, he said. They had liked Reagan and Bush for their anti-welfare policies and their toughness on communism, but these weren't issues any more. They weren't all that crazy about Clinton either. They didn't trust him not to raise taxes. But many were switching to the Democratic candidate for a variety of reasons, such as job losses, the fear of jobs going to Mexico or simply because they wanted change.

As the pace of the final weeks hotted up, the Clinton campaign achieved an extraordinary momentum. It abandoned the buses and took to the air in two Boeing 727s, one for the candidate and his entourage, the other for the media. The candidate's plane would take off first so that it could be filmed. The second followed and overtook it before the next stop to allow the camera crews to record the arrival. This process was called the death watch so that if the plane crashed, the networks would not miss it. In one thirty-six-hour period we travelled from Little Rock in the centre of the United States to Seattle on the Canadian border and then on to southern California, taking in stops in Colorado, Wyoming, Montana and Oregon on the way, and ending up in Las Vegas, Nevada. At each landing we tumbled onto the runway to form part of a moving organism around the candidate. Typically we rushed in a twenty-vehicle convoy to the nearest basketball gymnasium or school hall to be greeted by cheering and screaming crowds. Clinton would react with a slack-jawed, gee-shucks grin and a peculiar up-and-down movement of his hand as if shaking a cocktail in slow motion.

The thoughtful Clinton was replaced in the final days by a stump politician with a collection of populist slogans like: 'We want to take you into the future,' and 'Once in a generation we are called upon to make a decision like now.' This was not the time for taking risks. After each speech Clinton worked the crowds along a long rope-line, shaking hands and signing autographs for anything up to an hour. He had an unusual empathy with people. At Pueblo, Colorado, Mary Roman, an elderly woman in a pink cardigan, pressed a set of rosary beads into his hand and said she had been praying for him. He hugged her for a long time and his eyes misted over. Clinton created a sense of excitement which made one non-committed bystander, who had doubts about Clinton, say: 'You know I hope he wins, just so I can be happy with the whole country, even if it's only for two weeks.'

The controlled nature of the Clinton operation on the ground was in marked contrast to the anarchy on the Clinton media plane. It terrified the uninitiated, like the governor of Mexico's personal security guard, an Hispanic-American in white stetson with a .45 in his suit pocket, who squeezed into a seat beside me in Pueblo while his boss travelled on the Clinton plane.

'Unbelievable,' he muttered as he looked around him. The regular camera crews and photographers and the 'pencils', as the writing press was called, had plastered the plane's narrow interior with posters and suspended theatrical spider webs from the ceiling. An artificial arm dangled from the luggage rack above his head as if from a corpse. No-one bothered with air safety regulations. At each take-off, as the plane started its climb, the more flamboyant members of the camera teams surfed down the aisle on plastic trays, raising cheers as they banged into the toilet door. The stewardesses followed them, calling out cheerfully: 'Who wants drugs? Who wants drugs?' and passing out cough sweets and aspirin from little baskets.

George Bush took to the railway after the festival of darkness in Houston, trying to emulate Harry Truman, who in 1948 had toured the country by train and managed to defeat the hot favourite, Thomas Dewey, with a massive voter swing in the final two weeks. Bush called his train the 'Spirit of America'. As it crept slowly through Ohio and into Michigan, with most of us in the carriages dipping into Truman's biography, the crowd which gathered along the way was modest in size. George Bush was liked as a person but he was not popular as a president – and he was no Harry Truman.

The lack of enthusiasm for the President was notable when the 'Spirit of America' came to a halt beside a field in the Ohio village of Arlington where six hundred locals were having a picnic to celebrate their civic centenary. This was corn-growing country deep in the 'Buckeye state' and one of the Republican strongholds of the Midwest. The band played and high-school girls waved American flags, but most of the people remained sitting on the grass, even when the President appeared on the platform on the last carriage of the train.

At the back of the field a young vendor called Todd Mann leaned unhappily on a board covered with Bush campaign buttons. No-one was buying, he told me. Mann travelled to all political events in the Midwest selling badges. 'At this point,' he said, as Bush was finishing his speech, 'Clinton gets them so fired up they'd be fighting for badges.'

As the train made its slow, time-wasting progress north towards Michigan, small groups of people waved patriotically, but some made rude gestures and one man in a field near Toledo dropped his trousers and mooned his President.

A man dressed as a chicken began appearing at every stop with a sign saying 'Chicken George', a taunt about Bush's hesitation to agree to debate with his Democratic challenger. At Bowling Green in Ohio, Clinton supporters rattled Bush by heckling him noisily. Robert van Horn, a factory maintenance worker, distributed T-shirts proclaiming the 'Bush/Quayle Wrong Track Tour' and listing 107,000 Ohio jobs lost at Chrysler, Peter J. Schmitt, Frigidaire, NRM Steelastic, Eaton, Champion Spark Plug, Teledyne Monarch and Grimes Aerospace. 'There he is, the chicken,' an exasperated Bush cried as he spotted the now-familiar yellow suit. 'I'm not sure if that chicken is from Oxford, England.'

The line seemed to please him and the President took to using it at every stop. Clinton had been tainted, he implied, by something foreign, something intellectual, when he was at Oxford, infected perhaps with a germ of effete European socialism.

By this time Bush himself had recruited the Oxford-dominated British establishment to help in his campaign. Sir John Lacy, campaign director of the British Conservative Party, and his assistant, Mark Fullbrook, travelled to Washington to advise Bush aides on how the Conservatives had won the British general election with a weak candidate, John Major (who didn't go to Oxford, or anywhere) and with an economy in crisis. Sir John Lacy told his American counterparts they had made their main opponent, Neil Kinnock, leader of the Labour Party, the issue by hammering on the question of trust and taxes. They had used gimmicks like slide rules for distribution to voters which showed how much tax would be raised on specific incomes. The Republicans took notes and issued instructions.

Bush campaign organisers needed no prompting to go after Clinton on the character issue. Their only chance of victory now was to destroy their opponent. They chased a rumour that a classmate, who was now a Marine colonel, had said that in Oxford Clinton had once expressed the intention of giving up his US citizenship to avoid the draft. The colonel was located and denied the story but some Republicans did not want to be deprived of an 'October Surprise' which could swing the election. British officials were asked to check their files. Some of Jim Baker's political appointees at the State Department dug out the passport files of Clinton and his mother to look for damaging material. Directing this highly unusual exercise was Elizabeth Tamposi, an assistant secretary of state, who also went 'fishing' for Ross Perot's passport file. The searches were conducted after-hours at the National Records Center at Suitland, Maryland, where 3.2 million cubic feet of government documents are stored. Nothing was found, but when the full details leaked after the election, Tamposi was sacked.

Another seductive, and more ludicrous, suggestion was that Clinton had been at one time a stooge of the KGB. Fiery, right-wing Congressman Robert Dornan of California, raised this red flag in a series of late-night speeches in Congress in which he alleged that, on a student trip to Moscow in 1969-70, Clinton had come under the influence of the Soviet security forces. Dornan and three colleagues made such a fuss that they were eventually allowed to call on Bush in the White House to urge him to take up the question.

The result was one of the most shameful episodes of the campaign. On CNN's *Larry King Live*, Bush suggested that there was something sinister about the Moscow trip. 'I don't want to tell you what I really think,' he told King, adding that Clinton should 'come clean with the American people'. The President of the United States, whom viewers would trust as the country's Commander-in-Chief not to make such statements lightly, expanded on his charge of treachery by recalling that the Democratic candidate had 'demonstrated against his own country on foreign soil', a reference to Clinton's peripheral involvement in anti-Vietnam war activity in London.

Bush's below-the-belt assault was yet another misjudgement of the mood of the electorate, which wanted to hear a genuine economic debate. It raised more questions about Bush than about Clinton.

The smear tactic appeared to have been modelled on the innuendo heaped on Neil Kinnock before the British general election over reports that the Labour leader visited the Soviet embassy in London during the early 1980s. But Clinton was not Kinnock, who did have a socialist past to live down. In Britain voters blamed Margaret Thatcher rather than Major for the recession; in the United States they blamed

Bush. Moreover, where Kinnock was sometimes gauche and lacking in *gravitas*, Clinton's every gesture and action in public was now presidential, from his Kennedyesque jaw-clenching to his hairstyle.

The red smear gave Clinton an opportunity to render Bush speechless in one of three televised debates which were eventually held. He said to the President: 'Your father was right to stand up to Joe McCarthy. You were wrong to attack my patriotism.'

Televised debates in media-conscious America can affect the fortunes of a candidate in an unexpected way. Nixon's five o'clock shadow turned many voters towards the more telegenic Kennedy in 1960. Reagan deflated Carter in 1980 with his admonition: 'There you go again.' This time Bush needed to score convincingly in three pre-election debates to cut back Clinton's lead in the polls. Instead he was caught glancing at his watch and was wrong-footed when a black woman asked how the national debt affected him personally. 'I'm not sure I get it,' he replied.

'Bush just lost the election,' said Clinton's chief strategist, Jim Carville, who was watching the debate on television. 'Can you imagine if we had a candidate who did this. You'd be fanning me right now.'

Bush did get in one telling return. When Clinton rather smugly mocked Bush's plan to give James Baker control of the domestic economy, saying: 'The person responsible for the domestic economy in my administration will be Bill Clinton,' Bush retorted: 'That's what worries me.'

In the end, the October Surprise came from Ross Perot. Five weeks before polling day and seventy-six days after he quit, the jug-eared billionaire decided to get back into the game.

It is doubtful if he had ever really left it. After his abdication in July, volunteer leaders descended on Dallas for a post-Perot meeting and found that he wished to set up a political pressure group in place of the draft-Perot movement. At a heated encounter in the Sheraton Park Central Hotel, several people demanded that he be immediately drafted as a presidential candidate. Of those who pressed Perot, Alaska chairwoman, Donna Gilbert, was most insistent, writing the demand on a blackboard before Perot arrived in the room and getting the others to sign it. Perot's face darkened when he saw it. 'If anyone thinks I've quit they're going to be in for an October Surprise,' he said, but he would not commit himself further. He explained his reticence with the words: 'My family is my weakness, and if that leaves this room I'm out.' He also told his astonished loyalists that Boris Yeltsin had informed him about missing American POWs in Russia and if this revelation left the room he would deny it and leave the movement.

Perot in fact never closed the door on his campaign. In the days after he said he was quitting, the computer tycoon continued spending money to get his name on the ballot in all fifty states, hiring professional petition-gatherers in New York to replace the volunteers who had stomped on their petition sheets in disgust. In the next month Perot spent $4 million.

At the same time he supervised a messy purge of his most independent-minded chairpeople, including Donna Gilbert, who said later: 'I concluded that he was either a liar or a lunatic or maybe both at the same time.' Elizabeth Elmore, another disillusioned organiser from Los Angeles, said: 'What's left are the sycophants. The idealists have left or have been booted out.'

When the shake-up was complete Perot had a pliant, nation-wide organisation, which he called 'United We Stand, America' and his unwieldly campaign had been brought under control. Perot also gained a breathing space which got the media off his back.

It turned out he still had a sizeable reservoir of support around the country. His $5 book named after his new organisation became a best-seller when it was published in September.

To provide cover for re-entering the fray, Perot arranged for a poll of his volunteers, an exercise which *Newsweek* likened to asking admirers of Elvis Presley if they would like him to come back from the dead. They voted that he should run for president.

In his first two weeks after re-entry, Perot spent $24 million on sixty-second advertising slots and half-hour sales pitches in which Perot used Texas plain talk to show what a pickle America was in. To cut the deficit Perot offered a laundry list of measures which included a 33 percent tax on petrol, a 2 percent increase on income tax, sweeping defence cuts, a 10 percent cut in discretionary budget items, the slashing of agricultural subsidies, the elimination of social security for affluent retirees and cost-containment in health-care. Over a five-year period he planned to raise $350 billion in increased taxes and save $413 billion in spending cuts. An astonishing sixteen million people watched his first thirty-minute 'infomercial', in which Perot used a little conductor's baton and computer graphics to lecture his audience like a sales manager addressing a class of trainees. He began to rise steadily in the polls again.

Then Perot shot himself in the foot once more, this time with one of the strangest tales of the 'weird' election year. In a *60 Minutes* television interview, he said the real reason he dropped out of the race in July was to protect his daughter, Carolyn, from a Republican Party plot to disrupt her August wedding. Bush's operatives, said Perot, planned to publish a doctored photograph depicting his daughter as a lesbian by imposing her head on another body. He got out of the race and the wedding went ahead. 'I adore her, I would not risk ruining one of the happiest days of her life,' said Perot, adding: 'We even had the dogs in, the whole works.' He admitted he had no proof of his allegation but named as one of his sources an Arizona dress-shop owner named Scott Barnes. A former police officer, Barnes was a notorious conspiracy theorist who specialised in bizarre espionage stories.

Perot had forgotten the advice of his former campaign co-chairman, Ed Rollins: 'If anything you do makes you into a kook, you lose.' The independent candidate was once again 'Inspector Perot'. Bush said to a friend: 'The son-of-a-bitch is a psychiatric case.' Voters began turning away from Perot again. Few would want to have so credulous a president, who would take drastic action on the word of dubious sources.

Bush meanwhile travelled several times to Detroit to try to 'pick the lock' and cling on to the presidency. His desperation showed. At one memorable rally in Macomb County, I heard him call Clinton and Gore a 'pair of bozos'. Barbara Bush and his officials took him to task for not being 'presidential' and for going over the top. 'Jeez, you guys, lighten up, I was only trying to be funny,' said Bush. More telling was his persistent attack on Clinton on taxes. As the election approached, voters began to get the little slide rules purporting to show the extra tax they would have to pay, as if it was an official publication (eg salary, $42,000, extra tax $1,423.54). It was a fabrication, but effective. If Clinton was going to cut the budget deficit as much as he said he would, Bush claimed, this would mean higher taxes for everyone who earned more than $36,000 a year. In the end Bush was not too far from the truth, but, when the suggestion appeared in a Republican TV advertisement, Clinton was furious. Privately he called the commercial 'one of the most totally irresponsible in presidential politics,' according to a travelling companion, and told his aides: 'We've got to say he made it up. I want to put a fist halfway down their throats with this. I don't want subtlety. I want their teeth on the sidewalk.'

Bush's slash-and-burn tactics at last began to have their effect. Clinton began to slip in the polls in the final days. Bush became 'engaged' for the first time as Clinton's negative ratings climbed to fifty. The polls narrowed until, incredibly, four days before polling, Bush and Clinton were at thirty-nine points each. But any hope Bush had of pulling off a Truman-like victory were dashed when he was hit the same day by the real, long-awaited October Surprise. Documents were released by the special prosecutor in the Iran-contra affair showing that Bush not only had known about the deal hatched by Reagan's aides to swop arms for American hostages, something he had always denied, but had approved of it. Bush had been attacking Clinton for a 'pattern of deceit' in his public life. Now he appeared to be the slick one.

The centre of Little Rock was packed with thousands of people ready for a victory party as Clinton headed towards a convincing win on the evening of polling day, 3 November. It was a cold and gusty November evening with smoke from hot-dog stands blowing up across giant television screens erected on the back of trucks. People thronged the hotels to drink and whoop and to spot celebrities. The lobby of the Japanese-owned Excelsior Hotel became a heaving mass of bodies, throwing together rich white women in bare-shouldered gowns, poor black men in hooded parka jackets, politicians in $1,000 Armani suits and scruffy teenagers weighed down with campaign badges like Soviet generals. Black executives and white country youths stood shoulder to shoulder at specially-installed trestle-table bars in the huge foyer getting seriously drunk. It was a celebration not just of Clinton's victory but of Arkansas nationalism in this poor, rural state. People from Hope and Hot Springs mingled happily with the crowd. 'I never thought I'd see a president from Arkansas,' cried a black woman dripping gold ornaments.

The networks declared the race over at 9.50 p.m. Clinton won 43 percent of the vote, Bush 38 percent, and, surprisingly, Perot 19 percent. Like Mikhail Gorbachev in the former Soviet Union, George

Bush had been repudiated by his own people, as history turned to new leaders to address the challenges of a changed, new world. A delirious crush of people surged into the chilly street to join the throng already waiting for their Governor, now President-elect, to emerge from the Old State House nearby. Inside the stone building there were tears and hugs as the new First Family readied themselves in the lobby.

I found myself crushed against a wall on which were inscribed the words of one of Arkansas's most famous man-of-letters, Thomas Bang Thorpe, written in 1852. Nothing seemed more appropriate for the occasion than Thorpe's triumphal 'Happen! Happened in Arkansas!' Clinton, Hillary and daughter Chelsea joined hands and moved through the door with their junior partners, Senator Al Gore and Tipper Gore and their children, and a deafening cheer washed over them from a vast sea of faces illuminated by klieg lights. In the front of the crowd, Clinton's mother Virginia and her fourth husband, Dickey Kelley, waved like mad.

'My fellow Americans, on this day, with high hopes and brave hearts, in massive numbers, the American people have voted to make a new beginning,' Clinton declared. He introduced Hillary to the throng, saying: 'She will be one of the greatest first ladies in the history of the Republic.' More cheers. After they left for a series of parties in the Excelsior, the crowd lingered on singing 'God Bless A-mer-i-ca'. Campaign aides handed out huge American flags and groups of young and middle-aged people paraded them around, like Baltic nationalists waving their flags at independence rallies.

There was a sense that this was the final triumph of the Vietnam generation, of the young, now middle-aged, people who had opposed the war and who no longer had to endure the lingering disapproval of an older generation rooted in World War Two. The Cold War was over and the leader of the lone world superpower had emerged from here, the heart of real America from where there wasn't even a direct flight to New York or Washington. It was well past midnight before the streets emptied, leaving only a small band of revellers around a Texan group with long hair and guitars singing 'Power to the People' – and the first badge vendor appeared selling lapel buttons with the words: 'Clinton Victory Nite. I Was There'.

Chapter 13

THE BUBBLE-GUM
WHITE HOUSE

We are the World,
We are the children,
We are the ones
To make a better day.

LIONEL RICHIE, WE ARE THE WORLD, 1985

THE FIRST THING THE NEW LEADER of the United States did after
his inauguration in Washington on 20 January was to have John F.
Kennedy's old wooden desk moved back into the Oval Office.
America had got a New Age president with a strong sense of the
importance of symbols.

They also had elected a president with an emotional folksy style
who is a master of the rhetoric of pop-psychology, and still a 'good ole
boy' from Arkansas.

They elected a leader who wears a $29 Timex Ironman watch with
plastic strap, is a lover of Baby Ruth candy bars, decaffeinated coffee,
coke with ice, the music of Fleetwood Mac and Peter, Paul and Mary,
the novels of William Faulkner, late-night card games and jogging,
preferably to and from a McDonald's.

He is a communicator, a toucher and a hugger in a way that his
predecessor never was nor could be. His style of communication is
group-therapy. After his election, Clinton held a national economics
seminar at Little Rock which moved Robert Kuttner, an economics
columnist, to say to him: 'This has to be the defining moment of your
presidency. It is the president as leader, as explainer, as synthesizer.
This is a magical moment and I thank you for including me.' To which
Clinton replied, for once embarrassed: 'I hope that doesn't mean it's
all downhill from here.' Before his swearing-in, Clinton also attended
a 'Renaissance Weekend', a get-together of high achievers, at which
participants were encouraged to confess what troubled them. He took
notes at a session called 'What I've learned about love', as prominent
people talked about how they had overcome marriage problems. At

his first weekend with his new cabinet at Camp David, Clinton brought along two professional 'facilitators' to get people to talk about themselves; at one late-night session devoted to childhood fears, the President confessed to being humiliated when he was taunted about being fat at the age of seven.

The election of Clinton was a transfer from a passive presidency to an active one. It marked the exit of a president who liked to throw horse shoes and the grand entrance, stage left, of a president who played 'Your mama don't dance ...' on the sax at one of his inauguration balls.

At his stirring inauguration on 20 January the new President pledged that an era of deadlock and drift was over and that 'a new season of American renewal has begun'.

In the Clinton administration the cultural ethos is different. The composition of the team is politically correct to an exquisite degree, making it look, as Clinton promised, more like America. The eighteen-member Cabinet has four blacks, two Hispanics and five women. Attitudes are different. Everyone is a workaholic. The new people rent houses rather than buy. They are non-ideological liberals. The President is a champion of neo-liberalism, which has been defined as a commonsense revolt against the tendency of liberals to avoid the middle ground or the wisest answer if it offends any of their people or causes. Some criticise neo-liberalism as dangerous as it tends to assume that the right solution can always be found in the middle of the road. Put another way, Clinton is a well-intentioned consensus politician, a romantic disposed towards pragmatism, who wants to be liked.

Clinton has surrounded himself with young people, average age thirty-six. Only three out of ten people wandering the corridors of the White House are over forty. Put it another way: seven out of ten are too young to have served in Vietnam. This is the seventies generation, not the sixties. The White House mess has the air of a students' union, with a younger, looser crowd than there ever was in the Kennedy days. Clinton's communications director, George Stephanopoulos, is thirty-two. His press officer, Dee Dee Myers, is thirty-one. Nancy Soderberg, staff director of the National Security Council, is thirty-four. Mark Gearan, the deputy chief of staff, is thirty-six. Kathleen McGinty, director of the Office of Environmental Policy, is twenty-nine, and so is Thomas Kalil, special assistant to the President for domestic policy. Andrew Friendly, the President's personal aide, is twenty-four. In corridors where pumps and skirts were expected, sweaters, jeans and pant suits are fashionable.

To veteran observers like Helen Thomas of UPI, who has covered the White House since the days of the Kennedy administration, this is not all a good thing. One of the first acts of the young press team was to shut the media out from the inner rooms of the White House press office, occupied by Stephanopoulos. 'This didn't happen even in the worst moments of Watergate,' Helen Thomas told me. 'It's always the first sign of a presidency that will go wrong, when they think they can do things without anyone knowing.'

The free-flowing discussions and policy sessions going on inside the White House contrast sharply with the isolation and confinement of the media. An official delegation of White House correspondents went to complain to George Stephanopoulos about the new restrictions. 'He sat in the chair and chewed bubble-gum and blew bubbles and said he'd get back to us,' said one of the delegation, Laurence McQuillan of Reuters. In the meantime, Stephanopoulos told these senior correspondents he couldn't have them 'loitering' in his corridor outside. Nothing changed. In his first two months Bush held five open press conferences. In the comparable period Clinton held none.

'The only reason they put Lloyd Bentsen [seventy-two] in the cabinet was because they needed someone old enough to buy beer at the Seven-Eleven,' said Kate Couric of NBC, in a barbed comment as master of ceremonies at the annual congressional dinner of the Washington Press Foundation a few weeks after the election. Noting that Bill and Hillary Clinton failed to make an expected appearance at the dinner, Couric also quipped: 'We were so looking forward to meeting the new leader of the western world and her husband.'

Once in the White House, Hillary came into her own. The President and his wife made it clear that this was going to be a team presidency. The pre-Tammy Wynette Hillary Clinton re-emerged, calling herself Hillary Rodham Clinton once more. She asserted control by forbidding her husband's fun-loving mother Virginia Kelley and his half-brother Roger to give media interviews during the transition period.

The First Lady occupies an office in the West Wing of the White House as adviser to the President, breaking with the precedent where first ladies always made their executive quarters in the East Wing. Clinton appointed her to head a committee to prepare legislation to overhaul the $800 billion US health-care system, the most powerful post ever given a president's spouse. The First Lady has more aides than Vice-President Al Gore.

She will need all the help she can get. Clinton has given her the formidable task, one on which his presidency may be judged, of reforming a system which makes the United States the only advanced country in the world which does not provide basic health-care for all its citizens. The cost of medical treatment and drugs in the United States has become prohibitive for the average low or middle-income family. Health insurance costs are so expensive that private sector employers are abandoning the traditional practice of insuring their workers. Ford today pays more for health-care than it does for steel. Up to 1.2 million people are dropping out of the health insurance system every year. A large percentage qualify for state Medicaid benefits, aggravating the federal deficit. Others simply do without insurance and live in terror of serious illness. They cannot afford to pay for a family policy, the average cost of which has trebled in a decade to an estimated $400 a month. To put it in perspective: one in every seven dollars spent each year in the US goes to doctors, hospitals, insurance companies, drug companies and related services and equipment. Rising health-care costs are expected to account for half the increase in the deficit in the next five years, unless there is radical change.

The President's wife faces complex and inter-related problems. America has an ageing population which demands more medical care, and there is widespread abuse of programmes for the less well-off. Doctors fear litigation, and this makes them automatically apply the most expensive treatment. Also, financial arrangements reward the decision to treat a patient even if there is no evidence that such treatment will work. The First Lady will have to take on the powerful American Medical Association, insurance companies and the drug industries. Neo-liberalism will not be a solution. To look for consensus would be to do nothing.

Despite all this, Mrs. Hillary Rodham Clinton has not abandoned the more traditional role of White House hostess. She has changed the menus to emphasise American cuisine instead of French and, in the new politically-correct White House, imposed a total ban on smoking.

When the First Lady visited Capitol Hill to lobby on health-care reform she charmed and dazzled legislators with her intelligence and coolness and grasp of detail. She conducted interviews for the post of attorney general, which was reserved for a woman.

When Chelsea Clinton needed permission at school to get aspirin, the thirteen-year-old told the nurse: 'Call my dad, my mom's too busy.' (The nurse did and the President had time to chat for several minutes.)

There was little public opposition to the appointment of the President's wife to such a crucial role. Many felt her record as one of the top one hundred lawyers in the US would have qualified her for a place in a Clinton cabinet in any event.

James Carville assessed her power as a senior presidential adviser in this way: 'If the person that has the last word at night is the same person who has the first word in the morning, they're going to be important. You throw in an IQ of a zillion and a backbone of steel and it's a pretty safe assumption to say this is a person of considerable influence.'

Within a few weeks of the relative obscurity imposed upon her during the campaign, Hillary became box-office, with greater appeal than Princess Di on the cover of *People* magazine. Her approval rating climbed, with 62 percent saying in a poll taken about her new assignment that she would do a good job. She became a positive role model and her troubled marriage became a model one. A 3 foot by 2 foot photograph of a broadly smiling Hillary hangs at head height above the desk in the President's study off the Oval Office.

In the Clinton White House, as much attention is devoted to the presentation of policy as during the campaign. Government by focus groups has replaced campaign by focus groups.

It was Hillary Rodham Clinton who took the initiative in the confused days in the run-up to Clinton's first State of the Union message on 17 February when coverage of Clinton's emerging economic plan was dominated by negative speculation. She pointed out that they needed to return to the campaign message of growth, jobs and a cut in the deficit.

At the Camp David meeting she recalled the success of their tactics in selling education reform in Arkansas, which involved making people understand what Clinton was doing. The President's pollster, Stan Greenberg, was asked to find out from his focus groups whether Clinton had a 'read my lips' problem with his promise, which he was about to break, not to increase the tax burden on the middle class. The message which emerged was that he did not, but that voters expected Clinton to get on with fixing the economy. Greenberg set up a 'dial group' in North Carolina. Its members registered eighty out of an approval scale of hundred for the proposition that the middle class should pay more taxes.

The State of the Union address was the signal for a great battle to begin. It was a far-reaching agenda for renewal, a call to undo the Reagan revolution by increasing taxes and trimming spending. Clinton asked for an energy tax, an increase in income tax rates for individuals earning more than $115,000, a tax on social security benefits of well-off pensioners and a cut of $325 billion in the deficit over four years. He pleaded for reform of the US health-care system. 'Unless we change the present pattern,' said Clinton, 'by the year 2000 almost 20 percent of our income will be in health-care.'

The speech was a committee affair, which Clinton was still amending on his way to Capitol Hill. In the end the new President did the unthinkable. He ad-libbed much of the State of the Union address, the critical speech of his presidency. It was a masterly performance, a mixture of charming long-windedness and free-form oratory, with Clinton drawing on all his natural communication talents and long experience of front-porch campaigning to pull it off.

The successful implementation of the plan will depend on how deeply the nation perceives the deficit to be a national crisis in the months ahead.

Clinton found an unexpected ally in Ross Perot to keep the sense of crisis alive. After the election Perot began renewing his campaign for drastic fiscal action by promoting his organisation United We Stand, America through television advertising, rallies, mass mailing and appearances on talk shows, including, of course *Larry King Live*. On 2 March 1993, he came to Washington to testify to Congress, the common man from the Frank Capra movie, though his home-spun homilies were wearing thin. Clinton, with 43 percent of the vote, does not have an electoral majority, but together he and Perot won 62 percent of the popular vote, a convincing mandate for change.

The importance of the Perot phenomenon in American politics cannot be under-estimated. One in five American voters cast their ballots for a flawed candidate who articulated their rage against government in Washington. The Perot supporters are the 'risen people'. The real significance of their rebellion is that a sizeable proportion of Americans feel the two-party system has failed them. Bill Clinton is the last hope of old-style government being able to fix things. If he doesn't succeed he will not just lose the next election but the two-party system will be seen to have failed, with uncertain consequences for the future of the traditional political balance.

'If we have the vision, the will and the heart to make the changes that we must,' Clinton said in the State of the Union speech, 'we can enter the twenty-first century with possibilities our parents could not even have imagined, and enter it having secured the American Dream for ourselves and future generations.' To get his plan through Congress, Clinton needs to maintain the extraordinary engagement of the American electorate which he managed to achieve in the last stages of the 1992 campaign. Within twenty-four hours of addressing Congress he was on the campaign trail again, swinging through the Midwest and ending symbolically at the home in Hyde Park in New York State of Franklin D. Roosevelt, who also called for 'bold, persistent experimentation'. Such campaigning had two purposes: to build a constituency across the country for policies which will be resisted in Congress, and to win a second term in 1996. His return to the trappings of the campaign is an attempt to recruit the voters as allies in a struggle with Congress to pass his proposals, to create a public atmosphere where it will be difficult for a legislator on Capitol Hill to resist change.

The electronic town hall meeting also enables Clinton to have impromptu, intimate conversations with voters with the whole nation looking on, while the by-passed press corps is reduced to recording his soft, cajoling words from the television screens. It is presidency by seminar, with Clinton the nation's teacher.

Clinton had another reason for taking his message back on the road. The State of the Union address represented a retreat from a campaign pledge not to increase the tax burden on the middle class. (In Clinton's first major election speech in Chicago he had actually promised to work for a 10 percent reduction in the middle-class tax rate.) Clinton had broken other campaign promises, including a commitment to lift the US naval blocade around Haiti to prevent refugees fleeing to the United States. The new President wanted to assure the people that the situation called for the measures he took, and to explain that the plan represents hope for a better future. It is a tactic which worked in Arkansas.

It will work, too, in Congress. Speaker of the House of Representatives, Tom Foley, told me in an interview: 'If somebody asked me should the President keep his campaign promise on China, or on Haiti, or dealing with issues relating to American domestic policy, if he thinks that that policy on due consideration is not the right one ... then of course he should not keep his campaign promise. It is stupid and wrongheaded and wrongful to do a wrong thing against the interests and purposes for which those promises were given. With deference to George Bernard Shaw, there are two great sins in American politics, the sin of the candidate who doesn't keep his campaign promise, and the often greater and mortal sin of the candidate who does. And frankly in our history a lot of good has been done by candidates who were wise enough to revise their decision.'

The most immediate danger for Clinton is that if he fails to push his plan through Congress in his first year, the prospect of real reform of the health-care system, which will take years, will dim, as will his effectiveness as a president. The disillusion in the country will become deeper than before. For this reason, the majority of Americans voiced support in the days after the speech for what Clinton was trying to do. In Congress, government gridlock ended, with the House of Representatives passing his $16.3 billion economic stimulus Bill by mid-March.

The use of town hall meetings is also an effective way of combatting the fifth estate in the US, the – mostly-conservative – radio talk show hosts who set the agenda each week for national conversation. When Clinton sits on stage on the edge of a high stool and addresses a schoolgirl about health-care, he is offering an alternative to the views of Larry King, Brian Lamb, Jerry Williams, Mike Seagel, Diane Rehm, David Gold, Imhotec Gary Byrd, Rush Limbaugh and dozens of other radio personalities involved in call-in democracy, America's secular religion. Limbaugh, the scourge of the liberals, has taken to introducing his shows with the words 'Day 100 [or whatever the correct number is] of the hostage crisis: Clinton holding America to ransom.'

Clinton enjoyed in his first hundred days an extraordinary amount of goodwill from liberals and women's groups, generated by the victory he won for the progressive side in America's cultural wars.

There was an air of triumph when several hundred people, mostly women, many of them black, gathered after the election in Washington's Sheraton Hotel for the annual dinner of the National Women's Law Center, a body devoted to women's rights. The special guest was Anita Hill. When the Oklahoma law professor appeared, everyone stood up, even some of the normally stoic reporters around me at the press table, to give her a rapturous standing ovation. Sharon Pratt Kelly, Washington's black Democratic mayor, told the audience that Anita Hill had done for women what Rosa Parks had done for the Civil Rights movement. She had 'tapped an appropriate impatience, anger and energy among women which would benefit America in the twenty-first century and which had helped elect a Democrat to the White House and double the number of women in Congress.' Anita Hill too was caught up in the mood of the moment. 'We have not quite arrived,' she declared, 'but we are well on our way. We can make America America again.'

To these people, Anita Hill, as much as Bill Clinton, had changed the face of America. Just after the Senate hearings at which she testified against Judge Clarence Thomas, a *Newsweek* poll showed that only 27 percent of women believed she had been sexually harassed. By December 1992 the figure had risen to 51 percent. There was considerable political fall-out from the hearings. Senator Alan Dixon, one of the Democratic senators who voted to ratify Clarence Thomas as a Supreme Court judge, failed to win renomination as Democratic Senate candidate in Illinois, ceding his seat to Carol Moseley Braun, who had become the first elected African-American woman senator. She and Dianne Feinstein, a white senator from California, were appointed to the Senate Judiciary Committee, ending the days of white, male hegemony on the body which had humiliated Anita Hill.

One of the chief beneficiaries of the Anita Hill experience was EMILY's List, an organisation founded in 1985 to support pro-choice Democratic women candidates, the word EMILY being an acronym for 'Early Money Is Like Yeast'. (It makes the dough rise.) EMILY's

List raised $6.2 million in 1992, the largest by any single political action group, to support women candidates in House and Senate campaigns and its membership increased from 3,500 to 24,000.

'The Thomas-Hill hearings sparked a firestorm of determination to elect women to major political offices,' said its president, Ellen Malcolm. 'Whether you believed him or believed her, you looked at that Senate Judiciary Committee and said, this is what's wrong with the Congress, these guys are insensitive, they're arrogant, they're out of touch. If we had more women the place would work better.'

In the elections the total of women senators increased from two to six, of whom five were Democrats, and congresswomen, aged from twenty-nine to forty-eight, of whom thirty-six were Democrats. It was the highest-ever number of women to win seats on Capitol Hill though still only 11 percent of the total number of legislators.

The abortion and gay rights movements found themselves operating in a less hostile atmosphere with Bush gone from the White House. The new President ended the questioning of military recruits about their sexual status, though he faced opposition from the Chiefs of the General Staff and Congress members from both sides in the House when he expressed his intention of lifting the ban on homosexuals in the military and had to settle for a six-month review of the problems involved.

The two sides in the abortion struggle took stock after Clinton's victory. The public acceptance of abortion as a right is now more widespread than in 1980 and the prospect that it will be criminalised by the Supreme Court has receded. It diminished further when Justice Byron White resigned unexpectedly on 19 March 1993, weakening the Court's conservative wing. Clinton's first act was to cancel several abortion-related decrees made by President Bush. These had banned abortion referrals by government-funded clinics, experiments on foetal tissue, abortions in military hospitals abroad, US aid for foreign organisations which provided abortions and imports of the French abortion pill, RU-486. The struggle is taking on new dimensions. The RU-486 pill may lessen the pressure on abortion clinics but it faces major obstacles in distribution. Pharmaceutical companies will be pressurised not to produce the pill by threats of a boycott of their products by Catholic hospitals.

In the moment of defeat there was some consolation for the

anti-abortion side in a decision of the Supreme Court. It issued a judgement removing federal protection from abortion clinics. By six votes to three, the judges overruled the decision of Judge Patrick Kelly of Wichita in 1991, and used widely by other federal judges, that the Ku Klux Klan Act of 1871 gave federal courts the right to bar anti-abortion protestors from blockading abortion clinics. At the same time, Randall Terry, the head of Operation Rescue, and his accomplice were charged in March 1993 with refusing to obey a court order compelling them not to carry out a threat to present a foetus to Mr. Clinton during the Democratic National Convention in July, and faced six months in jail.

On 10 March, less than two months into the Clinton presidency there occurred a bloody event which forced both sides to re-think their strategies. In Pensacola, Florida, a chemical plant worker named Michael Griffin who had been picketing an abortion clinic, shot and killed the attendant physician, Dr. David Gunn with three bullets in the back.

The killing was the culmination of a decade of blockades, threats and firebombings of clinics across the US. The Catholic Conference reacted with horror, saying: 'Killing in the name of pro-life makes a mockery of the pro-life cause.' Randall Terry said, however: 'We must also grieve for the thousands of children he has murdered.' In 1992 Operation Rescue had distributed 'Wanted' notices with Dr. Gunn's picture and the words: 'We need your help to stop Dr. David Gunn.' It gave details of his schedules so that people 'could ask him to stop doing abortions'.

'We're going to have to be a hell of a lot more cautious,' said Linda Taggart, director of the Ladies Center clinic in Pensacola. But the first fatality of the war of the clinics seemed likely to result in a greater setback for the anti-abortion movement. It not only discredited the 'pro-life' cause, it gave impetus to a Bill in Congress to make it a federal crime to interfere with the work of the clinics.

President Clinton may ultimately be judged not on domestic but on foreign policy as he explores the uncharted territory of the post-Cold War world. He must determine whether it is in the nation's interest to try to reform the world through force and aid programmes. America can impose its will on smaller, weaker countries through muscle and technology, as it has done in Iraq and Somalia, but it can be frustrated in other difficult terrains. Mindful of Vietnam, the generals, under the direction of outgoing Chief of the General Staff Colin Powell, had taken the view: 'We do deserts, not mountains.' In the first months of the Clinton administration, they privately admitted that they were at a loss about what America's role should be in the face of world conflicts where human rights abuses occurred on the scale of World War Two. This created pressure to get involved for humanitarian reasons. With the collapse of communism, the United States is the only country in the world with the reach and military technology to impose its will on a faraway country.

In the absence of an overriding external threat such as that from the Soviet Union, Americans need compelling reasons for supporting an active role in the world. Clinton has to articulate the organising principle for US global leadership in the wake of the Cold War, as Will Marshall, head of the Progressive Policy Institute in Washington expressed it. This, simply put, is that foreign and domestic policies are interlocking and interdependent. It costs less to promote democracies than to arm for a Cold War, and democracies are less likely to engage in aggression or to develop nuclear weapons. Shortly after his election, Clinton said that substantial aid to former Soviet republics was vital, not just to sustain Russian economic reforms, but to nourish the US domestic economy. If democratic and market reforms failed because of lack of support and investment from the West, he pointed out, the US would have to increase defence spending. If they succeeded there would be a better prospect of global economic growth.

Clinton had the vision to make the distinction between a fledgling democracy in need of assistance from friends and a defeated enemy looking for handouts. His problem was finding the resources to implement a post-Cold War plan like the Marshall Plan, which helped rebuild Western Europe after World War Two.

'In principle, Americans are unlikely to welcome major expenditures abroad at a time when there are serious cuts or restraints on spending here at home,' said Speaker Foley in his office on Capitol Hill as Clinton began turning his attention to the former Soviet republics. 'Foreign aid or foreign investment is easier when the country is doing extraordinarily well, when there is prosperity, and when the government is not in the austerity mode,' he noted. 'Having said that, I think a case can be made that we have saved a very substantial amount on defence only because of changes in conditions in the former Soviet Union.'

But Americans have short memories. 'It's a public education problem because many people have kind of accepted the changes in the former Soviet Union, Russia and the other Russian republics as permanent and unchangeable,' said Speaker Foley.

A major threat to US security with which Clinton must grapple comes from within, from an 'America First' mind-set which goes beyond the Republican right wing and permeates the trade unions, and which cannot tolerate large expenditure abroad while public spending is cut at home. America also cannot be a world leader when its economy is weak, its health-care system almost bankrupt, its children poorly educated, and poverty and crime rates higher than elsewhere in the developed world.

Where Clinton has restored hope to many Americans that things will improve at home, his foreign policy gives hope abroad that the United States will replace its anti-communism with more practical support for democracy.

Clinton is not rigidly tied to an ideology, as was his predecessor. The passion has gone out of the left-right division in the United States since the Berlin Wall fell. The arguments and divisions are over foreign aid, protectionism, free trade, and intervention in regional wars, and they often cut across the old ideological divide.

The end of the Cold War has also meant the cooling of traditionally close US ties to its allies. The special relationship between the United States and Great Britain, for example, is not quite what it was in the days of Margaret Thatcher and Ronald Reagan. Clinton has not forgotten the questionable role played by colleagues of British Prime Minister John Major in trying to ensure his defeat in the presidential election, nor the way British officials co-operated in a search through passport files for evidence that he might have applied for British citizenship to avoid the Vietnam draft. Clinton tells jokes in public about Major, regaling guests at a Washington dinner once about how Major told him: 'You don't look at all like your passport photos.'

In deference to promises he made to Irish American voters, Clinton raised the issue of human rights violations in Northern Ireland at a frigid first meeting with the British Prime Minister in the White House at the end of February 1993 – and then rolled out the green carpet for

Irish Prime Minister Albert Reynolds on St. Patrick's Day three weeks later. He appointed Jean Kennedy Smith US ambassador to Ireland at the behest of her brother Senator Edward Kennedy – an act of atonement by the Senator for the debacle at Palm Beach when he took her son William Kennedy Smith for a late-night drink in April 1991. He nominated Boston Mayor Ray Flynn, a strong critic of British policies in Ireland, as envoy to the Vatican as a reward for Flynn's role in delivering the 'pro-life' Catholic 'Reagan Democrats' during the election. Neither appointment took into account the Anglophile State Department's concern to keep the British 'cousins' happy. Clinton, whose mother was called Cassidy, a common Irish surname, seems to find more congenial cousins among the Irish.

In his contest with Bush, Clinton won the Irish vote, the women's vote, the Catholic and Jewish votes, the gay vote, the black vote and the trade union vote. Clinton took every coalition category except that of white Protestants, his own category. He called for a new covenant between the American people and those who govern them, and proposed social and economic programmes which reflected the appeal of a Democratic Party which had re-discovered middle-class values. He captured all income classes except the very wealthy. The last two Democratic candidates for president took only the lower-income class vote.

And yet Clinton had luck on his side. Bush's popularity after the Gulf war persuaded prominent Democrats it was not worth running, which meant Clinton had a less daunting field to beat in the primary elections. He was fortunate that Patrick Buchanan destroyed Bush's credibility from within, and that the Republicans alienated minorities and moderate voters at their Convention in Houston. He was lucky that the Gennifer Flowers story, which could have destroyed his candidacy in the final weeks, surfaced early and was buried. He was most fortunate of all in the way the economic recovery which Bush had been promising held off until after the election, when the economy did at last show signs of renewed vigour. In the end, he won with less support from voters – 43 percent of the popular vote – than the losing Democratic Party candidate, Michael Dukakis in 1988, who got 45.6 percent of the vote. The disparity is explained by the presence in the election of Ross Perot who took votes from both Clinton and Bush.

With the local boy's ascension to the White House, Hope could no longer be considered a place in the centre of nowhere, as Mary Neill Turner of the Hemstead County Historical Society had once said early in the election campaign. It was now the centre of America.

Tourists come from far and wide, bringing new jobs for townsfolk to add to those provided by Champion Auto Parts, Hudson Foods chicken processing plant, Klipsch stereo loudspeakers, Cal Maine Foods and Fink and Company's jigsaw puzzle factory. A new Days Inn motel opened in January 1992, along with dozens of new bed and breakfasts and a Mexican and a Bar-B-Q restaurant, bringing the total of eating places to twenty-four. 'You can now get anything you want to eat here,' said Ivan Baker, chairman of the Economic Development Corporation, who travelled to Washington with a hundred Hope residents for the presidential inauguration. 'You can get fried catfish, steaks, barbecue, Chinese and Mexican, anything.' Every gas station and convenience store now sells Clinton coffee mugs and buttons and T-shirts.

Since Clinton's inauguration, no-one passing through Hope, which straddles Route 30 running from Little Rock to Dallas, is allowed to forget its claim to fame. A big hand-carved redwood sign saying 'WELCOME TO HOPE, BIRTHPLACE OF BILL CLINTON' has been erected in the main street. A more modest plaque appeared at the site of the old Julia Chester Hospital where Clinton was born but which burned down in 1990. It says, 'Birthplace of President Clinton'. When it went up, people started coming by with jars which they filled full of earth from the site to take home as souvenirs.

Even the local Republicans were caught up in the whole thing. 'Once he's a president he's not political,' Ivan Baker pointed out. 'He's a man of history. And this is his home town. And as he said: "I still believe in a place called Hope."'

Bibliography

Allen, Charles F. and Portis, Jonathan, *Bill Clinton, Comeback Kid*, (Birch Lane Press, 1992)

Allen, Thomas, *CNN Guide to the 1992 Election*, (Turner Publishing Inc., 1992)

Barlett, Donald L. and Steele, James B., *America, What Went Wrong?* (Andrews and Mcmeel, 1992)

Buchanan, Patrick J., *Right from the Beginning*, (Regnery Gateway, 1990)

Duffy, Michael and Goodgame, Dan, *Marching in Place, the Status Quo Presidency of George Bush*, (Simon & Schuster, 1992)

Faludi, Susan, *Backlash, The Undeclared War Against Women in America*, (Anchor Books, 1991)

Faux, Marian, *Roe v. Wade*, (Mentor, 1988)

Goldman, Peter and Matthews, Tom, 'How He Won, The Untold Story of Bill Clinton's Triumph', (*Newsweek Special Election Issue*, November/December, 1992)

Green, Mark, *Changing America, Blueprints for the New Administration*, (Newmarket Press, 1992)

Hacker, Andrew, *Two Nations, Black and White, Separate, Hostile, Unequal*, (Scribners, 1992)

Kennedy, Paul, *Preparing for the Twenty-first Century*, (Random House, 1993)

Koon, Stacey, *Presumed Guilty, The Tragedy of the Rodney King Affair*, (Regnery Gateway, 1992)

Limbaugh, Rush, *The Way Things Ought To Be*, (Pocket Books, 1992)

Mason, Todd, *Perot, An Unauthorised Biography*, (Business One Irwin, 1990)

Marshall, Will and Schram, Martin, *Mandate for Change*, (Berkley Books, 1993)

Morrison, Toni, (editor) *Race-ing Justice, En-gendering Power, Essays on Anita Hill, Clarence Thomas and the Construction of Social Reality*, (Pantheon Books, 1992)

Phelps, Timothy M. and Winternitz, Helen, *Capitol Games*, Hyperion 1992)

Phillips, Kevin, (Boiling Point, Democrats, Republicans and the Decline of Middle Class Prosperity, (Random House, 1993)

Polsby, Nelson W. and Wildavsky, Aaron, *Presidential Elections*, (Free Press, 1991)

Ralston, Jeannie, 'The Great Divide, A Frontline Report from the Battle over Abortion', (*Life*, July 1992)

Reich, Robert, *The Work of Nations*, (Knopf, 1991)

Romm, Joseph J., *The Once and Future Superpower*, (Morrow, 1992)

Rowan, Carl T., *Dream Makers, Dream Breakers*, (Little, Brown, 1993)

Sheeran, James Jennings and Haas, Pamela J., 'The Palm Beach Book of Facts and Firsts', (*Palm Beach Society Magazine*, 1989)

Staff of the *Los Angeles Times*, 'Understanding the Riots', (*Los Angeles Times*, 1992)

Tribe, Laurence H., *Abortion, The Clash of Absolutes*, (Norton, 1992)

Warner, Judith, *Hillary Clinton, The Inside Story*, (Signet, 1993)

Weiss, Murray and Hoffman, Bill, *Palm Beach Babylon*, (Birch Lane Press, 1992)